BY REASON OF INSANITY

BY REASON OF INSANITY
A Glimpse into the Lives and
Minds of the Criminally Insane

Richard R. Sternberg, Psy.D.

International Psychoanalytic Books (IPBooks)
New York • http://www.IPBooks.net

Published by IPBooks, Queens, NY
Online at: www.IPBooks.net

ISBN: 978-1-949093-59-9

ACKNOWLEDGMENTS

There are many who have provided invaluable assistance in the creation of this book. Readers who offered not only their time but their thoughtful critiques include Lewis Aron, Ph.D., Kathy Bernhard, Jerold Gold, Ph.D., Lauri Klein, Ph.D., Deborah Klener, Ph.D., Jacquie Rosenblum, J.D., Marshall Silverstein, Ph.D., Jill Shalan, Ph.D., Michael Simon, Louis Sternberg, J.D., and Harris Zwerling, J.D., Ph.D. All gave generously of their time, but I must make specific mention of several. Kathy Bernhard was one of the earliest readers and therefore very helpful in shaping the work. Louis Sternberg, my son, was one of my most severe – and therefore one of my most helpful – critics. Jerold Gold, Jill Shalan, Marshall Silverstein and Michael Simon all read the many versions of each chapter as well as chapters that were ultimately not included in the book. Their advice, encouragement and support were invaluable. Harris Zwerling's contribution was remarkable; after reading the entire manuscript he took it upon himself to set down on paper a systematic and extensive critique, commenting on all aspects of the work from the overall tone to minute but important detail. I greatly appreciate both his effort and his consistently sound advice.

I was also fortunate enough to receive a great deal of help with regard to preparing a book proposal and negotiating the publishing process in general. Lewis Aron, Ph.D., Kathy Bernhard, Jerold Gold, Ph.D., Steven Kuchuck, Ph.D., Elizabeth Lyon, Susan Beth Pfeffer, Gerald Sorin, Louis Sternberg, J.D., and Ben Yalom helped me to find my way through this foreign and rather intimidating domain. P.J. Dempsey, whom I first contacted as a professional editor for help with the book proposal, gave as freely of her time and advice as if she had been a lifelong friend.

As much help as was offered by all of these people, three must be given special mention because it is unlikely that the book would have reached publication without their help. Jill Shalan, a colleague at the Kirby Forensic Psychiatric Center and a friend before, during and after our time there, was a source of endless support during our years of working together in that institution. Her reading and re-reading of every chapter and the thoughtful opinions she offered were invaluable. But perhaps more importantly, she had earlier shown interest in reading my forensic reports for the hospital, and her constant insistence that my writing had merit was an important impetus to my decision to make an attempt at a book. Without her persistent encouragment, it is doubtful that the book would exist.

Marshall Silverstein offered advice, support and encouragement throughout the writing and publishing process. He was persistent – relentless, actually – in pushing me to complete the manuscript and find a publisher. I owe him much gratitude.

Above all, though, is the debt that I owe to Judith Rubinstein Sternberg, my wife, best friend, first-line editor and possibly the world's foremost grammarian. She read every word of every revision of every chapter. More, though, she gave me a reason to write the book.

To the memory of my family that is gone

My parents, Louis & Constance

My brothers, Robert, Eric, Glenn and John

And

To my wonderful family of today

My wife, Judith

My son and daughter-in-law, Louis & Janna

My son, Alan,

and

Our newest and most adorable addition,
my grandson, Blake

AUTHOR'S PREFACE

This book grows out of my experience as a staff psychologist in the Kirby Forensic Psychiatric Center, a maximum-security psychiatric hospital in New York City. The book includes the life histories of four individual patients, as well as one chapter on the hospital as an institution.

One of the greatest difficulties involved in the creation of this book was in finding a way to accurately capture the personalities and psychopathology of these four individuals while preserving their confidentiality and concealing their identities. Although their crimes and the legal proceedings against them are a matter of public record, the knowledge and understanding of them that I gained as a clinician in the hospital is privileged information, necessitating that the patients be disguised.

Simply changing their names would not suffice; I have therefore altered certain facts about their lives and the specific circumstances of their crimes. Furthermore, detail about their early lives was often unavailable in the records and unobtainable from the patients, and I thus allowed myself a degree of artistic license in creating these narratives. However, regardless of these changes and fictionalized elements, I have made every effort to accurately portray the personality tendencies and psychiatric disorders that characterized these individuals and led to their antisocial actions. Although some detail may not be factual, I endeavored to make it fully consistent with the psychological realities involved. This, in fact, was of crucial importance to me as it has been my aim to present stories that are not only engaging but are also informative about personality and psychopathology.

On the other hand, the brevity and lack of personal-historical detail in the clinical vignettes in Chapter Three made concerns about confidentiality unnecessary. Aside from name changes, these stories have been told as accurately as my notes and my memory allow.

In my years at Kirby, I learned a great deal and found the work endlessly fascinating. If the reader finds the book half as interesting as I found my experiences in this unique setting, I will be well pleased.

Contents

BY REASON OF INSANITY

Manolo Gonzalez, Donald Lane, David Reardon and Ronald Walensky all have two things in common: all were acquitted of serious criminal charges, and all have been incarcerated for many years – or decades. These seemingly contradictory statements are reconciled by the fact that all were found not guilty by reason of insanity or – as the statute actually reads – not responsible by reason of mental disease or defect. They have been confined not in prisons, but in the Kirby Forensic Psychiatric Center, a maximum-security forensic psychiatric hospital on Ward's Island in New York City. In the past, such facilities were known as hospitals for the criminally insane.

People hold several erroneous ideas about the insanity plea. Many believe that this defense is very common, that it is often successful, and that those so acquitted "get away with" their crimes – that a successful insanity defense amounts to a free pass, a "get out of jail free" card. People hold these ideas, but the ideas hold little reality. The defense is, in fact, employed in less

1

than one percent of criminal cases and is successful in far less than half the attempts. And, a successful insanity plea certainly does not mean avoidance of consequences for the crime. Very much the contrary. It is true that people who are acquitted on these grounds generally do not spend time in prison. However, they are incarcerated in secure psychiatric facilities, institutions that have more than a little in common with prisons. And they often spend far more time in these uninviting confines than they would have in prison, had they been convicted.

Furthermore, regardless of whether they ultimately spend more time in such a prison-hospital than they would have in prison, there is a particular kind of hell that attaches to their incarceration that does not pertain when one is convicted and sentenced to a term of imprisonment. In New York State, insanity acquittees are not sentenced; they are committed or "retained" for given periods of time. Such periods of retention never exceed two years. However, the retention can and will be repeatedly renewed until such time as the patient is deemed by the courts to be no longer "dangerously mentally ill." That is to say, although it is possible that he could be released in a much shorter period of time, the patient might well be retained for the remainder of his life. And he never knows when – or if – he will be freed.

The public generally devotes far more thought and debate to the legitimacy and fairness of the insanity defense and its application than it does to an understanding of the individuals who raise it. Given that issues of justice and public safety are involved, this is both unsurprising and appropriate. But the understandable concerns for morality and security perhaps divert attention from what may actually be more interesting questions, questions about those who are acquitted on these grounds, questions such as, Who *are* these people? What are they like? How did they come to be that way? What have they done? And *why*?

This book is an attempt to provide partial answers to these questions.

Kirby is a bizarre and fascinating institution and in it I came to know several hundred of the most extraordinary human beings I've ever met; choosing from among them the very limited number of individuals I would portray in this book was a difficult task. I have not necessarily selected the most lurid or sensational cases, but have instead chosen individuals whose histories, crimes, personalities and psychopathology make compelling stories and are wonderfully depictive of various aspects of mental illness. It is my hope to illustrate some of the ways that the human mind and soul can be distorted and deformed, bringing to life for the reader specific individuals who exemplify various aspects of psychopathology such as delusion, hallucination, sexual obsession and impulsivity, paranoia and the utter lack of moral constraint. The four life histories include two individuals whose psychoses led them to commit murders of people they loved, one individual who raped and committed all manner of sexual crimes while believing himself to be a romantic lover of women, and one individual who committed offenses of virtually every kind and was incapable of loving anyone – a psychopath's psychopath.

All psychological phenomena exist on a continuum. The individual who is mildly depressed or slightly anxious or a bit too easily moved to anger suffers from an exacerbation of tendencies that can be found in the healthiest among us. And the more severe forms of psychopathology serve well to demonstrate the essential nature of their milder counterparts. Individuals such as the denizens of Kirby, then, must be seen as being of great worth in terms of what they can offer to our understanding of ourselves.

Yet these four are not people you would wish to know personally. They are people to be avoided. Whether by dint of their lifelong personality tendencies or by virtue of psychoses that transformed otherwise gentle individuals into murderers and mutilators, they are dangerous; it is with good reason that they are locked behind Kirby's walls and razor-wired fences. You would not wish to know them, yet they are surely worth knowing about. They are worth understanding, not only for mental health professionals, but for all those who have a curiosity about human nature, all those who might wish to have a better understanding of themselves, as well as of the people around them.

This book then provides an opportunity to "meet" and to "know" such people from a distance. The severe psychopathology and frightening violence contained in these portraits can be experienced in safety, yet offer a window not only into such "insanity," but into the more mundane varieties of human aggression and emotional suffering. Believing that Kirby's patients – as they actually are – have a great deal to offer in helping us understand everyday forms of human misery, I have attempted to present unvarnished views of their psychopathology and antisocial behavior, neither vilifying nor whitewashing, and keeping in sight their essential humanness.

It is my hope that, in addition to gaining a glimpse into the lives of some fascinating characters and learning something of a special kind of crime – the crime committed by reason of insanity – readers will come away from the book with a greater understanding and appreciation of the emotional problems that they encounter in their own lives – both in themselves and in others.

Allow me, then, to introduce Messrs. Gonzalez, Lane, Reardon and Walensky.

CHAPTER ONE
DONALD LANE

When She Was Good

There was a little girl, who had a little curl
Right in the middle of her forehead,
And when she was good, she was very, very good,
But when she was bad she was horrid.

She stood on her head, on her little trundle bed,
With nobody by for to hinder;
She screamed and she squalled, she yelled and she bawled,
And drummed her little heels against the winder.

Her mother heard the noise, and thought it was the boys
Playing in the empty attic,
She rushed up the stairs, and caught her unawares,
And spanked her, most emphatic.

(Henry Wadsworth Longfellow, American Poet, 1807-1882)

THE YOUNG MAN INSISTED he was innocent. His mother was not dead, he insisted. He would never hurt, much less kill, his mother. He would protect his mother. He loved her. In the end, he protected her. By killing her. Allow me to explain.

Donald Lane had always loved his mother, had always been a good son. He was her youngest child, and his mother doted on him; he, in turn, was devoted to her. She watched over him, did

7

all she could think to do for him, and he was an appreciative, loving son. They enjoyed each other's company, spent much time together, and got along famously. It was always so. Except when it was not. Donald loved his mother dearly and usually felt that she was the best mother in the world. But sometimes he seemed to believe that she had turned against him. And then he'd turn against her. He had two dramatically different ways of feeling toward her, two opposing ways of seeing her and treating her, and never the twain could meet. When she was his loving mother, all was sweetness and light and he could not do enough for her. When the sweetness and light turned bitter and dark, he hated her. When she was good, she was very, very good, and when she was bad, he killed her.

Committed to Kirby after being found not guilty by reason of mental disease or defect, Mr. Lane fell into a pattern of stable and predictable behavior. He caused no trouble, committed no violence and bothered no one; he was almost invisible. He slept. When he could, he slept in his bed. When the patients were en route to some organized activity - going to the dining room or the yard or the treatment and recreation floor - he could be found slogging along in line, looking as if he neither knew nor cared where he was going, looking almost as if he were sleep-walking. At most other times, he would assume his place in the day room, curled up in a chair in the corner, sleeping - or, at least, appearing to sleep.

Mr. Lane, like all patients in Kirby, was assigned to a number of therapy groups. Such groups were a daily component of life at Kirby, and were often considered an annoyance by patients and staff alike. There were substance abuse groups, symptom management groups, anger management groups, legal issues groups (for those who were still facing criminal charges), general discussion groups, and men's issues groups, among others. All groups were equally farcical. A somewhat acerbic colleague described his experience as a group leader in a humorous, but not wholly inaccurate manner. He said that he would go into the day room to announce the start of a group. Of the ten patients who were assigned to this group, five would simply ignore him, continuing to sleep in their chairs, not bothering to open their eyes. Of the remaining five, three would tell him to go fuck himself. The other two would accompany him to the group room. Once inside, one would talk to the walls and the other would yell at him about being unfairly held at Kirby. Group therapy.

Mr. Lane could be counted upon to be among those who simply ignored the announcement. He did not wish to be bothered; he did not wish to interact with either patients or staff. When he was unwilling, he was unwilling; there was no discussion.

"Mr. Lane, it is time for the group to start."

"Leave me alone."

"The group is important for you. Don't you want to work toward getting out of here?"

"Leave me alone."

"You might feel better if you spent a little time talking with people."

"Leave me the fuck alone," he growled, before turning over in his chair and facing into its back, graphically demonstrating that the conversation was at an end and that he would be left alone, whether I liked it or not.

It seemed particularly sad in his case. A young man, in his early twenties, who might be in Kirby for many years or decades to come, he had very quickly taken on the look of the living dead that characterized so many of his older ward-mates. He was on antipsychotic medication which often has a sedating effect, making the patient feel lethargic and unmotivated, and, in all probability, this contributed to his chronically somnolent state. In spite of his occasional irritability in the face of demands made upon him, one might have seen him as generally becalmed by his medication. However, it was clear that he was not simply drowsy, that he was not truly quiescent. And his lack of tranquility was consistently revealed when he took a notion to share his thoughts at greater length.

Each patient at Kirby has a treatment plan, a plan devised by the treatment team and periodically updated in a team meeting. Sometimes the patient would be invited to join the team meeting so that he might have some input into his treatment plan. Although patients did sometimes refuse such invitations, they often would attend, seeing it as an opportunity to voice their complaints, make various requests, or simply to be the focus of attention. On occasion, Mr. Lane would attend his treatment planning session, albeit with some reluctance; and in the meeting he would speak as if wanting to end the session quickly, allowing him to return to his habitual state of withdrawal as soon as possible.

However, on occasion, he had something to say, something that dramatically demonstrated that, his sluggish and listless behavior notwithstanding, he suffered from no mental lassitude. Indeed, not only was his mind active, it was frighteningly and

10

destructively so and, roused from his somnolent state, Mr. Lane would inform his listeners of their impending doom.

"Mr. Lane, how do you feel about your current medications?"

"They suck. I don't care about my medications. I'm getting out of here in a few days and all of you will be gone. This fucking place will not exist. It'll be blasted out of existence. The F.B.I. is coming and they'll fucking blow you all to bits and I'll be out of here. The Marines are coming for me within three days."

"But in the meantime, we'd like to know if you are still having the side-effects that were bothering you before."

"They're going to really fuck you up. And I'll be free and you won't be able to hold me in your jail anymore. You're going to all be put on trial and put in jail."

"Nevertheless, Mr. Lane, we'd like to hear how you've been feeling. Are you still having problems with constipation?"

"This illegal prison is going to be blown up, and you'll all be dead. Or else you'll finally be the ones in prison. You're the ones who are supposed to be prisoners and the F.B.I. will get me out and you'll be the prisoners."

Thus, in keeping with his longstanding delusion, he would inform us that as a member of the F.B.I., he communicated by computer with their headquarters in Washington, D.C., and with Marine facilities in Quantico, Virginia. He was to be rescued from Kirby by a squad of Marines immediately before the hospital was to be "blasted out of existence," and all its employees "pulverized into dust."

Over the months, when summoned to meet with the team or when forced to participate in some activity when he would prefer to sleep, his response was consistent. Kirby and all its staff were on the brink of extinction; it was only a matter of time before his allies in the F.B.I. would swoop down, rescue him from our grasp, and destroy Kirby - edifice and employees alike. He clearly felt that we were some sort of malevolent organization, unfairly and sadistically victimizing him, and needing to be annihilated. Unfortunately for Mr. Lane, he was prone to such sentiments, and it was such sentiments that led him to Kirby in the first place. His anger and his sense of victimization had started long before, Kirby being merely the latest in the series of individuals and entities seen by Mr. Lane as villainous persecutors.

* * *

As a child, Donald was very close to his mother, obviously attached to her, obviously dependant upon her - overly so, in the opinions of his sisters who loved him as the baby of the family, but thought him overindulged. He had always seemed to be his mother's favorite and, after his father left the family when Donald was four years old, she devoted herself to him as if she wanted her attentions to him and her adoration of him to absorb her, to drown out the loneliness and emptiness she felt.

But she was subject to periods of deep depression during which she would take to her bed and leave her son to the care of his eldest sister, Jennifer. She was six years older than he and was a good sister to him, but she could not replace his mother, and Donald suffered during these periods, which sometimes lasted for weeks. As the days wore on during a period of depression, he became irritable, developed stomach aches and seemed somewhat listless. He would visibly brighten when his mother felt well enough to leave her bed and be up and around the house.

The pattern continued for years. At first, it was as if their moods varied in tandem. When his mother became depressed, Donald moped. Furthermore, the mood spread to his sister who perhaps resented the burden of responsibility placed on her when her mother became depressed. And Donald, rather than recognizing or appreciating Jennifer's efforts on his behalf, seemed only to resent her for her trouble. In fact, she sometimes felt that he held her responsible for his mother's disappearance, as if she had intentionally usurped her place.

As the years went on, young Donald's moods took on their own variation, independent of his mother's. She, in fact, became less subject to debilitating depressions, her mood and her presence in the household becoming more stable and consistent. Donald did seem to respond to her more predictable availability, and continued to feel very close to her, perhaps unusually so. He would sit in school, feeling anxious to see his mother at the end of the day, and even into his adolescence, they would spend their evenings together. After dinner, they would watch TV or play cards or just be in the same room together, he doing his homework, she reading, paying the household bills or knitting – an activity which she always enjoyed and in which she was quite skilled. She made beautiful blankets, scarves, ski hats and sweaters for her daughters, Jennifer and Danielle (the middle child), as well as for her neighbors and relations; but it was clear to all that she most enjoyed working on something for her beloved Donald. She would carefully choose colors and patterns that she knew he liked and put a great deal of careful attention into her creations. He may not have been a particularly well-dressed child, but he had a collection of beautiful sweaters and scarves, lovingly created by his doting and dedicated mother.

And Donald always loved using and wearing the things she made. On his bed he kept a blanket that she had made, and he was sure to wear one of his many scarves whenever it was cold enough or even, on occasion, when it really wasn't. Most of all, though, he loved the sweaters that she made. Of these, there was quite an assortment in both style and color, and Donald liked them all. They were, in truth, very important to him for several reasons, aside from the fact that they were beautifully made, handsome articles of clothing. He seemed to feel that wearing one of her creations was like having her with him and was a sign of what a special and talented mother he had and of how much she loved him. He would beam with pride and pleasure whenever he received a compliment on one of his sweaters, something which occurred with great frequency.

Even into his teen years, when he began to dress in ways which his mother could not appreciate, he would often wear one of her sweaters. He wore them simply because he loved them, and the fact that he did helped his mother overlook the ripped jeans and untied sneakers which she certainly did not favor. In fact, there was little that gave Janet Lane more pleasure than seeing her son wear one of her creations and knowing that he loved it. It was plain that the making and wearing of these garments was an expression of the mutual devotion of mother and son.

Of all his sweaters, there was one, a blue v-neck with a red and white argyle pattern on the front, which Donald loved above the rest. Janet had made it for him when he was about nine years old and he wore it often. Over the years, he continued to wear it in spite of the fact that it had become a bit ragged; he continued to wear it even when it became too small for him. Although he remained, as an adolescent, slight of build and short of stature, he nevertheless was taller than he had been when his mother knit the sweater, and, by the time he was fifteen, the arms of the sweater ended far above his wrists. But he would not give it up. Janet often told him that she'd make him a sweater of any kind and of any design he'd like to replace it, but he continued to wear it and insisted that no sweater could be as good. Finally, working on it in Donald's absence, she made a painstakingly-exact replica of his beloved sweater in a more appropriate size, and put it on Donald's bed for him to find upon his return home from school.

Finding it there, neatly folded on his pillow, he ran back into the living room and embraced his mother with an almost overwhelming surge of gratitude and affection. "Oh, Mom. You have to be the greatest mom in the world! You always like making new designs and I didn't want to ask you to make another one of the same sweater, but you knew! I thought it would bore you, but... you're just so good to me. But I'm never, ever going to throw the original away. I'm just going to fold it up and keep it in my drawer, on top of all my other sweaters. I'll love it forever."

Nothing on Earth could have made Janet Lane happier, and with her eyes tearing up, as were his, she held him tightly and felt that all was right with the world.

Donald did love his new sweater and was happy that he could wear it without worrying, as he had with its predecessor, that it was ill-fitting. He wore it often and let his mother know how much he appreciated her thoughtfulness. And he cherished the original, keeping it, as he had said he would, neatly folded on top of one of the piles of sweaters in his dresser drawer. Other clothing came and went, but there the sweater remained.

In addition to enjoying the time spent with his mother, Donald had friends and hobbies and did well in school. It would seem that, aside from the absence of his father, his life was complete. But all was not well with young Donald. There seemed to be another side to him, a dark and unpleasant side, a side that no one in the family understood, but that all dreaded. As loving and lovable as he could be, he could be equally sullen, morose and irritable. At such times, he was unapproachable. Any attempt to speak to him was met with a frightful surliness that was difficult to comprehend in one who, a short while before, had been so affectionate and agreeable.

It was sometimes clear what precipitated such moods as, for example, the first time Janet went out on a date with a man. Donald was eleven at the time, and his family remembered the incident well. The man was a very congenial, likeable middle-aged man, a businessman in the local community, and he went out of his way to be pleasant to Janet's children. The others responded well, but Donald would have none of it.

When he first came to the house, the man made a point of trying to befriend Donald. "Well, hello, Donald! I've heard a lot about you!" he said, smiling and holding out his hand to the boy. Donald, arms tightly folded and mouth tightly frowning, looked at him for a moment, wheeled around and marched into his room, closing the door emphatically behind him. His patient mother, after giving the man a look of appreciation for his attempt, walked to her son's door, knocked lightly, and gently asked, "Donny, please come say hello. Mr. Brooks has been looking forward to meeting you!" Donald's "NO!" was immediate, loud and resolute. "I don't want to meet him!"

Realizing that he was unlikely to relent, Mrs. Lane left Donald to his anger, hoping that it would be short-lived. He did come out of his room when his mother and her despised friend left the house, but the matter was not at an end; Donald did not quickly return to his more pleasant self. For the next several days, he would not speak to his mother who, understanding her son's fears in the situation, made every effort to please and reassure him, but her efforts fell flat. If she spoke, he turned his back; if she cooked for him, he refused to eat. And, in spite of the cold weather, he did not wear any of his sweaters for days. Then, as abruptly as the mood came, it went. He awoke one morning, cheerfully ate the breakfast that his mother prepared and, before leaving for school in his favorite sweater, hugged her tightly and kissed her goodbye.

At other times, the immediate cause of a mood change was as mysterious and confounding as the nature of the change. What was clear, however, was that whatever the trigger, the family was at the heart of his impenetrably black thoughts. It was not only that he would not speak with them, but he could sometimes be seen looking at them, looking at them in a way that he never could or would when he was "himself." There was anger in the look, yes, but more than that, there was a look of victimization, a look that seemed to say that he saw his family as strangers who, somehow, had abused or mistreated him. The family came to speak of it as his "we done him wrong" look.

There were times, too, when the immediate precipitant of his shift into sullen animosity was clear, although the family might be astounded at its triviality. If, for example, his mother, who was apparently an excellent cook, should happen to overcook something on the dinner menu, Donald might react with furor out of all proportion to the offense. On one occasion that Jennifer recalled, he cut into his steak and, finding that it was a bit too well-done for his liking, he slammed his fist on the table and pointedly glared at his mother with unmistakable hostility for several tense moments before pushing his chair back and storming out of the room.

His mother, feeling utterly at a loss as to how to cope with such behavior, simply sat there, feeling on the verge of tears. Jennifer, however, even if feeling a bit intimidated, spoke up.

"Donny! What's the matter with you? Mom made us a wonderful dinner. So it's slightly too well done. What's the big deal?"

"You can eat that garbage if you want to! I'm not eating it. If Mom wants me to eat dinner she can try to get it right!"

It was on this occasion, in fact, that Jennifer realized something about her brother's fits of rage. She saw that he was not simply angry; he was indignant, he felt deeply injured. It was not that Donald was unable to tolerate small frustrations; she knew, for example, that he was capable of real persistence in the face of difficult homework assignments. And his epicurean inclinations were not such that the steak's imperfection, in itself, was intolerable to him. No; it was that he was profoundly offended. It was as if he felt that if his mother cared anything about him, she would not allow him to be disappointed in what she served him to eat. To Donald, the slightly overdone steak was a declaration of indifference to him by his mother, a declaration on which he choked more than he would have on a steak that had been burnt to a crisp. And, if swallowed, such a steak surely would have been easier to digest than his mother's terrible insult.

In his teens, Donald's means of venting his anger underwent a change – very much for the worse. In his earlier years, he would make angry accusations about being treated unfairly, retreat to his room, scowl and sulk, and sometimes refuse to eat or do his household chores. His family found these behaviors unpleasant, but far less so than what supplanted them. The first incident of destructiveness, when Donald punched a hole in the wall of his bedroom, came as a surprise, and the family hoped that it was a one-of-a-kind event. It was not. The escalation was not sudden or rapid, but occurred over a period of years. Punching a hole in the wall was followed in the next episode by breaking a chair, which was followed by overturning the breakfast table, covered with food, and breaking off one of the legs. Interspersed were more minor outbursts – slamming doors, yelling obscenities or banging his fists on the walls. On one very memorable occasion, the one which led to his first receiving psychiatric attention, Donald made a crucial shift, a shift which was looked upon at the time with great alarm and, in later years, with sad recognition of what it foreshadowed.

He was about fifteen years old. Danielle had gone to do some food shopping for the family after taking requests from all about their wants. When, back at home, as she was unpacking the groceries, she noticed Donald looking for something. "Oh!" she said, "I completely forgot the ice cream. Sorry, Donny. I'll be sure to get some tomorrow." When Donald didn't reply, she looked in his direction and, to her alarm and dismay, saw the familiar transformation overtake him. It was as if she could see it progress, making its way downward from his face into and through his body; his eyebrows lowered, his eyes narrowed, his mouth tightened, his jaws clenched; his breathing became shallow and rapid, his neck muscles tensed and his whole body went rigid. As his fists clenched, the words exploded from his darkened countenance.

"DAMN YOU! Why is it always my things that you forget?! I wrote it down! I told you! You got everything else for everyone. Why is it always my things!"

Everyone watched, hoping that his anger might not follow its usual pattern of intensification; but they were more than disappointed. They stared in paralyzed fear and disbelief when Donald raised his arm to hit Danielle. Jessica's sharp intake of breath and his mother's "NO!" were simultaneous with Donald's swing. Danielle's reflexes saved her from the blow, but it might have been better had they not. Now fully enraged, out of control, Donald grabbed a steak knife from the counter and moved toward Danielle as she pulled away. Both Jessica and her mother shrieked, Danielle bolted for the door and fled but could not close the door behind her in time to stop Donald from pursuing. As Donald chased Danielle, Jessica chased Donald, not really knowing what she'd do if she caught him. Janet, meanwhile, rallied from her immobilized terror and called 9-1-1. In the street, Jessica saw Danielle running and, with great

20

relief, saw Donald trip on something on the sidewalk, falling to the ground, the knife flying from his hand. She stood and watched as her brother, lying there, let his body go limp. He then slowly stood up, leaving the knife on the ground, and began to walk back toward the apartment, his look of dark bitterness and agitation remaining, but the uncontrolled fury abating. When the police arrived, they found Donald sitting on his bed, staring at the floor.

With the family's urging, the police took him to the hospital, foregoing the possibility of arresting him. His stay was brief; antidepressants were prescribed, and he was discharged within a few days. Donald, however, resisted treatment; he fought against taking his medication, complaining of unpleasant side-effects. Furthermore, he did not feel that he was depressed; he felt that his family sometimes mistreated him. How would medication help? Janet was unsure of the better course: should they allow him to be unmedicated with whatever risks that might entail, or should they insist on compliance and face his inevitable surly response?

They had spent long hours discussing the situation while Donald was in the hospital. At first, they were appalled – and terrified. What if Donny hadn't fallen? Oh, my God; what would have happened?! He would have stabbed Danielle! But as they talked on – and on – commiserating together, then worrying together, then comforting each other, the terror seemed to lose its razor-sharp edge, the fear began to shrink to more manageable proportions. Somehow the horror subsided and, slowly, they began to feel more optimistic. Could he really have stabbed Danielle? No, it couldn't be. He couldn't really have "done anything." And anyway, surely he had learned a lesson. And Jennifer added that, looking back, she wasn't sure that Donny tripped; she thought maybe he had just flung himself on the ground, knowing that he couldn't possibly really hurt his sister. Of course he wouldn't really hurt her! So when Donald refused to take his medication, they thought it might be better to just let it be. Ultimately, since Donald's episodes of dark mood and violent outburst were the exception, and his affable, good-humored state of mind the rule, they decided they would not press the issue.

Unfortunately, as is so often the case for individuals who are ultimately committed to Kirby, Donald's psychopathology deepened and his belligerence and anger escalated. Unlike some of his fellow Kirby residents, his violence never seemed motivated by cruelty or sadism; he never seemed to want to hurt anyone just for the pleasure of inflicting pain. Rather, he was aggressive towards others – whether verbally or physically – only in response to his belief that they were mistreating him. He did not again – until much later – attack anyone with a weapon, but he flew into rages, yelling, pushing people, and occasionally destroying property. His perceptions of others and how they were treating him became ever more distorted.

This applied to friends, as well as family. In the early years of school, he did well enough academically and had a few friends, but even then he spent inordinate amounts of time alone or with his family. As he entered adolescence, he fell in with a small crowd of youngsters, apart from the mainstream, who were angry and resentful and generally considered by their peers to be strange.

As the high school years went on, although Donald continued to do passably well in school, he seemed to have an increasingly hard time maintaining friendships. He would frequently make passing comments to his family, comments which they often found incomprehensible, about how someone who had seemed to be a good friend had betrayed him or turned out to be something other than what he had seemed. He would never elaborate on these comments, and his family understood that he did not wish to be questioned. In this, as in many other aspects of his behavior, they had come to the conclusion that tolerance and allowance of his idiosyncracies was the best policy.

Unsurprisingly, given his great sensitivity to slights of any kind, his problems with girls were even worse than his troubled relationships with male friends. His sexual interest in girls was evidenced by the collection of pornography that Danielle once found under his mattress, but he showed no inclination to date. His feelings on the subject, however, could only be surmised as he was even more secretive in this regard than he was in general.

When he graduated from high school, it was with a mixture of sadness and relief that his mother sent him off to an upstate college. Although she could not deny to herself that there would be less tension in the household with Donald away, she knew she would miss him dearly. And so she did. She thought about him and knitted for him and found herself going into his bedroom, just to feel near him. Once, on a whim, she opened his dresser drawer and smiled to herself when she saw that his beloved sweater, the original blue v-neck with the red and white pattern on the front, ragged and unwearably small, had accompanied him to college.

Donald, meanwhile, was not faring well at school, finding himself isolated and depressed. He lived in the dorm and had a roommate, Kevin, but they did not get on well. Kevin found Donald strange and moody and Donald, for his part, did not like Kevin and made no attempt to hide his antipathy. Kevin would go out with friends and, at first, made a point of inviting Donald to join them. But Donald made it clear that he wasn't interested and Kevin, ambivalent about bringing him along in the first place, soon stopped inviting him. And when Kevin had friends in the room, Donald would make a point of either leaving or burying himself in a book, giving the unmistakable and accurate impression that he wanted nothing to do with them. It was not, however, that he preferred the company of other students; he made no friends, participated in no activities and, in fact, soon stopped going to his classes. Once or twice, recognizing that his roommate had a problem, Kevin tried to draw him out, tried to see if he could get Donald to open up to him so that maybe he could help him make a go of things. His efforts, though well-intentioned, were not only unsuccessful, but were rebuffed in a manner that effectively discouraged further attempts. Kevin gave up.

Never one for whom things came easily, Donald was unable to adjust to the demands of college life. He found he could not regulate his time and his schedule and had trouble getting out of bed for class. It was only with great difficulty that he could do any work, and he found he could not maintain interest in his studies. His social life was, if anything, even more dismal. He did not feel able to approach other students or even to respond appropriately when approached by them; he spent all his time alone. He was failing – academically and socially – and became

24

unable to manage even the most routine daily activities such as feeding himself and keeping clean. Having always been moody and somewhat isolated, never an emotionally stable or contented person, he now retreated further into his own private world, but it was a retreat that provided no respite and no refuge. It was more an involuntary withdrawal than a tactical regrouping, and it led to a wholly uncontrolled fall, a fall into the tragic chaos of psychosis.

Kevin was a first-hand witness to Donald's increasingly strange and puzzling behavior. He had long taken notice of the inordinate amount of time that Donald spent in bed, his isolation and his failure to attend class, but, after his early attempts, Kevin took no action to get help until matters took a turn for the worse. Standing in the hallway one day, about to open the door to their room, Kevin heard an animated conversation from within and was surprised, thinking that Donald had company. Although he could not make out the conversation, he could hear that Donald was angry or agitated and he paused, wondering if he should interrupt. A moment later, however, when he heard Donald loudly yell, "Shut up. Don't say that!" he thought he'd better go in. The surprise he'd felt upon hearing conversation from the hallway was rapidly replaced by a far greater one upon finding that Donald was alone. The obvious question flew from Kevin's mouth before he could even stop to think, and in spite of having grown somewhat used to Donald's unfriendly manner, he was startled at the brusque "Mind your own damned business!" that was hurled back at him.

Although Kevin surely found this unpleasant and curious, he had grown used to thinking of Donald as strange and did not trouble himself overly much about it. Even as the situation continued and he repeatedly found Donald talking to himself, he dismissed it as simply a byproduct of his obvious loneliness. Similarly, when Donald began wearing a baseball cap at all times, even in bed, Kevin shrugged to himself. Other behavior, and the way that Donald began treating him, he found more difficult – in fact, impossible – to dismiss.

Returning to the room late one night, he found Donald looking through his (Kevin's) dresser drawers. He somehow found it hard to believe that Donald was interested in stealing anything – Donald seemed uninterested in his own or anyone else's possessions and had no evident use for money – but he nevertheless wanted an explanation.

"What the hell are you doing?" he demanded.

Acting and sounding like the injured party, Donald replied, "I'm looking for it... and you'd better tell me where it is!"

"Where what is? What are you talking about?"

"As if you didn't know!" Donald said, bitterly. And as Kevin stood in stunned silence, Donald walked over to the television and began examining it carefully before saying, "It's not in your clock radio, but I want to see that damned portable radio you're always carrying around... and any other electrical shit you have!"

In those days, days predating the now omnipresent cell phones, laptops and iPods, the electrical devices a student might have in his dorm were few and Kevin, realizing that something was very wrong with his roommate, decided to grant the request. While looking for his portable radio, Kevin noticed his clock radio on the floor – fully disassembled. Although he felt a brief surge of anger, the sight only served to further convince him that he was not dealing with a rational person and he made two quick decisions: he would sleep in a friend's room that night and he would speak to the dorm's Residence Assistant first thing in the morning.

And the sight that greeted him when he returned to the room in the morning certainly did nothing to make him doubt the wisdom of those decisions.

He had awakened in a strange room, but quickly recalled where he was and why. He thought he would waste no time; he would seek out the R.A. before his first class, stopping only to get a change of clothes from his room. But, entering the room, thoughts of his clothes quickly vanished. He could not immediately take in the scene in its entirety; he stared for moments at Donald, watching him work frantically, taping layer upon layer of newspaper to the windows with masking tape. Transfixed by the sight, it was a few moments before he thought to look around the room. When he did, he realized that Donald had pulled the telephone out of the wall, leaving the torn wires hanging loosely. Pieces of glass and plastic littered the floor, remnants of the telephone, radio and televisions which Donald had broken or disassembled; some of the electrical components they had contained were piled in the middle of the floor. Donald had apparently interrupted his task of putting these components in his clothes trunk, which he had lined with aluminum foil, when it struck him that covering the windows was a task of greater urgency. His change of clothes forgotten, Kevin immediately sought out the R.A. and the wheels were set in motion for Donald to be evaluated in the University Counseling Center.

BY REASON OF INSANITY

Returning to his room after speaking with the R.A., Kevin felt regretful that he hadn't done more to help Donald. Perhaps earlier in the semester he could have tried harder to help his roommate come out of his shell; perhaps later, he could have made more of an effort to encourage Donald to tell him what was troubling him. He knew that Donald had never shown the slightest interest in friendship with him, but Kevin was not an unfeeling young man and he decided to make one more effort to reach out to his troubled roommate. He was quick, though, to see the futility of the task. He was dismayed, if not terribly surprised, to find, upon asking Donald – in his most gentle and compassionate tone of voice – what was bothering him, that Donald immediately grew surly. He insisted that Kevin knew full well what was bothering him, and that he was, in fact, complicit in the attempt to spy on him and torment him. It was only when Donald began talking about the F.B.I.'s efforts to manipulate his thoughts through electronic and telepathic communications that something clicked for Kevin, and he remembered the descriptions of paranoid schizophrenia that he'd read in his high school abnormal psychology text. Now frightened, he became considerably more so when Donald removed his baseball cap. Revealing a shaved portion of his scalp covered with ugly red scabs, Donald angrily explained that he had been unsuccessful in trying to find and remove the electronic device that Kevin had implanted in his head.

* * *

Schizophrenia, in its more severe forms, takes a truly horrific toll on its victim. Among the most obvious and dramatic symptoms are hallucinations and delusions. Delusions, such as Donald's convictions about the F.B.I. and its attempt to control his mind, are false beliefs which have a hold on the individual such that he is unable, in the face of all the logic and reason that he can muster, to discount them. Hallucinations, by contrast, are false perceptions; they are experienced by one of the five senses in the absence of any external stimulus. One sees, hears, smells, feels or tastes things that are not there. In schizophrenia, the most common modality of hallucination is auditory, and the most common type of auditory hallucination is that of a voice or voices, speaking to or about the afflicted individual. In a very real sense, Donald, when heard by his roommate in animated and often angry conversation, with no visible personage present, was not talking to himself. He was talking back to hallucinated voices.

The fact that a schizophrenic engages in conversation with his hallucinatory voices is of great significance, and is an indication of how hallucinations differ from illusions. Anyone can experience an illusion – see or hear something that is not actually there. Light or sound can play tricks on the mind, fatigue can diminish perceptual accuracy. But the non-psychotic individual will doubt what he is perceiving if the experience is not in accord with his understanding of reality. A non-psychotic individual, if he hears a voice in the absence of other people, may dismiss the experience or look for the source of the sound, but he will not simply accept it as a disembodied voice. That is to say, he is able to exercise reality-testing; he is able to check what he seems to be perceiving against his understanding of reality and will not simply endorse as real something which he believes not to be within the realm of the possible. The schizophrenic, to great and dreadful consequence, loses this ability.

The schizophrenic, in fact, loses the ability to make a number of extremely important distinctions. He loses the ability to differentiate between real and unreal, inner and outer, and self and non-self. The last may well be the most horrible visitation of the disease; imagine the terror that an individual feels as his sense of himself as an intact entity begins to slip away. The schizophrenic individual loses his boundedness, his psychological skin, so to speak, and exists in an amorphous, shadowy world in which there is, psychologically speaking, no floor beneath his feet. He lives in a state of chronic terror, always in danger of ultimate dissolution. It is this "de-differentiation" of self, this inability to sustain a sense of oneself as a whole, distinct and separate entity, as a particular person in a particular place, that underlies most, if not all, of the many unfortunate manifestations of this remarkable and appalling illness.

The inability to make this primary, most fundamental of distinctions underlies the loss of the ability to make other distinctions, distinctions made effortlessly and unthinkingly by most people. The delusion, for example, results from an inability to distinguish inner from outer in the sense of a confusion between feelings and thoughts, on one hand, and objective – external – reality, on the other. We all have thoughts, fears, wishes, fantasies – sometimes enjoyable, sometimes unpleasant – but we are able to make the crucial distinction between mental activity and external events, an ability which the schizophrenic loses as he slips into psychotic darkness. For him, thoughts are realities, inside is outside. Hallucinations, similarly, are manifestations of the inability to distinguish between imagination and reality, between inner sensation and actual perception; a thought becomes a voice or an image with an external existence, as opposed to the strictly internal existence that it has for the non-psychotic person. The schizophrenic individual has a tendency to lose or blur boundaries in any number of ways. If someone sneezes in the presence of a schizophrenic, the schizophrenic may say, "I must have a cold." Concepts and words are fused, sometimes in remarkably creative ways as, for example, when a schizophrenic patient who had been arrested for assault and sodomy informed me that he had been charged with "assaultomy."

Furthermore, this unboundedness is surely a factor in the very common schizophrenic delusion – as exemplified by the tormented Donald – that one is being penetrated and controlled by alien forces. His desperate efforts to ward off the malevolent influence of the F.B.I., as manifested by his covering the windows, searching televisions and telephones for secret transmitters, and his self-mutilating attempt to remove an electronic device from his head, were necessitated by his feeling of being helplessly subject to being entered and taken over by something outside of himself. Such experiences of utter powerlessness, and the delusion of being influenced against one's will are part and parcel of the terrifying descent into paranoid schizophrenia.

* * *

After coming to the attention of health professionals, Donald was admitted to a nearby hospital and put on a regimen of antipsychotic medication. After discharge, he withdrew from school and returned home, where the difficulties that the family had known before his departure for school were soon eclipsed by the new problems they faced. Aside from their sadness about Donald's illness, which they struggled to understand and adjust to, they were faced with emotional outbursts from Donald, especially when he discontinued his medication, as he was inclined to do, outbursts that surpassed, in strangeness and incomprehensibility, any that they had previously encountered. Certainly, there were times that he was calm and quiescent, and during these times he was almost – not quite, but almost – the same sweet, loving young man who he had generally been in the past. But those periods, increasingly rare, were but brief respites from the ever more frequent displays of anger, moodiness and, now, outlandish behavior, behavior which his family found alien, bizarre and profoundly disturbing.

Among the more minor and tolerable such behaviors, although still difficult for the family to understand, were repeatedly disconnecting electrical devices, turning all the television screens to the wall, insisting on wearing dark glasses at all times, even at home, demanding that no one say his name aloud, drawing indecipherable symbols on his bedroom wall, and covering his bedroom window with multiple layers of aluminum foil and electrical tape. More annoying and costly were the occasional outbursts during which he destroyed radios and televisions and ripped telephones from the wall. And his loud conversations, seemingly with himself, which sometimes

32

escalated to screaming, were nerve-shattering, all the more so when his monologic "dialogues" involved reference to torture and murder.

Often, the behaviors were not destructive; but that is not to say that they weren't disturbing. There was, for example, the time when he "realized" that his psychotherapist was working with the F.B.I. One evening, after a period of pacing agitatedly around the apartment, sweating profusely and looking desperate, he pressured Danielle into accompanying him to his therapist's office building. Walking rapidly down the hall, almost running, pulling his sister after him, he pointed to the metal stripping under each of the office doors and, triumphantly, showed her that his therapist's was the only door on that side of the hallway with a silver, rather than gold-colored, strip. Her confused look only frustrated him further, and he angrily informed her that he didn't for a minute believe that she didn't know the terrible significance of this discovery.

For his mother, however, the worst moments were when he looked at her with hatred and accused her of working with his tormentors. This, she could not stand. For her, the memory of her youngest child, her darling son, as the sweet, affectionate, adorable little boy he had been not that many years earlier was still very much alive. She could not long listen to him denouncing her as an agent of the government, having betrayed him and being determined to destroy him, without dissolving into tears.

His sisters surely felt injured by his bitter accusations, but not as deeply. They could even, at certain moments, see the humor in his explanations of why they, along with "the Clintons, the F.B.I. and the Catholics" wanted to do him in. They all knew, he would sometimes say, that he was "transposed," and were hellbent on destroying him and all others who were transposed. He never took seriously his sisters' claims to be ignorant about such matters, but he did sometimes denigrate their intelligence while adding that his enemies in the F.B.I. were determined to harness the enormous power of his brain for their own nefarious purposes.

There were a couple of hospitalizations after Donald's return from school, but as later became so painfully obvious, neither they nor his outpatient treatment contained and controlled his illness in the way that was needed. During each hospitalization, he would be medicated and improve, showing less fear and paranoia and being more grounded in reality. But, as is so often and so often tragically the case, Donald disliked his medication; he complained that it made him feel tired, groggy, like his "head was wrapped in a towel," and blurred his vision. And, shortly after being released from the hospital, he would stop taking it. After the first hospitalization, his family was very pleased with his improvement and accepted his assurances that he would keep taking his medication. By the time he acknowledged that he had stopped taking it, he was well launched into his psychotic flight – angry, paranoid, accusatory, delusional and, as was always his tendency when overtly psychotic, destructive of electronic devices.

After the second hospitalization, the family was more alert to the importance of Donald's medical compliance, but they still had difficulty recognizing the early warning signs of psychosis and wanted to avoid unpleasant confrontations with Donald. Donald, himself, upon discharge, did not want to have to return to the hospital, or at least so he said. But either the medication side effects or something in Donald that wanted the freedom, such as it is, of psychosis, made it difficult for him to comply. His outpatient psychiatrist perhaps didn't see him frequently enough, or perhaps didn't pay enough attention or, most likely, was simply not able to detect the process of decompensation – the regression to psychosis – until it was too late. Donald, after all, could make attempts to hide his symptoms in the early stages of such regressions. In any event, he was able to slip past all the various guardians of sanity, ultimately, with tragic and irreversible consequence.

By this time, Donald was very isolated and barely functioning, even during the periods when not overtly psychotic, and his family found it hard to see him living as he did - almost vegetating. His mother began pushing him to go to school, find a job or, at least, participate in a hospital's day treatment program. Donald resisted, first passively, by saying he would look for work, but doing nothing, then actively, by openly refusing. He became more belligerent, there were more arguments, the tension and discord escalated, relationships became increasingly strained. But even in the midst of this, he and his mother were sometimes able to have good moments, spending time together and enjoying each other's company. Over all this time, Janet continued to knit, perhaps now having even more reason to do so, as she found it soothing and relaxing. As always, she continued to make things for Donald, and, although he left the house infrequently, he would usually wear something she had made when he did.

Eventually, Donald again stopped taking his medication. His paranoia again escalated. He spoke of the F.B.I. wanting his brain, he made accusations towards family members, he disassembled or destroyed telephones, televisions and radios – all of which had been replaced multiple times in the months since his return from school. And he looked at his mother with hatred. Furthermore, he began looking at her in a new and strange way, as if he were trying to figure out something about her, almost as if he didn't know who she was. In fact, he made comments to Jennifer about their mother being an impostor, comments which his sister found disturbing, but not much more so than many of the other things he said at such times.

He had been sitting silently with Jennifer one evening while their mother was out shopping. He seemed angry, sullen, deeply disturbed; she could see his eyes moving around the room suspiciously and she could hear his breathing become more rapid; but as long as he was quiet, family members were loathe to disturb him. Suddenly, though, he looked directly at Jennifer and blurted out, "So, who do you think she really is?"

"What?"

"That woman. She looks like her ... but they can do that. And I know better."

"Who? What on Earth are you talking about, Donny?

Donald glared at her for a moment, his face darkening in anger, then abruptly stood up and marched to his bedroom, slamming the door behind him.

Jennifer, of course, found this conversation strange and disconcerting. Then again, most of what her brother did was strange and disconcerting and the family had become somewhat anesthetized to it; broken-hearted, but anesthetized. Soon thereafter, though, something caught everyone's attention.

Janet Lane didn't often go into her son's room anymore. The covered windows, the strange writing on the wall disturbed her, and she never knew what new and incomprehensible sign of psychosis she might find. One day, however, for whatever reason, she ventured in. What she saw made her gasp and run out of the room, unable to speak. Jennifer, seeing her mother run out, entered the room herself – albeit with considerable trepidation. With a sick feeling, she saw on the bed the newest sweater that her mother had made for Donald – cut to pieces.

The family knew that the time had come for Donald to be hospitalized, but didn't quite grasp the urgency. The next morning, no one was at home except Donald and his mother. She was in the kitchen, standing by the stove, cooking and talking on the phone. Donald quietly walked up behind her holding a heavy plumber's wrench. He raised it high in the air, paused for a moment, then brought it crashing down on his mother's head. She crumpled to the floor, dead.

In the days and weeks that followed, Donald Lane was interviewed by many people – detectives, prosecutors, mental health experts retained by the defense, mental health experts retained by the prosecution and, finally, by the judge who adjudicated the case and readily agreed to the finding of not guilty by reason of mental disease or defect. In his psychotic confusion, Mr. Lane's story varied in many ways from one telling to the next. It was, however, consistent in two important ways: he told everyone that he had committed the act, and he told everyone that he had not killed his mother. His mother was alive, he insisted; he had killed only an android impostor, planted by the F.B.I. One of the reasons that the authorities, including even the district attorney's office, readily accepted his sincere belief in this story, was the circumstances in which he was found by the police after the murder. Sitting on the floor next to his mother's lifeless body, he was busily at work, deeply absorbed in his task – opening his mother's skull and carefully probing her brain with an ice pick, trying to locate the electronic transmitter which, he had no doubt, he would find within her robotic interior.

Mr. Lane insisted throughout the legal proceedings that his mother was alive and still held to that belief when last I saw him at Kirby. Once an individual is hospitalized on an insanity finding, he is held until he is no longer deemed to be dangerously mentally ill, and a sine qua non of such a determination is an admission by the patient of what he has done. As it was to all insanity aquittees in Kirby, this was explained to Mr. Lane on multiple occasions. He understood full well that if he wished to be to be released from Kirby, he would have to acknowledge that he had killed his mother, but never did he waiver in his insistence that his mother was alive. He would never kill his mother; he had killed only an android.

* * *

In 1923, Joseph Capgras, a French psychiatrist, described a peculiar delusion held by one of his patients, the delusion that her husband and others had been replaced by impostor "doubles." Since that time, Capgras Syndrome, as it is known, has become recognized as a delusional pattern, found most often in patients with schizophrenia, although it has been known to occur in other conditions. There are other misidentification syndromes, one example of which is prosopagnosia, a disorder in which the afflicted person is unable to recognize faces, even of those near and dear. One of the essential differences between Capgras and most other misidentification syndromes, including prosopagnosia, is the fact that the individual afflicted with the latter understands that the difficulty is within himself, that he has a problem in perception and recognition. The Capgras sufferer, by contrast, has no such insight and adamantly insists that his highly implausible belief is accurate. He cannot entertain the notion that he has a problem such that a loved person no longer generates a sense of familiarity and somehow seems, in spite of his appearance, to be someone else. Rather, he insists that the person whom he knew is now, in actuality, someone else, that he has been replaced by an impostor.

Why and how would such a delusion arise? The answer, unfortunately, is not a simple one, and might seem strange to those unfamiliar with such ideas. Let it sink in. And bear in mind that, if the explanation seems strange, it is surely no more so than the delusion.

The capacity for emotional ambivalence – the ability to simultaneously feel conflicting feelings towards self or other, to appreciate that one can be good in some ways and bad in others – is a developmental achievement, one that is attained by people to a greater or lesser degree. It has been suggested, and indeed seems likely, that the newborn first organizes his experiences in terms of pleasure or displeasure, good or bad, largely related to feelings of hunger and satiation, and that thenceforth his world is cognitively and emotionally organized around those polarities. The infant thus comes to see people as either pleasure-giving or displeasure-giving and does not grasp that the same person can occasion both feelings. People can be good or bad, loving or hateful, one *or* the other, but not both – at least not at the same moment.

At a very early age, the child *remembers* his mother. He recognizes her, as is evidenced by his obvious reaction upon seeing her – the happy smile that is evoked by her appearance. But it might be asked, how is this experience of recognition brought about? How is it made possible? A seemingly unavoidable answer is that the child develops an internal or mental image of the mother, and when the mother appears, her appearance is quickly checked against that image for concordance and, if the concordance occurs, a smile bursts forth. If the appearance is at too much variance from the remembered image, a different reaction occurs.

This internal image – or "object representation," as it is known in certain schools of personality development – is of great emotional importance to the child. His memory of his mother, his expectation that she will appear to provide for him, take care of him, and love him, is essential to his sense of well-being, his ability to have a basic trust in his world. His real mother comforts him when she is present; his memory-mother comforts him when he is alone. Thus, this internal object – the mental representation of mother – must be a *good* object, a loving object, otherwise the child is in grave psychological danger. The child, however, sooner or later will feel some discomfort which the mother cannot relieve, or the mother will fail to appear when he cries in hunger, or she will directly frustrate him by refusing him something that he wants. This experience creates another kind of

40

memory, another kind of internal image, the image of the bad, hateful mother. This internal object brings bad feelings, strong displeasure, and the child, in his emotionally primitive way, hates this internal object, this bad mother, and feels hated by her. The object is destructive and dangerous. In order to preserve and protect the internal image of the good, loving mother, it must be segregated from, kept distinct from, the image of the hateful, destructive mother. This is of dire importance. Should the two images bleed into one another, the memory or image of the good mother will be spoiled or poisoned, so to speak, by the destructiveness of the bad, hateful mother. This fundamental and archaic mental/emotional complex, a product of the child's rudimentary grasp of the nature of things, fueled and rendered highly charged by the primitivity of his internal experience, the barbarity of his fantasy life, is the prototypical basis of an emotional difficulty with which we are all faced throughout life.

As the child ages, this underlying cognitive and emotional organizing schema or framework changes in how it is manifested. A toddler's world revolves around his parents, he clings to them and feels that they are the source of all goodness and comfort – except when one of those same parents frustrates him. The child will then become enraged, cry, turn red in the face and scream, "I hate you," or "I'm going to run away," or "I don't want you to be my mommy anymore," or otherwise declare his intention to terminate their relationship and strike out on his own. It does not take great powers of observation to recognize that the child, at that moment, has lost all good feeling toward the parent who has become, in his eye, an evil tyrant. Ten minutes later, when the child is smiling lovingly at his mother it is not because he has reconciled himself to the fact that "sometimes mom has to do things that displease me," it is because the feeling has passed and been wholly replaced by another; the good mother has been restored to him; the wicked witch has been transformed back into the loving angel.

The human tendency to split the world into good and bad is readily observable in all forms of culture. The fairy tales which we read to children have great emotional power largely because they are contests between good and evil. There is a central character who becomes threatened by an evil villain and is ultimately rescued by a brave hero. The tendency, however, persists long past childhood, which is readily apparent in any consideration of culture, high, low or in between. Drama and literature, from comic books and cartoons to classic fiction, deal with issues of good versus evil. In more mature forms of culture, however, there is a greater appreciation of the reality that all individuals and groups embody mixtures and blends of traits – noble and base, generous and miserly, loving and hateful, courageous and craven, or any other polarity of characteristics that can be seen as more or less admirable. Superman versus Lex Luthor is not far removed from the brave prince versus the ugly troll, but the complex character of more serious fiction who struggles with conflicting tendencies within himself, showing that he is in some ways "good" and in some ways "evil," surely is much more so. The adult who fancies himself too sophisticated, and cannot allow himself to enjoy the satisfaction of seeing good conquer evil is shortchanging himself, often due to one or another kind of emotional inhibition. But an adult who cannot be open to considering more complex varieties of tension and conflict and to experiencing a broader range of more subtle emotions is, at least to some degree, developmentally stunted.

In everyday experience, we have the same tendency to organize the world into good and bad. This can be seen in the way we view the many sets of opposing groups, ideas and forces that we encounter. There is always a tendency to see the groups to which one has allegiance as being the "good" side, and to demonize the other. Impassioned Republicans and Democrats, for example, have a tendency to vilify each other – each seeing the other not merely as holding a differing political philosophy, but as being in some way malevolent and ignominious. Even in the arena of spectator sports, where outcomes have little practical effect for most, fans tend to feel a hatred for their heroes' rivals, turning them from competitors into villains.

The same tendency also applies to our personal lives. Less emotionally mature individuals – of whatever age – have less capacity to appreciate the complex blending of personality traits in themselves and others, and continue to see the world in stark contrasts of good and bad. The fact that age in no way ensures advancement beyond this level of emotional development is clearly demonstrated by a nonagenarian patient in my private practice who remains stuck fast in the land of characterological purity. She herself is surely "a good person," as she reminds me in every session, and virtually any mention of an individual in her world, be it close relative or almost total stranger, is concluded by her decree about the category to which she has assigned that person. A supermarket check-out girl who is friendly toward her or who gives her extra coupons will be accorded the status of "a good person"; while the man at the deli counter who failed to meet her standard of politeness or who gave her insufficiently-lean roast beef is "no good... a rotten one." This woman splits the world into the good people and the bad people, and she tries mightily to maintain this view of life. On one occasion, however, her son, who is most definitely in the "good" camp, somehow tired of his mother's remarkably self-absorbed behavior and became enraged at her. Never have I seen this woman as upset as she was in the session following this incident. With horror, she told me how her son had "turned into a monster... I didn't know who he was," and she repeatedly spoke of his being "a different person," saying, "that was not my son." As time passed, she would occasionally refer to this incident, and was always sure to say, "I hope he never comes back... that monster!" Although she most certainly understood that the "monster" was actually her son, and would have said so if asked, on an emotional level, she did not experience it in that way. She was affecting what might be called a temporal split; that is, she was dividing her son into two: the "good son," who he usually was, and the "monster," that he was for a brief moment. There was no need to ask her if she ever wondered whether the "good" son actually held feelings of animosity towards her that he generally kept under wraps; she could consider no such possibility. Furthermore, the question would have placed a great strain on our relationship; she would have been deeply offended by the question, and would have asked me if I was saying that her son was "really" a monster. In fact, she might well have decided that I had temporarily "turned into" a monster, or even that she was discovering that I had actually been a monster-in-disguise all along.

One might well ask, why would the notion – or even the question – of her son's harboring the slightest ill feeling toward her in his "good" state be so intolerable to her? The answer lies in the fact that she has, at least in some important ways, never outgrown the archaic state of mind that pertains in the infant who must segregate his "good" and "bad" images of his mother. In order to love and feel loved by the good mother, the good mother must be kept pure of the badness of the bad mother. In this primitive manner of thinking and feeling, the badness of the bad mother would destroy or spoil the goodness of the good mother, and the infant would no longer feel able to love or be loved by his mother. For my elderly patient, to realize that her son, somewhere inside, held antagonistic feelings toward her, would be to become unable to love him and unable to feel that he could love her. He must be pure.

This – for the reader who has had the patience to remain with me – brings us back to Mr. Lane.

* * *

Throughout his life, Mr. Lane had had trouble tolerating any displeasing behavior on his mother's part without turning against her. He expected her to be giving and loving at all times, in all ways, and in all things, and he experienced a strong emotional reaction when disappointed. It is not that he came to a rationally-based decision that a particular behavior on his mother's part was unacceptable and that he should, therefore, demonstrate his disapproval. Or, if he did have such a thought process, it was a mere rationalization, a reaction to, rather than a cause of, his much more immediate and visceral emotional reaction: She is bad.

This was the pattern throughout his life. Had he not become afflicted with schizophrenia, he would quite probably have continued to have a somewhat tempestuous relationship with his mother, with periods of loving closeness alternating with periods of angry estrangement. But, as happens in schizophrenia, an ordinary emotional problem assumes outsized proportions and bizarre manifestations. As discussed above, a feeling or thought is often transformed into a delusion or a hallucination, and it is generally those feelings or thoughts that are troubling, with which the schizophrenic individual is preoccupied, that are so transformed. Another Kirby resident, for example, was troubled by the feeling that he could not possess his mother for himself. This feeling was transformed into his delusion that his mother had become a prostitute. Mr. Lane's delusion came about in a similar way. His feeling about his mother, when she became bad mother or "not my good mother," was concretized – transformed into the delusion that she was actually someone else, an impostor, an evil pretender, a malevolent deceiver.

Would Mr. Lane have killed his mother had he not been psychotic? This is unknowable. As we have seen, his anger and his violence escalated over a period of pre-psychotic years, and he did, at least once, threaten his sister with a knife. However, complicating the question is the fact that Mr. Lane might well have been suffering from a more covert form of psychosis long before his arrival at college. Nevertheless, he had never previously hurt anyone before murdering his mother. Destroying property and even threatening violence toward others are not the same as injuring someone. They are actions that may tend toward serious violence, but the fact that they tend toward it does not mean that they will reach it. There are individuals who, over many years, repeatedly or persistently destroy property or threaten others or even commit minor acts of violence, but never escalate to more seriously injurious behavior. There are forces within an individual that contribute to his destructive tendencies and behaviors, and forces that impose restraint. It often seems that each individual has his own limits – a line that, under ordinary circumstances, he cannot easily cross. Just where Mr. Lane's line would have been in the absence of schizophrenic delusion is unanswerable.

There are many other questions, interesting questions about Mr. Lane's story, which cannot be answered. Of how much influence on Mr. Lane's personality were his mother's repetitive bouts of depression and the virtual disappearances from his life that they brought? Neither of his sisters developed such debilitating problems, but then, neither of his sisters was as young as he during that period. It may be tempting to say that this here-again-gone-again pattern in his relationship with his mother might well have been "the" cause of his failure to outgrow the perception of others as all good or all bad; but life events and personality development rarely involve such clear-cut, one-to-one patterns of causation. Another unknowable is the question of whether, had he the opportunity, Mr. Lane would have gone further in his mayhem, killing his sisters whom, perhaps, he might also have seen as "androids." In this regard, it is interesting to note that, once she fully understood what had happened, Danielle remembered a particular incident with great horror. She recalled how her brother had, just a few days before the murder, insisted that she allow him to scrutinize her hands and arms, inspecting them in what seemed some bizarre medical examination. He looked closely at the skin, touching it, rubbing it and studying it. This frightened her slightly at the time, but she dismissed it as just one of her brother's many incomprehensible behaviors. It seemed far less innocuous – chilling, in fact – with the hindsight she now had.

What more Mr. Lane would have done, had he not been arrested, I cannot say. What can be said is that Capgras syndrome, a strange and unusual phenomenon – even within the world of psychosis – has led to murder in more cases than just Mr. Lane's, with motivations quite similar to his. It is surely a frightening thing to feel that a loved one has been replaced by a sinister impostor, and there must be an overwhelming urge to take action of one kind or another to bring back the person whose place has been usurped. I believe that that is, essentially, what Mr. Lane did. Long before he was schizophrenic, Mr. Lane could not reconcile, could not integrate, his love for his mother and his disappointment in her, his anger at her. Afraid that his hateful feelings toward his mother might destroy her or his good feelings for her, he split her into two individuals, the good, kind, loving mother with whom he shared happy moments, and the frustrating, displeasing, anger-inducing bad mother at whom he directed his rage. He protected the good mother by keeping her apart from the bad mother and his feelings toward her. For most of his life he had at least an intellectual understanding that the good mother and the bad were, of course, the same person. Unfortunately, his psychotic loss of reality and the power

and primitivity of his needs reified, corporealized this split and personified his "bad mother" feeling into the perception of an actual, concrete, alternate identity. He had to protect his feeling for his mother, protect the existence of his internal "good object," by creating a different "mother," a receptacle for all his hateful feelings. Then, her badness was simply too much, too pure, too dangerous, and she had to be killed. All in the service of protecting and preserving his loving and beloved mother, the mother who had held him, comforted him, smiled at him and made him beautiful garments.

All his life, Mr. Lane had been pushed and pulled by his chaotic feelings, never being able to achieve an emotional stability. But once he reached Kirby, there was a great consistency to Mr. Lane's behavior. In fact, a never-ending sameness seemed to settle upon him and his life, as it does upon many of Kirby's residents. He was consistent in his withdrawal from both patients and staff and in his reluctance to participate in any hospital activity. He was consistent in his statements – when he did speak – about his great value to the F.B.I., the imminence of his rescue and the annihilation of Kirby. His comments implied that he was consistent in, in fact, endlessly lost in, his fantasies of destruction – probably fending off the fears of the loss of the sense of self, of impending psychic annihilation, that are at the heart of the tragedy of schizophrenia, by turning them into fantasies of the obliteration of his enemies. Sameness and consistency. And my best guess is that there he sits, still today, lost in fantasies of cataclysmic destruction, while Jennifer and Danielle continue to mourn the loss of their mother – and of their beloved little brother. Mr. Lane, himself, might seem to have forgotten his family except for yet another of his consistencies: whenever the patients went out to the yard, Mr. Lane could be seen wearing a sweater, always the same sweater, a blue v-neck with a red and white argyle pattern on the front.

CHAPTER TWO
MANOLO GONZALEZ

Rape & Romance

IT WAS LOVE AT FIRST SIGHT, a beautiful romantic experience that both would treasure forever. How often does it happen, after all? A young man spies a lovely young woman in distress and comes to her aid. They instantly feel captivated with each other and share an afternoon of passion – spontaneous, thrilling, and perhaps the start of an intense and extraordinary love affair. From his point of view. From hers, brutal, vicious rape.

They found a secluded spot and sat, gazing into each other's eyes. Slowly, tenderly, they began kissing. The passion built and our young man haltingly began undressing his new-found sweetheart. Naked, they held each other, gently touched each other, kissed each other from head to toe and, finally, consummated their passion. From his point of view.

From hers, he threw her into the dark room, pushed her down on the couch, ripped her clothes from her and, despite her desperate struggling, her tears and her pleas, despite her begging him to take all the money and jewelry in her possession

51

and let her go, he viciously, forcefully and painfully penetrated her orally, anally and vaginally.

After the love-making, they lay in each others' arms, dreamily looking at each other, softly whispering of their love, and feeling profound gratitude for having found each other. Slowly, gradually, the sexual excitement was rekindled and they again made ecstatic, impassioned love. He said.

He shoved her back onto the couch when she tried to flee, held her – painfully – by the arm while he waited to become able to repeat his assault, and then did so with, if anything, even more sadistic force than before. She said.

Their passion spent, and knowing that they each had places to go, they tore themselves away from each other, dressed and prepared to leave the room. Before leaving, they embraced tenderly, then stood holding hands and gazing at each other before finally exchanging phone numbers, sharing one long, last kiss and parting. Maybe.

Or, maybe, as soon as he released her, she grabbed her clothes and bolted from the room, not even pausing to dress until gaining some distance from him. She ran home and called the police.

The fact that our young man was ultimately arrested and charged with several felonies, and that the police records described a terrified, hysterical and badly bruised young woman reporting a vicious assault would seem to indicate that it was the young woman's vision that held more reality. But not for Manolo Gonzalez. He was a lover, not a rapist, and he was shocked to see the police sketch of himself on the evening news – in spite of the fact that he had been a sexual predator for years, with virtually countless arrests for indecent exposure and sexual assault.

How does a rapist come to see himself as a lover – a tender, sweet, romantic admirer of women? Surely an interesting question, but not as interesting as a more fundamental one: what happened to a good-looking, intelligent, likeable young man, one with no trouble attracting young women, one with a talent that foretold a promising career? What would make such a young man cast aside all the personal and vocational success that his future could have held in favor of a life of sexual depravity, a life of desperation and degradation, a life of degeneracy and humiliation, a life that ultimately led to confinement in a hospital for the criminally insane? And, to return to the first question, how does that man, finding himself in such circumstances, continue to see himself in this absurdly sanitized manner – without even the "benefit" of psychosis to help him accomplish his remarkable feat of self-deception? Perhaps a look at the course of the evolution of Mr. Gonzalez from pleasantly ordinary young boy to Kirby inmate will yield at least a partial answer to these questions.

Born in New York City, Manolo Gonzalez was the third of four children, with a younger sister and two older brothers. His father, Hector, was a construction worker who sometimes worked and sometimes preferred watching TV and drinking beer. The family's financial circumstances certainly didn't improve when Hector abandoned the family, but Alicia, Manolo's mother, was a registered nurse and a hard worker, and the family maintained a lower-middle class lifestyle, living in the upper part of Manhattan.

At the time his father left, Manolo was five years old; his older brothers, Armando and Wilfredo, were fifteen and thirteen, respectively, and his younger sister, Sandra, was three. Single mothers do not have an easy time of it, but with the help of her older sons, Alicia Gonzalez rose to the challenges of supporting the family and running the household; order prevailed, and the family endured.

Hector Gonzalez had never been very attentive to any of his children and Manolo had little observable reaction to his absence. He seemed happy enough as a little boy and he and Sandra, as the two babies of the family, were watched over by their older brothers as well as by their mother. The older children functioned as quasi-parents to the younger ones, but Manolo and Sandra were playmates and very much enjoyed each other's company. Manolo loved Sandra, yes, but Sandra had more than just love for her big brother; she adored and revered him. She felt the sun rose and set on him; in her eyes, he could do no wrong. He was her favorite playmate, she wanted to be with him, she wanted attention from him, she thought he was just IT. As the older one, Manolo was not taken with his sister in quite the same way. He played with her and was certainly fond of her, but he was sometimes cruel to her, in the ways that an older sibling can be expected to be cruel. She wanted all she could get of him and he sometimes wanted to be left alone. He would tell her she was a pest and run away from her – and the tears would flow. She idolized Manny, her big brother.

In time, things changed.

The eight-year-old Sandy still looked up to the ten-year-old Manny, but was not quite as openly, unashamedly adoring.

And the ten-year-old Manny was a bit more patient with the eight-year-old Sandy, although becoming more interested in his male friends and often leaving Sandy feeling dejected; the basic pattern of toddlerhood persisted into later childhood, even if in adulterated form. And, if Sandra's idolization was in some ways dimmed in the years between three and eight, it was, in other ways, heightened.

Within the home, Manolo had been Sandra's companion and teacher. Two years of age makes a considerable difference in the abilities of toddlers and young children, and Manolo was able to show Sandra all manner of wonderful things. He could tie his shoes; he could make paper dolls and fly paper airplanes; he could whistle with his fingers; he could read comic books; he could even climb up on the kitchen counter and reach the cookie cabinet. What was not to admire?

Sandra's attachment knew no bounds and, at times, she suffered the consequences. When Manny started school and Sandra was still at home, the hours dragged by in his absence. An hour before he was due home, she would begin running to the door, checking the hallway to see if he was approaching and, oh, what joy, when he would at last be with her again. But a whole new dimension of hero worship was occasioned by Sandra's entrance into elementary school when she, at last, attained the status of "big girl" and went to school with Manny every day. First, there was the official recognition of his exalted status. She saw that while she was in first grade, Manolo was in the third. Third grade! But his shining armor did not attain its greatest luster until the incident that occurred several months after the start of school.

Tommy Langerman, a boy in Sandra's class, the biggest boy in the class, somehow decided that she would be a good bullying prospect, and he began teasing her, calling her names and pulling her braided hair. After he had persisted for a few days, she was sufficiently angered to try hitting him. This was not a successful counteroffensive. Tommy laughed at her. However, when, later that day, she told Manolo about what the boy had been doing, her hero became furious and after school taught the bully quite a lesson, a lesson that included a punch in the mouth and real blood! Tommy Langerman bothered Sandra no more, and Manolo was consecrated as her Champion, her Warrior Protector, her White Knight.

But a few years after this incident, two of Manny's other interests began to come between him and his sister. One pulled him away from her somewhat; but it was to be expected that he'd develop enjoyments that might make childhood games recede in importance, and the pursuit was innocent. If it pulled him away from Sandy, it did nothing to tarnish his image in her eyes; it may, in fact, have burnished it. The other was darker; it was sinister. It drove a wedge between the siblings and, in the process, did great damage to Manny's image, first blemishing and then blackening it. The angle of the wedge was not steep; it widened only gradually, over an extended period of time, but widen it did. A wedge is driven into an object, separating it into parts, pushing each ever further from the other, but wedges may vary in their ultimate width as well as in the smoothness of their surfaces and the friction and abrasion they cause as they do their work. This wedge not only reached a great width, but it was rough, it was coarse; it entered harshly, rudely and painfully; it did not separate neatly or cleanly or gently; it ruptured, it corrupted, it destroyed.

Manolo's more benign distraction was art. He loved to draw. He had taken delight in it from the time he was old enough to hold a crayon and enjoyed nothing more than coloring – sometimes in appropriate places, sometimes not. He was the unhappy recipient of several spankings, well-earned from his mother's point of view, for decorating the apartment walls with his handiwork. She always encouraged him to draw, but felt that he should be a bit more judicious in his choice of canvas. And by the time he was ten, Manolo not only knew where to draw, but how. He took in all he could from art classes at school, but that seemed to be the least of what he did to develop his skills; he was largely self-taught. He drew. He drew what he saw around the apartment. He drew what he saw in the street. He copied pictures that he found in books. His talent was obvious, and he invested prodigious amounts of time in nurturing it. Equally obvious was his need for praise.

Upon completing a drawing, he would immediately bring it to his mother, his sister and whoever else happened to be available for an appraisal of his work. He listened intently to their comments and, although he did seem to want to learn from the critique, the hurt and disappointment he felt at anything less than a rave review was unmistakable. His mother recognized this and tried to be as complimentary as she could, regardless of how she felt. Sandra, on the other hand, made less effort to be tactful. She generally thought that whatever he did – artwork or anything else – was wonderful; but if she should make a comment to the effect, for example, that she didn't like this drawing as much as some other one, he could not hide the deflation he felt. As she got older, Sandra would say, "Oh, Manny. Don't be so sensitive. It's great!" and her brother would brighten.

Family members were not the only ones to appreciate his talent. In school, he entered and won art contests and consistently garnered praise. As he grew from childhood into adolescence, his work advanced apace. His carefully executed work revealed a considerable artistic gift. And it not only became more mature and sophisticated in technique, but more focused in medium and content. He gained skill with a number of media and with varied subject matter; he was comfortable with pen and ink as well as watercolor and oils. But by the time he was fifteen or sixteen, his preferred medium was pencil, and it was with his pencil that he showed the most skill. He would try his hand at any number of subjects – portraits, landscapes, genre scenes, still lifes – but he had a clear favorite; he loved to draw buildings.

His interest may not have been surprising, given that he grew up in Manhattan, an island of building of all kinds, crowded together. He drew modern office buildings, stylish old apartment buildings, cathedrals, townhouses and tenements; he drew storefronts and street scenes and skyscrapers. And it was in this vein that his talent shone most clearly. He seemed to somehow be able, in a manner belying his young age, to capture architectural detail with both exactitude and beauty, whether in the geometric intricacies of fire escape-clad buildings of his neighborhood or the elegant and opulent ornamentation of a church. These subjects became his mainstay, and he would consistently return to his architectural renderings after each brief foray into other areas.

This was his love, this was his passion. Other subjects were simply that – subjects; his buildings were labors of love. Whatever their particular meaning to him, his profound emotional investment in these works was evidenced in more ways than one. Not only were his bedroom walls covered with his studies, neatly and thoughtfully arranged in groupings, with the most prominent positions being reserved for his best and most favored works, but the works themselves, the care with which they were done, the wealth and precision of detail, the painstakingly created geometrical symmetry, the overall beauty of form all bespoke an ardor for his work, an infatuation with the objects he was representing as well as of the act of recreating them.

It was his evident aim, an aim which he accomplished well, to create works that would overwhelmingly impress the viewer, works to be taken in with awe and admiration. Most of his architectural interpretations, although they varied in specific subject, medium and size, had in common the perspective from which they were drawn, that of being viewed from the ground, as if one were gazing up at a structure of enormous dimension and breathtaking majesty, a structure which filled the sky, captivating the viewer and making him acutely feel his own smallness as against the immensity of the edifice. The viewer was intended to feel awed and overpowered.

With time, although he maintained his love of fine art, Manolo's interests centered ever more on architecture and he gradually began to feel that he would like to see his work in three dimensions, leading him to determine that he would become an architect, a designer and builder of monumental works – bridges, skyscrapers and, as befit his Catholic upbringing, cathedrals. Most felt that he could not be more suited to the calling.

Manolo was a pleasant sort and all seemed well throughout childhood and into adolescence. He was a friendly and considerate boy, an amiable youngster who enjoyed his friends, did his schoolwork and was a good son to his mother. The family's homelife was generally serene, even if the boy's teasing of his younger sister did sometimes seem excessive. But any tendency to cruelty was counterbalanced by his wish to be liked. He appeared to want approval and acceptance much more than he wanted to be hurtful, and any concern felt by his mother, or resentment felt by his sister, was more than ameliorated by the kindness and attention that he would bestow upon Sandy, taking care of her, helping her with her homework and sometimes taking her out for ice cream sodas or other treats. All seemed willing to dismiss the occasional moments of mild cruelty, outweighed as they were by his obvious devotion and generosity.

But the family's untroubled existence, or what appeared to be such, was to be profoundly shattered as Manolo's wholesome childhood gave way to a deeply troubled adolescence. The change did not occur all at once and, even when his problems had progressed to a considerable degree, they were not apparent to most. The love of art and of drawing continued and he remained congenial and amiable; he had friends in school and, for a while, did his schoolwork conscientiously. Furthermore, he was outgoing, good-looking and athletic, and easily attracted the attention of girls. Teachers liked him, as well, especially his art teachers, who enthusiastically encouraged him. His life, as seen by others, may well have seemed ideal. He had work he loved and did well with peers, male and female. He had motherly love and brotherly love and the adoration of his sister. But, somehow, none of this was ever quite enough.

Manolo had other needs, needs which could be satisfied neither by his artwork nor by any amount of applause for it; not by the comradery of his friends nor the love of his family. It may be impossible to say when these needs first began to take hold; surely, they did not spring into existence fully formed, the embryonic stages probably dating back into very early childhood with origins that were unrecognizable as such, seeds that took root subtly and without Manolo's awareness. But once his problem made itself apparent, Manolo found an overly simplistic explanation for his difficulties, as people often do. It was not that the event he designated as responsible for his downfall was not significant or that it was not a turning point; it was both. But it is highly unlikely to have had the extraordinary causative power that Manolo ascribed to it.

He was about twelve years old. It was a summer night, a hot summer night. Deciding to combine a little fresh air with some drawing, Manolo took his sketch pad and went out on the fire escape. He walked up a couple of flights, seeking the best vantage point from which to view the street, but something distracted him. Glancing in a window, he saw a half-dressed young girl admiring herself in the mirror. He froze. Then he pulled away from the window, concealing himself as best he could while continuing to stare at the girl. He was transfixed; breathlessly transfixed. He forgot about his sketching and stood motionless, gazing at the girl until she covered herself and left the room. He then roused himself from his mesmerized state, returned to his apartment, closed himself in the bathroom and masturbated, reaching orgasm for the first time in his life. Manolo later said that it was this experience that "caused" him to become an insatiable voyeur. Highly unlikely, that; but there was no doubt that the incident had a profound effect upon him, apparently functioning as a catalyst, an activating agent, igniting something that had been forming, more covertly, within him. And this experience, this distraction from his evening's sketching, was a microcosm of his life to come, a life in which aberrant sexual needs, relentlessly demanding needs, oppressively tyrannical needs, distracted him – tore him – from what might have been a far more comfortable and satisfying life, a life of family and friends and work.

The flame ignited by the experience leaped into existence and burned brightly, but it was, at first, a small flame. Like a flame started in a corner of a fire-resistant building, it took hold, but was limited in scope and spread slowly. Manolo began to spend an occasional evening out on the fire escapes, prowling, hoping for a chance to relive his moment of intense excitement. But pickings were slim and the time spent on fire escapes in his neighborhood bore fruit only infrequently.

He sought other alternatives, opportunities that would be more reliable and, before long, he began positioning himself at the bottom of stairways in subways and other settings in order to get quick glimpses up girls' skirts. This approach yielded results greater in predictability but lesser in reward; it did not satisfy. Manolo would later say that it was this frustration in his fledgling attempts at voyeurism that turned his thoughts to his sister, but this, along with much, if not most, of what Manolo said about his sexual proclivities could not be taken at face value. He always had reasons; he always had stories. In any event, though, it was at this time that he began to see his sister as a source of satisfaction for his singular needs and, in so doing, began the slow but steady process of alienating her, weakening her affection, adulterating her admiration and debasing himself in her eyes – he began the process of driving in the wedge.

As children, they had shown the normal sexual curiosity and, several times, had "played doctor," examining each other's body. But this was a mutual endeavor, even if Manolo tended to be more enthusiastic about it than his sister. Now, it was different. The first time that Manolo walked in on Sandra while she was dressing, she fully accepted that it was an accident and thought it was just his shock that prevented him from immediately retreating. And, for a time, he was able to limit his attempts to catch her undressed and to create the impression – and perhaps believe himself – that it was accidental. Walking in on her in the bedroom or the bathroom, he would apologize and withdraw, but it began to seem to Sandra that he always lingered a few seconds more than necessary, staring wide-eyed before backing away. But just as he did not want to admit to himself that he was using his sister as an object of voyeuristic satisfaction, she was loathe to face the reality. After several incidents, however, she found it harder to accept that they were unintended despite Manolo's convincing attempts at feigning innocence.

Finally, there came a night when the truth of the situation made itself plain; it could no longer be evaded or disguised. And, in spite of the many dents that the armor of her White Knight was to sustain in the months and years to follow, a full decade after this incident Sandra recalled it as being perhaps the most painful to her. It was certainly not that she saw it as the most reprehensible of his many and varied deviant acts, but it was the moment at which she could no longer deny that her beloved Manny was not the paragon she'd believed him to be.

She was about twelve or thirteen years old at the time, old enough to feel intense self-consciousness, along with her anger and revulsion when she awoke to find Manolo standing over her as she lay in her bed. He had pulled the covers off her and, as she was lying there in only her underwear, he was staring down at her with his hand in his pants, rubbing himself. She instantly pulled the covers up not only over her body, but over her head, as if to try to make herself disappear, as if to remove herself altogether from the room and the awful situation. Through the blanket, she yelled at him in a sort of loud whisper, "Get out! Get out! Get out!" She was outraged and her idolization of her brother was insufficient to cloud her understanding of what was happening; but, as upset as she was, she could not bring herself – at the moment – to call her mother's attention to the situation.

The next morning, Manolo approached her. Looking at her, then looking away, then looking at her, hoping that she would say something to show that she wasn't angry, asking with his eyes, he finally said, "You know, Sandy, what happened last night... you got so upset... but I didn't really know what I was doing... I think I was half asleep... maybe I was sleep-walking... and I just saw you lying there... when you woke up I realized what was going on...."

"You didn't just see me lying there! You took the covers off me! How could you do that? Ugh! I can't believe you did that!"

64

Manny persisted. And by the time the conversation ended, she had convinced herself – sort of – that he really hadn't been fully awake and that maybe – maybe – she had thrown the covers off herself in her sleep. Could she be sure? Maybe she should believe him? ... But later in the day, away from Manny and the influence of his reassurances and protestations, to which she was all too susceptible, she realized – at least for the moment – that this was a fully intentional attempt by her brother to arouse himself using her as stimulus.

Childhood idealizations do not die easily; the death is often slow and painful. The emotional storms of the teenage years attest to the difficulty that adolescents have in relinquishing their childhood perceptions of their parents as perfect and omnipotent. And Sandra's admiration for her big brother did not die easily. Her anger would surge every time she learned of some act he'd committed that she felt was revolting, especially on the relatively few occasions when she was the victim, but she'd try to find ways of excusing or minimizing his culpability and, with his ardent cooperation in the attempt, she'd try to convince herself that he "wouldn't do it again."

But he always did "do it again" ... in some fashion. He did learn to curb himself in some ways, to be a bit more discriminating in his choice of venues to use for the satisfaction of his penchant for voyeurism. He found Sandra's anger and her lingering resentment unpleasant, leading him to resolve to avoid using her as an object of sexual gratification or, at least, to avoid allowing her to catch him at it. Other consequences of his behavior led him to a resolution to further restrict himself.

At some point it occurred to him that the girls' locker room in school was the motherlode of voyeuristic delight, a treasure trove he could not forego. On the first of the two occasions in which he was caught peering into this fount of flesh, his behavior was dismissed as boyish mischief and there were no consequences. On the second occasion, caught by an angry gym teacher, his transgression was taken more seriously and some minor consequences were imposed. Regardless of the relative insignificance of the consequences themselves, the incident made something click for Manolo. He did not want to be hated or held in contempt; he wanted to be liked and admired by those he knew. So he resolved at that time to be more discreet about his illicit activities; he would shield himself from the disdain of those in his daily life. He would refrain from any untoward behaviors in school and, at home, would never again involve his sister unless he felt that his behavior could be dismissed as accidental – a decision that would prove taxing, but would nevertheless spare him from certain consequences of his behavior.

Other changes were to follow.

Manolo's earliest experimentation with deviant sexual practices was, as we have seen, devoted to voyeurism. And I have revealed that the trail ends with his incarceration in Kirby after being charged with a forcible rape. But there were many years in between, and Manolo's progression from innocently happening upon an undressed girl while out on his fire escape to being arrested for a savage rape was gradual and proceeded step-wise through a number of phases, encompassing a variety of sexual aberrations. And, as his criminality escalated, it was accompanied, seemingly inch by inch, measure for measure, by his escalating capacity for self-deception, his ability to distort and disguise within his own mind not only the motivations for his actions but their very nature, as well.

In all, the voyeurism that began that fateful day on the fire escape caused only relatively minor problems; the exhibitionism which supplanted it had far greater social and legal consequences. Actually, the purely voyeuristic phase did not long endure. Soon after it began, he began to feel that he would like to have the power to enthrall women, much as he had found himself enthralled by them. He was so greatly excited by the sight of naked girls, why should they not have a similar reaction to him? Would it not be just as exciting – maybe even more so – to expose himself to young girls? At first, though, he was hesitant and, unsurprisingly, his sister seemed the most available female. Where, outside of his home, might he "accidentally" be seen undressed? So he took advantage of what his situation had to offer. On a few occasions, he "forgot" to lock the door to the bathroom and would stand there naked waiting for Sandra to walk in. He had success on a couple of occasions, but it took a great deal of patience. Furthermore, after just a few such incidents, Sandra began knocking before entering the bathroom even if the door wasn't fully closed. And his resolution that Sandra see any such incidents as accidental was unsuccessful; after the bedroom incident, Sandra no longer accepted his protestations of innocence.

Nevertheless, the urge to see had now been eclipsed by the urge to show and Manolo's urges always seemed to win out in the end. So, hesitatingly at first, and with abandon later, he gave license to that urge. The first time he sought to satisfy the urge with someone other than his sister occurred when he was about fourteen years old. In the early evening, he walked to a park near his home, not quite knowing exactly what he would do. After wandering aimlessly for a while, he saw two young girls sitting side by side on the ground, and knew what to do "without thinking," as he later explained. As he approached them from behind, he unzipped his fly and, stimulated by the thought of what he was about to do, he was fully aroused by the time he quickly walked in front of them. The girls, roughly of his own age, stared for a second, then screamed, leapt up and ran. Manolo quickly closed his pants and walked rapidly in the other direction, his heart pounding with an excitement he had never known before. He went home and masturbated, feeling not only highly aroused but, somehow, triumphantly victorious, a feeling which he did not understand, but which he found intoxicating.

If there had been before that evening any possibility of turning away from his aberrant urges and satisfying himself with his artwork, the praise it brought him, and the ordinary pleasures of an adolescent boy, it faded away into oblivion along with the last moments of sunlight on that spring evening. The events that followed were then as if ordained, the personal darkness descending upon him as inevitably as nightfall. The thrill of it all, as he later explained, was more than he could resist. There was the thrill of "the chase," as he came to think of it, of seeking and spotting and closing in on an unsuspecting girl. There was the thrill of public nakedness, of his genitalia being uncovered in public, even if no one was looking. But the ultimate thrill came when he suddenly presented himself in front of his prey, watching her attention be drawn to his erection, seeing her shock and knowing that she would, if only for the briefest instant, be transfixed – before she could turn her back, run, scream or otherwise put an end to her moment of capture. Nothing could compare to it. Not the pleasure of having an attractive schoolmate show interest in him, not the approval and applause that his artwork won for him, not the warmth and comfort of home, family and friends. Nothing. He had discovered an experience that was for him a jolt of ecstacy, a rush of intense pleasure and excitement, a flood of adrenaline. It was as addictive as any narcotic and the young Mr. Gonzalez would not be denied his dose.

The analogy to drugs, in fact, holds in several ways. The "experimenting" gradually gives way to more regular use, but the user does not recognize the fact that the drug is insinuating itself into his psyche, gaining ever greater control of his emotions and robbing him of the clarity of thought and the perspective on himself and his life that previously guided him. So it was with Mr. Gonzalez. As emotionally powerful as was his first foray into exhibitionism, and as inevitable as it was, in retrospect, that he would grow ever more dependent on the experience, he didn't, or couldn't, or wouldn't acknowledge, at first, that he was hooked. He thought of it as merely something that he did for some "extra fun" on an occasional basis, a sort of teenage mischievousness. But it was a "mischievousness" that grew in importance to him and that usurped his life inexorably and unrelentingly. At first occasional, it eventually became a regular part of his weekend activity. Then, before long, he could not endure the five weekdays without exposing himself and he would succumb to the urge once or twice during the week. Within two years of his first exhibitionistic experience, it had become a daily practice and he could no longer deny to himself its hold on him and its centrality in his life.

I do not mean to say that he had given up interest in other areas of his life, only that their importance to him could not surpass – or even equal – that of exhibitionism. But he maintained his involvement in more ordinary pursuits. Although a mediocre student who showed little interest in subjects other than art, he continued attending school and did enough work to progress from grade to grade. His drawing remained of great importance to him. He enjoyed art class as well as mechanical drawing, and his work continued to impress. As always, he focused on monumental structures, usually viewed from a vantage point which made them appear all the more overwhelming, and, as always, he sought out and enjoyed the praise that he received from both teachers and students. His mother, if no one else, noticed that he seemed to drink in the approval as if plagued by an insatiable thirst.

He spent time with friends and was, in fact, fairly popular. Furthermore, he was a good-looking young man and had no trouble attracting girls. He also spent time with his mother and siblings and created the appearance – if one did not look too closely – of a normal, well-adjusted high school student. And he tried to think of himself in that light. During and immediately after school, he would attempt to remove from his mind his exhibitionist urges and thoughts of his nightly wanderings, and for a time he was able to do so, thus succeeding in leading a double life. By day, a popular high school student, he spent his nights wandering through the city, at first exploring and discovering, then haunting those areas which offered the greatest opportunity to indulge his passion. He would leave home in the evening, find suitable targets, manage to place himself directly in front of them and expose himself, masturbating as he did so. This was his practice in all seasons of the year. In warm weather, he would wear shorts or sweat pants that could quickly and easily be pulled down; in winter, he wore coats that, in classic "flasher" fashion, he could quickly open to expose himself. The next morning, he would return to being a high school student, interested in school, friends and drawing. But a sensitive balance scale comparing the relative weight of his emotional investment in each of his two lives would have shown a slow but steady and unstoppable progression in favor of his nightly thrills. He came to recognize that he was in the grip of urges that he could not – and did not – control.

So a point came at which Manolo could no longer deny the compulsivity of his exhibitionism; he knew that he could not stop and he could not dismiss it as a passing interest. But if he could not deny the reality of his nightly wanderings or the necessity of indulging his urges, he could disguise and obscure his motivations, and find ways to cloak sordid and antisocial actions in fanciful and romantic garb. And his self-deception became as much a part of his way of life as his exhibitionism; they formed a partnership, as it were, allowing him to give license to his urges while maintaining a self-image with which he could be comfortable. After all, his actions were his actions, but certainly their motivations and emotional meanings were subject to interpretation.

He came to believe that he was a great lover of bodily beauty – his own and that of females. He would favor attractive girls with a display of his own sex organs for them to admire and in the hope that they would reciprocate. By so displaying himself, he would attempt to seduce them into returning the favor, and their mutual admiration and arousal would culminate in enjoying watching each other masturbate. He managed, in this way, to purify his motivations, washing away their antisocial nature and replacing it with a bizarre sense of romanticism. This idea he apparently gave serious credence, a credence which somehow withstood endlessly repeated disconfirmation. Girl after girl would respond not with amorous appreciation, but with shock, anger, fear, disgust, irritation or hostility, but he was undeterred in his behavior and undaunted in his self-deceit – even after his "romantic" overtures had led to arrests – numerous arrests, costly arrests, humiliating arrests.

And these arrests cost Manolo something beyond the value of coin; they cost him the respect of his family. Until his first arrest, his mother knew almost nothing of his sexual adventures. She had been informed by the school of the locker room incidents, but after her initial embarrassment in the meeting with school personnel and her anger at Manolo in the days that followed, she seemed to put the incident out of her mind. Armando and Wilfredo were in total ignorance of their younger brother's proclivities. They had long since moved out of the family home and, just as Sandra had decided against informing her mother about Manolo's attempts at brotherly voyeurism in order to spare Manolo the embarrassment, his mother had foreborn telling her older sons about the locker room incident. With the arrest, if the pun can be excused, the problem was exposed; such sensitivity and delicacy of feeling were now neither necessary nor possible. Manolo's perversity presented itself to his family as blatantly and inescapably as Manolo had presented himself to his victim.

Alicia's son, Armando and Wilfredo's younger brother, Sandra's older brother and erstwhile hero, had been caught by the police after prowling Central Park, stealthily approaching a fourteen year-old girl, exposing himself and masturbating within inches of her face. Furthermore, he was deprived of even the opportunity of claiming that this was a one-time incident, the product of a sudden, uncharacteristic and inexplicable urge; having now been apprehended, Manolo was identified by several other girls and young women who had, in recent days, reported similar incidents to the police.

The incident was of such significance to Sandra that, years later, as she sat in my office in Kirby, she recalled her reaction in a way that gave me the feeling that it might as well have happened that morning. Even though by now she knew that her brother had committed violent rape, the memory of how she felt after his first arrest for indecent exposure was as keen as ever. She said that each time she thought of it, it was like a knife slashing through her brain, and she spoke of it as one would of a fresh, exquisitely painful injury. It seemed that each of the awful words that needed to be said – arrest, exhibitionism, victim, masturbating – had to fight its way out of her mouth, fight its way through the resistance not only to say, but to acknowledge to herself, the facts involved. And as our conversation proceeded, Sandra clearly showed that, indeed, it had been and still was a terrible struggle for her to face the tragic facts.

73

At this time, Sandra was studying to become a physician's assistant. She was a bright and articulate young woman but nevertheless had great difficulty finding the words to express her sadness, her disappointment, her shame. She seemed to feel a need to put these feelings into words, just as she needed to talk about her other feelings about her brother. She wanted to say that there was more to him than what the records showed, that he had been something better, that he had been a kind, thoughtful and creative youngster, that he was more than just a sexual predator.

She offered many memories of the early days, memories that made her happy and memories that made her sad and some memories that pulled her from one emotion to the other. She told me, for example, about the incident that occurred when she was in first grade when Manny, her brave defender, had taught Tommy, the class bully, a lesson, taught him that anyone who bothered Sandra would end up with a fat lip and would learn that to bother her meant to face the wrath of her protector, her big brother. As she began the tale, she couldn't help but laugh, laugh at herself and how seriously she took the whole incident as a little girl; as she concluded, she couldn't help but cry, cry about her brother and how he had fallen.

She told me with poignancy and obvious pain about her struggle over the years to come to grips with the reality of her brother's "problem... his... his sick... perversions." She wondered, in retrospect, how she had managed for so long to exonerate him in her mind of all guilt despite his repeated arrests for indecent exposure and other offenses. Each time, she would feel angry, disappointed and disillusioned and would have trouble looking her brother in the face. But within days, the feeling would somehow recede. She shook her head slowly and laughed ruefully in recalling how, within a few weeks of an arrest, she would feel surprised and shocked when something reminded her of the incident. At times, she said, she doubted her own knowledge and felt that she might see that the awful event hadn't really happened at all if she could just shake herself and make it go away, like throwing off the lingering remnants of a bad dream. But it wasn't a dream. It was never a dream. It was always the excruciating and all too real fact that her brother had committed another shameful, degraded and degrading act.

"I don't know," she said, "I just couldn't face it. I loved him. I admired him. It just was just so hard to let it be real. It was impossible. It couldn't be. And I don't really understand... each time something would happen, it wouldn't just change him in my mind, it changed me. It's like I would become not the sister of a smart, talented, strong and charming big brother, but the sister of a... a... a CREEP! And it changed *me* into something different, not just him... It wasn't just that I couldn't look him in the face... I couldn't look at myself in the mirror!"

"And, you know what? I think my mother really was the same. It was almost like there was some sort of conspiracy in the house. Manny always tried to act like nothing had happened, like he still expected us to see him in the same way. And we just did. It's not that he made us... we just wanted to. But I remember one time, I must have been about sixteen years old, when my mom and I were sitting in the kitchen talking. By this time Manny had been arrested several times - for flashing... Oh, God!... for groping girls... in the subways - and the pattern was pretty clear. It was hard to think that it could end in any way but something like this... like being in a jail or in this... hospital. Nothing was working, not the mandated treatment programs, nothing. He would make promises, but... But, anyway, we were talking, I was talking about my future. So I was saying something about someday when I'm a doctor or a physician's assistant and Manny's an architect. Then I caught my mom's eye and we both immediately looked away. She got up and started busying herself at the stove and I walked out of the room. It was really something, now that I think of it... a moment when reality crashed in on us and we had to find some way to deflect it. Maybe there's something wrong with us, too, not just Manny. Or maybe some things are just too hard to face.

"I don't know. You know, I was really making it much harder on myself. After each incident, Manny would act like nothing happened or, even worse, he would try to tell me that he's just a guy who really likes girls, who feels very attracted to them and wants them to be attracted to him. I really couldn't listen to him say that, and I would say, 'Oh, Manny! Please stop it! Just don't talk about it! Please"! And then I would go about forgetting about it, pretending it hadn't happened. But then, the next time something did happen, I would get angry at myself for being disappointed again - like an idiot. I would vow that I wouldn't expect anything more from him. I'd tell myself that this is what he's like and I just have to get used to it. I would try to think of ways to not let myself start pretending that it wasn't going to happen again. I had some pretty crazy ideas, like making copies of the court papers and hanging them on my wall, or just making a big sign that said, 'Manny is a flasher and a groper.'

But I couldn't do it. I couldn't do it to him and I couldn't do it to me. I felt like there was no way out, no way for me to drive it into my mind once and for all. I guess it was just too painful. And sometimes I'd even start thinking about what if he did something worse... like what he ended up doing... and I would feel like I was driving myself crazy. I would start thinking... and I would feel that if he ever did... it... RAPE someone... that it would be my fault... somehow. Then I just couldn't take it and I'd start pushing it out of my mind and, before you knew it, it all started to seem unreal to me. Maybe it's me, or maybe it's just the way the mind works. I really don't know. When I think about Manny, I just don't know anything."

Shaking her head slowly from side to side and staring into the distance, she asked aloud, but more to herself than to me, how it could have happened, "How could Manny, my wonderful big brother... how could it... how could he... how did he go from being Manny to... " and, as the tears came and her body slumped, she whispered, "to someone I'm visiting in a hospital for the criminally insane?"

* * *

The sexual paraphilias, what used to be known as perversions, are relatively few in number and among the least understood of psychiatric disorders. They include exhibitionism, voyeurism, fetishism, frotteurism, pedophilia, sexual masochism and sexual sadism. The reader most probably has at least a passing familiarity with these terms with the possible exception of frotteurism, which refers to touching and rubbing against nonconsenting persons, most typically perpetrated in crowded places – busy sidewalks, subways or buses – places in which the individual increases his chances of avoiding arrest. All are characterized by intense, repetitive urges to engage in the particular behavior.

But this is merely descriptive. How are these urges explained? What underlies them? If they are conglomerates of more elemental urges, what are those component parts? We all have sexual urges, but what drives an individual to seek sexual satisfaction in such aberrant and in some cases antisocial and self-defeating ways?

In trying to understand Mr. Gonzalez's motivations, the first question to be asked is, what, essentially, did he *do?* Obviously, he exposed his genitals to women and that is certainly an important part of what he did. However, equally essential was the act of imposing himself on these women without their consent. He allowed the women he targeted no choice in the matter, in effect capturing them, or at least their attention, for a brief moment. I believe that this aspect of the behavior was as fundamental, perhaps more so, than the act of displaying his genitals in itself, and that his motivations cannot be fully understood without its consideration. To the extent that he could lay aside his claim to be trying to court women, Mr. Gonzalez insisted that he exhibited himself for sexual gratification. And there would seem to be little reason to doubt this. However, for Mr. Gonzalez, sexual urges are fused with others – including the need to take command of women, to appropriate them as objects for his own use, and to hurt – or at least discomfort – them.

Mr. Gonzalez repeatedly said that, in exposing himself, he hoped that his female observer would feel attracted to and excited by him. Some authors and clinicians have considered exhibitionism to be a contorted form of courtship and, in at least some sense, there seems little doubt that it is. While exhibitionists generally recognize and acknowledge that their actions will evoke irritation, anger or disgust from most women, there does seem to be an underlying wish to excite and attract – even if in the more rational part of the mind the exhibitionist knows better. In this regard, Mr. Gonzalez differs from other exhibitionists only in the degree to which he accepts and clings to his wishful thinking, using it to purify his self-image. Although his ideas about the mutuality of the experience – that he and the girl would enjoy displaying themselves to each other – cannot be accepted at face value, there is no reason to believe that he was not seeking and realistically expecting *some* kind of reaction from her. He yearned to be stared at and admired, yes; but if the admiration was to be denied him, the forcible seizure of attention was not. Whether any of his victims actually ever felt admiration or arousal is a matter of conjecture, but what is a virtual certainty is that they *noticed* him, that he had an *impact* on them, that he attracted their attention in a forceful manner and evoked a powerful response from them, a *visceral* response, an *emotional* response, a decidedly non-casual response. Although they may have shown themselves to be disgusted or infuriated, in all probability, in the vast majority of cases, the initial, albeit brief, reaction was one of shock; their attention was commandeered, captured, wrested from their voluntary control. Perhaps a moment later the girl would turn and run or report him to the police, but for at least one brief moment, he had her full and complete attention.

I believe that it was this experience that held such dire importance for Mr. Gonzalez, that became an absolute imperative, that became as irresistible to him as any need can be to a human being. I believe that it was for this transitory, ever-so-brief experience that Mr. Gonzalez sacrificed all else in his life. This experience was, ultimately, much more than a sexual one. Although he was seeking sexual gratification, sex and sexual interest was also a tool, a device, a means of instrumentation for Mr. Gonzalez, a useful medium through which to exact from others that which was most essential to him: attention, acknowledgment, recognition and, crucially, a sense that he could take possession of these priceless commodities on his own terms, at his own whim.

That conclusion, however, is at best only a partial answer to the question of what drove Manolo Gonzalez's behavior. A fuller answer requires an attempt to understand what made that attention and recognition of such compelling importance to him, an attempt which necessitates a momentary departure from the subject of Mr. Gonzalez himself and a brief foray into the issue of human narcissism in general.

In recent decades, a line of research has developed which, through use of frame-by-frame video analysis of mother-infant interaction, attempts to elucidate the nature of this relationship in its earliest days. The research clearly and consistently demonstrates how remarkably attuned infants are to their mothers' facial expressions, how they closely and intensely monitor the movements of the mother's face and respond accordingly. The research reveals much about the specifics of how the infant responds to the mother, the ways in which the infant seems to attempt to regulate the interpersonal transactions – for example, breaking away from the mother's gaze if she locks onto his too intently or for too long, or seeking the mother's gaze if she is insufficiently attentive. But my point, at the moment, is simply that this research confirms the fact that the human infant is intensely focused on social interaction within weeks of birth.

To me – as well as to these researchers and to virtually all psychoanalytically-oriented mental health professionals – it seems unarguable that it is in this context, in his earliest interpersonal relationships, in the first years of life, that the child develops the deepest layers of his sense of self and the most fundamental patterns of interpersonal attachment that will ultimately lead to his becoming the adult he becomes. In interacting with those around him, the child learns who and what he is, what it means to be him, what it means to be a human being, what his place is among others, how others see him and respond to him and how he will treat and respond to others. It is the sense of self that the child develops in the earliest years, in the pre-verbal years, that will form the core of his personality. This sense of self, all the more unalterable in later years due to its pre-verbal origins, will be to one degree or another adequate or lacking in solidity and stability, to one degree or another adequate or lacking in cohesion and integration based largely on the contingencies within his interpersonal world. The sense of wholeness and goodness – or the lack thereof – the overall emotional comfort as well as the capacity for close, warm and satisfying interpersonal relationships of the adult-to-be will be largely set – almost in stone – by the time the child enters elementary school.

Certainly, there can be modifications and refinements in later years; it is only the most fundamental characteristics that are determined in the earliest years. However, while the branches of a tree can grow in many different directions, the overall shape of the tree is determined by its trunk and the main branches, those that grow out of the trunk first and at the lowest levels. The further the branches are from the trunk, the less they affect the overall shape of the tree. Similarly, there are many different personality traits and adaptations to life that can develop out of a given underlying personality structure, but the general direction of the personality and the limits of the possible variations are determined by the earliest layers of personality just as the overall shape of the tree is determined most by its trunk and main branches. And, just as a malformation in the trunk of a tree will have a greater effect on its overall structure than will a malformation of an upper branch, it is the "malformations" in the deepest levels of personality that have the most deleterious effects on the overall personality structure.

A tree with a trunk that has been forced to bend, that has somehow been prevented from growing as straight and tall as it might, can compensate by developing higher branches that grow in an upward direction, somewhat compensating for the misshapen lower portion, but it can never be the fully upright, well balanced and well proportioned tree that it might have been. It is the lot of the human being with a weakness in his sense of self to forevermore strive to compensate for that weakness. It will be the fundamental existential problem with which he is faced.

This is certainly not to say that human beings fall into two camps, those with weaknesses or difficulties in the sense of self and those without. Humans are far too complex for any such simple categorizations. All people have narcissistic needs; all people must find ways to live with themselves and what they feel, all people must strive to find their place in the world of people, must find a way to satisfy their interpersonal needs, must find a manner of relating to the world around them – even if that way is to turn away from all others like the hermit in his mountain cave, or against all others like the chronically violent criminal or, for that matter, the lawful but hateful misanthrope. But it might be said, as a general statement, that the greater the weakness or difficulty or conflict within the individual's sense of self, the more likely that he will be driven to extreme, maladaptive, dysfunctional or antisocial methods of trying to overcome his existential problem.

If we now return to Mr. Gonzalez, keeping the above in mind, we can look at his exhibitionism in a new light. Rather than dismissing his behavior as "crazy" – which it well may be, in a manner of speaking – or as "perverse" – which, according to Webster, it certainly is – we can acknowledge both its craziness and its perversity, yet attempt to understand it in more human terms. Certainly there is a sexual aspect of Mr. Gonzalez' behavior and, as we will later see even more clearly, a sadistic aspect. But I maintain that the most fundamental, important and imperative aspect of his behavior is the need to be seen – the need to be acknowledged, recognized, attended to – and to feel that he has the ability to make this happen at his will. My sense is that it is by these means that Mr. Gonzalez assures himself, so to speak, of his own existence, solidifying – if for but one brief instant – his sense of self.

I know virtually nothing of Mr. Gonzalez's earliest years, and little enough of his adolescence and early adulthood. I was unable to get to know him well enough to have a sense of the impact of an absent father or a distracted and overwhelmed mother. Perhaps in response to these parental deficiencies he came to rely too much on a younger sister for that which only an adult could give. This is speculation; I have little knowledge of his formative environmental influences and even less about the contribution of his inborn, constitutional endowment. What I do know of him, however, is enough to show me that he has been involved in a lifelong struggle to make himself over in his own eyes, to see himself as something that he very much feels he is not. In fact, how he unconsciously sees himself can be inferred from his behavior and his self-deceptions; it is the inverse of his idealized self, as the shape of a bronze sculpture is the inverse of the reproduction mold which created it. Mr. Gonzalez wanted to impress, to win over, to arouse admiration, to be seen as powerful, lovable and exciting. My assumption is that his actual self-perception is that of someone who is small, unnoticed, unappreciated, unattractive, unappealing, uninteresting and virtually transparent. He is a more extreme and more antisocial version of the character celebrated in the song "Mr. Cellophane," from the musical "Chicago," a character whose anguished plaint is that "no one even knows I'm there." When he leaps out in front of a woman, his erection exposed and within inches of her face, Mr. Gonzalez is no longer made of cellophane; he has attained opacity – the look on the woman's face tells him that he is solid, he is seen.

That Mr. Gonzalez harbored such an ugly and enfeebled self-perception is borne out not only by his compulsive need to attract attention in this way, but by a very interesting fact, a fact which at first glance might seem puzzling. In the long-term relationships that he had with young women, he would never allow himself to be seen naked. How can this be explained? How is it that a man who evidently took such pleasure in displaying himself that he repeatedly exposed himself to the possibility of arrest would be unwilling to be seen undressed when he was able to do so with impunity and to his heart's content?

Perhaps this can best be answered by drawing parallels to other individuals. There are many people who are seemingly outgoing and bold in one situation, and uncomfortable and withdrawn in others. I have known, both as patients and as colleagues, individuals who are quite outspoken in business or professional meetings. They are eager to speak and eager to be heard, perhaps too much so, sometimes seeming to need the spotlight at all times. However, when their professional mask can no longer be employed, when they are in social situations, they shrink, sometimes feeling intense discomfort and self-consciousness if they should become the center of attention. People in show business are renowned for their problems in intimate social relationships, with a divorce rate that probably exceeds that of any other walk of life. Actors and other entertainers often say that they are most comfortable on stage, that is, when they are being admired from afar, when they are performing before an audience as actor, singer, dancer, comedian, etc. When they are offstage, when they no longer have the distance from the audience, when they are stripped of the protection and shelter afforded them by their role as performer, it is a different matter indeed. When they must be seen as human beings, as themselves, in personal relationships, they have all manner of difficulty. Nor is this syndrome limited to Hollywood. Politicians, for example, often feel a desperate need for the adulation of the crowds, but have great difficulty in more intimate circumstances. Perhaps the most famous example in the world of politics is Richard Nixon who drove himself relentlessly to be president, to be at the center of the world's stage, while known by his associates to be intensely and painfully shy.

A patient of mine exemplified this situation quite clearly. A strikingly good-looking middle-aged man, he craved attention. He was preoccupied with his wardrobe and spent hour after hour shopping for clothes and combing through catalogs, assembling beautiful outfits with as much loving care as was ever devoted to such interests by the vainest of women. He lived to be noticed, especially to be noticed by women and to be seen by them as attractive. He worked for a large corporation and loved nothing more than to feel the eyes of the women on him as he walked through the offices. However, until he gained some self-understanding in therapy, he was utterly frustrated and perplexed by the fact that he went to such lengths to attract attention from women but, when women showed interest in him and approached him for conversation – rather than admiring him from afar, as they often did – he would blush, sweat and feel such intense discomfort that he had to remove himself from the situation with great haste. At one transitional point in his therapy, he came to see himself as a brightly-polished but empty shell.

The performer or politician on stage, or my patient as he strode through his office, presents a persona to his audience and thrives on the admiration. Deprived of the cover of that persona, he is left with only himself and whatever problems he has in his sense of self. Mr. Gonzalez's stage act was his exhibitionism; when deprived of this persona and reduced to being something closer to his actual self, he could not tolerate being seen and hid his body from sight. Ironically enough, his exhibitionism could thus be seen as his cover, the mask he wore in presenting himself to the world for admiration. It served him well, in a sense, although at great cost.

* * *

To his dire misfortune, Mr. Gonzalez could not be satisfied with exhibitionism. It left him hungering, wanting, yearning. He had more pernicious needs, needs with yet greater costs – both to himself and to others. Although he sacrificed a great deal for it himself, his exhibitionism was of limited harm to others. Most victims reacted to it as an assault, but one of limited harm, and the law treated it accordingly. It is unlikely that one who restricted himself to such activity would find himself within the confines of Kirby, and it was not his exhibitionistic needs that earned Mr. Gonzalez his bed in the hospital. It was his need to possess and control women in a more physically direct manner, his need to overpower them, demean them and cause them pain that brought him to Kirby and to my acquaintance. Voyeurism and exhibitionism were the hors d'oeuvre which ultimately served only to whet his appetite for his main course: brutal rape.

There are certainly many paraphiliacs – exhibitionists, voyeurs or others – who never feel a need to progress beyond those offenses. Others, however, eventually lose the thrill that they had previously obtained from their actions and need to escalate. Mr. Gonzalez fell in the latter camp. He had apparently become addicted not simply to the action of exhibitionism in itself, but to the thrill that it provided, the excitement of momentarily controlling his victim, of imposing himself on her in his way. As the situation became routinized, it lost some of this thrill, and he had to escalate in order to experience the same ecstacy of power. So escalate he did.

The escalation of aggression and sadism took place gradually, as it so often does. For a period of time, he was content to force himself on women without physically hurting or controlling them beyond usurping their attention. Before long, however, the thrill began to pale and he needed more. His days were increasingly devoted to his attempts at sexual gratification, but exposing himself many times in a day and repeatedly masturbating left him dissatisfied and frustrated, and he knew that he would have to find new means of slaking his seemingly unquenchable thirst.

He had long felt that he would like to have physical contact with many of the women he came across during the course of a day. He didn't exactly *decide* to give in to this urge, but when he one day somehow "found" himself touching the buttocks of a girl on a crowded subway car, he enjoyed the experience and soon added it to his repertoire of furtive sexual satisfactions. He learned that if he chose a sufficiently crowded subway or bus and was sufficiently subtle and careful in his touching, he could carry out his activities with little risk of trouble. If a girl turned upon him with an angry expression, he could simply look innocent and pretend that the touching had been accidental.

So, onward and upward. He expanded his modus operandi and began to regularly engage in this limited frotteurism as a prelude to exposing himself and masturbating. But it was not long before he again felt the nagging frustration and knew that he would have to become bolder and more blatant; he would have to escalate from "accidental" brushing against girls to openly grabbing and groping them. And he resorted to his by now standard self-deceit and thought that he would simply be making advances towards women whom he found attractive; he would be more forthright about his ardor and perhaps some of them might respond positively. If not, he would simply be a rejected suitor – certainly not an abuser or a violator of women. Unsurprisingly, most women did not seem to find his advances to be romantically enticing, and he quickly met with hostile reactions and a few experiences of physical retaliation. But he was undeterred. He found this new thrill to be irresistible and, as it rapidly took on the characteristic compulsivity of his exhibitionism, he developed a technique which afforded him the maximum satisfaction.

He would dress in lightweight shorts or sweat pants, with no underwear, and seek out attractive women in the subway system – the subway system which he now knew quite well, having been frequenting it for both licit and illicit purposes for years. He would enter a subway car, seek out an appealing target and position himself next to her. Then, staring her in the face, he would reach up and grab her breast with one hand while reaching behind her with the other, grabbing her buttocks, and pulling her to him, enabling him to rub his body against hers.

He explained to me that he would try to choose a spot near the subway car door, and would wait until the train was approaching the station, so that "just in case" the woman wasn't receptive, he could make a quick getaway. He might repeat the routine a few times, or alternate it with exposing himself, but whichever his preferred activity of the evening, he would spend hours roaming the city, often frequenting familiar areas, those best suited to his purposes, seeking out attractive marks for his antisocial predilections, all the while telling himself that he was simply a great lover of feminine beauty, an ardent admirer of female face and form who, because he was born with a great abundance of romanticism and passion, could not limit himself to just one girl.

He did try.

Exhibitionists – "flashers" – are often thought of as – and often are – fearful, timid, overly shy men who are too frightened of women to be able to establish relationships. Not so our Mr. Gonzalez. As I have said, he was an outgoing and attractive young man who drew the interest of many young girls, basked in their attentions and, over the years, had several relatively enduring relationships.

These relationships were – or were intended to be – part of his "normal" life, the life which included attending school, playing sports, drawing, and spending time with friends and girlfriends. Whether his commonplace existence be thought of as a deceitful disguise, a superficial veneer or simply half of a life, Mr. Gonzalez maintained it for years. It was not easy for him, but he carried it on through high school and into his ultimately aborted attempt at college. He maintained it, and for ever more abbreviated periods of time, tried to limit himself to it. But he could not. He eventually realized, in fact, that he was not only unable to live within the constraints of his daylight world, but that his interest was forever tilting more towards his secret endeavors. Over time, and in spite of whatever efforts he might have made to stave off its inroads, the dark side of his life steadily encroached on its mundane rival. More, it was not only that ever greater amounts of his time and interest were invested in his nightly wanderings, but he became unable to keep his daytime world pure; he found that he was increasingly prodded and harassed by urges to expose himself in school, and that his relationships with his girlfriends were becoming contaminated by urges which he could not subdue.

There was one incident, when he was about seventeen, the details and exact nature of which are unclear, but which almost resulted in a charge of attempted rape, attempted "date rape," as it has become known. Mr. Gonzalez insisted that it was simply a misunderstanding, that he felt that the girl's resistance and protestations – her "No, no, no!" – were just an adolescent pretense of virtue, not intended to be taken seriously. Her story differed. The reader, having learned something of Mr. Gonzalez's interpretations of his own actions in other situations, cannot be accused of undue cynicism if he finds himself feeling doubtful of our young man's credibility in the matter, but the extent of his coercion is unclear; the girl acknowledged that when she screamed and forcefully and determinedly pushed Mr. Gonzalez away, he did not persist. She terminated their relationship

91

and later said that her parents urged her to press charges, but ultimately she demurred. Subsequent events render a verdict in this incident irrelevant to the issue of whether Mr. Gonzalez must be considered a rapist. But I am getting ahead of myself.

As is often the case with antisocial behaviors, as time passes, not only does the behavior escalate, but the pace of the escalation increases. Ever greater thrills, derived from ever more antisocial conduct become the guiding principle. So frotteurism did not long satisfy Mr. Gonzalez, and he sought greater excitement. He had always felt frustration that none of the girls he "tried to seduce," as he thought of it, responded in kind. Perhaps he should give them more of a chance; perhaps his hit-and-run style did not give women a fair chance to appreciate his charms. Yes, he thought, he would prolong the interaction and go further in his attempts to establish intimacy and promote a mutual appreciation. His first such attempt was on a warm evening in Central Park. He was not sure himself just what he would do, but he trusted his instincts – instincts which he had now been honing for several years. Even when he saw the young woman jogging alone and realized that she was a perfect prospect, he did not have a clearly formulated plan – but, as he expected, his intuitive flair for his avocation served him well.

Instead of jumping in front of her and exposing himself, he grabbed her from behind, dragged her from the jogging trail into the bushes and pulled her to the ground. When she was lying on her back, he straddled her, pinning her arms to the ground with his knees. He then pulled down his shorts and began to masturbate. As he later said, he didn't really know just how he managed the feat; the girl was trying to scream, he had to hold her arms down with his legs and cover her mouth with one hand while masturbating with the other. Apparently, the excitement – the greatest he had yet experienced – provided enough adrenaline to save the day, and he was able to subdue his victim while furiously stimulating himself. By this time he had a plan for the encounter's denouement, and he executed his newly-devised plan flawlessly, ejaculating on the girl's face. Incredibly – astoundingly – he later said, with apparent sincerity, that he felt great disappointment when the girl, released from his hold, screamed and cried as she ran away.

Disappointment notwithstanding, he knew, as he later said, that he had been "playing in the minor leagues" until that evening. The excitement, the exhilaration of the experience was like nothing he'd ever known, and he quickly lost interest in his "minor league" activities. Finally, he would no longer have to rely on memory and fantasy to reach orgasm. With his new-found method, he could climax while committing the act, rather than fleeing and delaying final satisfaction.

This was a new and intoxicating experience for Mr. Gonzalez. Certainly, he had had orgasms during sex with his girlfriends. He had enjoyed sex with them and found it satisfying – to a degree. But something was missing. He could not explain it to himself, but something was missing.

In Robert Louis Stevenson's wonderful and insightful classic, Dr. Jekyll and Mr. Hyde – a book which can be read in an hour and yet contains a great deal of wisdom about psychopathology – Dr. Jekyll creates and drinks a potion which transforms him from a serious, sober and staid physician into a depraved, sadistic and licentious miscreant. When restored to his former self, Jekyll is repulsed and appalled at the thought of his own actions as Hyde. But as he repeats his "experiment," he comes to find the experience liberating and exhilarating, and finds himself increasingly drawn to alter himself, to shed Jekyll's constricting decorum and propriety in favor of Hyde's dissipation and savage self-indulgence. The turning point, however, comes only when Jekyll, to his horror, finds that he has transformed into Hyde *without drinking the potion.* Hyde has proven irresistible, Jekyll is a devitalized and enfeebled also-ran.

Perhaps Mr. Gonzalez should have read Stephenson's cautionary tale about poor Dr. Jekyll's life, because something of this nature, although certainly in more prosaic form, occurred in his own.

For years, Mr. Gonzalez had successfully kept separate his two lives – the high school Dr. Jekyll and the Central Park Mr. Hyde. Although troubled by wayward urges during the day, he was able to resist, postponing his perverse behavior until night fell and he could drink his potion. He was able to maintain his innocent and inoffensive persona with the girls he dated, suppressing his baser desires and sequestering them to his nightly prowls.

But then, there came a time when he could not. In contrast to Jekyll, however, Mr. Gonzalez, characteristically, was unable to recognize the cold reality of his darker side, refusing to acknowledge what had been so horrifyingly plain to his girlfriend.

The young lady had been enjoying her relationship with Mr. Gonzalez, a relationship which had been sexually active for months. She appreciated his outgoing personality, enjoyed his sense of humor, and admired him for his drawing and his talk of becoming an architect. Their sex life was exciting, as well, and she was not troubled when he occasionally got a bit rough, dismissing it as a sign of his excitement and his appetite for her. She would later say that she sometimes was taken aback by a certain look in his eye during sex, but it evidently did not trouble her excessively. It was a different matter entirely, however, when, one evening, in the midst of their passion, her lover began to strangle her. She tried to pull his hands away, but he tightened his grip. She tried to push him off her, but could not. As she panicked, desperately gasping for breath, she saw him smiling, smiling with that look in his eye, a look of sadistic brutality. She had already started to feel herself passing out when he released her.

She never again allowed herself to be alone in Mr. Gonzalez's presence. He was offended by her reaction and unsurprisingly insisted that he was "only playing," and that he thought she "would like it." He was capable of Hyde's callous ferocity, but not Jekyll's painful honesty.

And so, over time, Mr. Gonzalez moved inexorably along his trajectory of escalating sexual aggression, shedding restraints, inhibitions and limits as he progressed. From voyeurism to exhibitionism, from frotteurism to sexual assault, an increasingly ruthless path culminating in brutal rape. The assault committed by Mr. Gonzalez, described at the outset of this chapter from the two vastly differing viewpoints of the participants, resulted in his arrest for rape and led to his incarceration at Kirby and my acquaintance with him. This was his first arrest for rape. Was it the first rape he committed? Mr. Gonzalez would say that he committed no prior rapes. But then, he would say that this incident was not a rape; it was a seduction, and he acknowledged a number of previous seductions.

How should such statements by him be understood? They were not delusions, at least not in the sense that others described in this book suffered them. Mr. Gonzalez usually held fast to this way of seeing himself and his actions, and his insistence was not simply for public consumption or for purposes of manipulation of his circumstances. In fact, he well understood that his release from Kirby – if ever such a thing were to occur – would require that he openly acknowledge that he had raped, and demonstrate that he had some understanding of his problem and a realistic determination to alter his behavior. At least during the time that I knew him, he never attempted to show that he had such an understanding. No, he would insist on his innocence, insist that he sought consensual relationships with women – that his exhibitionism was meant to arouse a woman's interest in him and that his rape was actually a seduction.

Mr. Gonzalez might almost have wished that he could be actually delusional, but he was not. He had a need to see himself and to portray himself to others in a certain light, but – fortunately or unfortunately for him – he actually knew better. If drawn into a serious conversation about his behavior, he would insist on his innocence. But if the matter were pursued and he eventually realized that he was convincing the listener only of how dishonest he was, that he was only earning contempt, he would relent. In response to a persistent interviewer, his denials might gradually wither and, over the course of the conversation, might follow a pattern such as, "I was seducing her ... I was trying to seduce her ... I wanted to seduce her ... I thought I was seducing her ... Okay, I wanted to think I was seducing her ... I wasn't ... I raped her." This admission, however, was made only

96

in response to feeling under some form of acute emotional siege, only in response to feeling that he was cornered and that the only way out – the only way he could gain a more favorable emotional response from his listener – was to acknowledge the fact of his brutality. Remarkably, if the topic were dropped and later revisited, his first response would be to again speak of himself as a lover, not a rapist, as if he had not made the admission ten minutes earlier. Unlike a delusional individual, he knew full well that he was deceiving himself. But the need to do so was nevertheless so great, the effort required to admit his guilt was of such proportions, that his denial reflexively reconstituted itself the moment the pressure was off – much as a stretched rubber band snaps instantly into shape when released.

The reader may wonder why Mr. Gonzalez was in Kirby, rather than in a prison. After all, he did understand the nature and illegality of his actions – technically making him ineligible for a finding of not guilty by reason of insanity. But technically ineligible or not, a plea agreement was reached and Mr. Gonzalez was deemed "insane" at the time of the offense and committed to Kirby where, to the best of my knowledge, he remains. He is among the many who may have outsmarted the system – outsmarted the system and outsmarted himself – and ended up spending far more time in Kirby than he would likely have spent in prison.

The details of how this plea agreement was reached may not warrant inclusion in our tale, but the same cannot be said of another issue, the question of how Mr. Gonzalez was caught. Within a day or two of the rape, a police sketch of Mr. Gonzalez was shown on television. The sketch was far from perfectly accurate; it might, in fact, be described as misleading. Furthermore, many such sketches appear on the TV screens and newspaper pages of New York City and Mr. Gonzalez's appearance was in no way unusual. Yet it was only two days after the sketch appeared that a team of detectives and uniformed policemen arrived at the Gonzalez residence and arrested Manolo. The authorities did inform him that they had received "a report" that he was the man depicted in the sketch, but they divulged nothing further. I cannot say that Manolo was plagued by curiosity about the identity of the informer, but it did cross his mind with some regularity. During our conversations, usually after a period of trying to act as though he felt he'd done nothing wrong in his "encounter," as he called it, he'd puzzle about who could have been able to identify him. My impression, consistently, was that he wanted to know not so that he might some day exact revenge upon whoever it might be, but because he felt hurt, injured, saddened that someone who knew him personally would want to turn him in, that a personal acquaintance could possibly feel that he should be arrested.

To my knowledge, he never learned the informer's identity. The records contained no information in that regard and, when I first became familiar with the case, I didn't concern myself much with the question. But I now have a suspicion, a strong suspicion, a suspicion that it was Manny's loving sister, Sandra, who, in a moment that must have been torturous, called the police. She said nothing of this when we spoke, and I resisted the urge to ask. But I believe that, knowing full well that it was her brother whom the victim and the police artist had tried to capture in the sketch, and unable to tolerate the possibility that failing to take action might lead to another girl being similarly victimized, she did what she thought she must – in spite of the agony she surely felt. Her desperate wish to deflect awareness of her brother's predatory nature was overborne by her sense of decency; her intolerance of facing the reality of his actions was outweighed by her unwillingness to allow them to continue.

The transformation of her image of her brother was now complete; the brave defender of damsels in distress, the noble avenger of victims of elementary school bullies had himself become a villain, a dangerous predator, a vicious defiler of women. Her White Knight had fallen from atop his gallant steed face first into the mud. In her moment of truth, Sandra could not pretend otherwise. And, at long last, she found a way to make the idea sink in.

* * *

The Kirby Forensic Psychiatric Center is not a place for those who require the niceties of refined deportment. Its inhabitants are often entirely unconcerned with the norms of polite conduct, and staff members must either adapt or seek employment elsewhere. In Kirby, the frequently-heard term "inappropriate behavior" does not mean using the wrong fork; when it doesn't mean violent assault, it means behavior of a coarseness, crudeness and offensiveness to be found in few other environs; it means indifference to the most fundamental customs of personal hygiene and interpersonal civility.

A frequently encountered characteristic of severe mental illness is a profoundly regressed primitivity, a primitivity that eradicates any interest in social propriety. Psychotic individuals, for example, are often preoccupied with the body and its products; they may not only lack the ordinary sense of disgust for bodily waste products but may display a great interest in them, taking pleasure in smearing or playing with their feces. One patient, in fact, apparently deemed his waste to be of such value that he fought mightily to keep it in his possession, storing it in his locker. Once staff became aware of this unfortunate habit, a great battle ensued, a battle of wits in which the patient schemed to find hiding places for his treasure and staff endeavored to defeat him in the attempt. Another patient was not permitted into the bathroom unless accompanied by staff; he could not otherwise be dissuaded from defecating in the shower stall.

Psychotic individuals sometimes cannot tolerate wearing clothing, almost as if desperate to return to an archaic state of feral existence, and will remove any garments that staff might attempt to induce them to wear, often disrobing so repeatedly and with such determination that staff eventually surrenders to what is seemingly the greater strength of will.

Public masturbation, too, is commonly seen in the day rooms of certain psychiatric wards, but this is often masturbation of a different kind than engaged in by Mr. Gonzalez; it is done not for the effect it has on those in one's presence, but in utter indifference to them. Such is the milieu, not in the psychiatric wards of private hospitals to which people may retreat for a few weeks for treatment of depression or an initial psychotic break, but in the Kirby Forensic Psychiatric Center as well as the in the back wards of state psychiatric facilities, warehouses for the severely and persistently mentally ill, for those poor souls who are beyond the reach of even today's potent and effective psychotropic medications.

And such is the milieu where Manolo Gonzalez would now live for an undetermined number of years, quite possibly for the remainder of his very young life. The reader may wonder how he fared in this setting, a setting very unlike high school, college and the streets of New York City which had until now been his domain. The unfortunate answer is that, although his environment was new and different, his patterns were old and unchanged. Mr. Gonzalez did not make a very good adjustment to Kirby any more than he had adjusted well to a life of freedom. Yes, it is true that his choices and options were now far more limited, his opportunities for sexual predation greatly curtailed, but his life was thematically unchanged. Simply being incarcerated did not put out the fire; nor did the medications that were prescribed. The needs that relentlessly drove him to his deviant behavior in the outside world accompanied him undiminished to his place of confinement.

It is true that if one were to see Mr. Gonzalez at a given moment in his new home, he might appear to be doing quite well. He might, for example, be seen in a ward meeting, speaking for the patient population, presenting their concerns to staff members in a cogent, articulate and persuasive manner, perhaps helping to change ward conditions or earn new privileges for the patients. Even more impressively, he might be seen helping patients to be more tolerant of necessary restrictions and more understanding of staff concerns. At other times, he might be found serenely playing chess or some other board game or simply engaged in quiet conversation with a wardmate or a staff member.

Or he might be found working on a drawing, one to be kept in his portfolio or, if deemed to be of sufficient worth, to be taped to his small share of wall space in the dormitory. He might, in fact, appear to be an ideal patient, a model, a perfect exemplar of cooperation, collaboration and appropriate behavior. But, as the reader has probably surmised, at another moment Mr. Gonzalez might be found exposing himself to a young female nurse or, if able to engineer the opportunity, grabbing or groping her until forcibly pulled away and placed in restraints. And it was always my impression that, in his periods of quiescence, well-behaved though he may have been, there was something troubling about his demeanor, something that made me feel that his appropriate conduct came at a great cost to him. He had a look that seemed to fluctuate between strain and emotional deadness – a look that was replaced by a fully-alive excitement once the self-imposed restraints were lifted.

Nevertheless, sexual assaults notwithstanding, Mr. Gonzalez was in many ways strikingly unlike the more primitive or violent patients on the ward and he presented staff with a problem of a different and, in some ways more difficult, variety. The very inconsistency of his behavior is what often led to their discomfiture. Interestingly, the problems he created for female staff members were not entirely unlike, in kind if not in degree, the problems he had created for Sandra.

It is true that staff members were instructed to maintain a consistent and professional stance toward patients; they were to be neither overly familiar nor unnecessarily harsh. But humans being humans, the actuality did not always conform to the ideal and Mr. Gonzalez was well able to complicate staff members' attempts to maintain a clinical stance. He could readily evoke from staff members feelings of congeniality and friendliness and went out of his way to do so; he was well able to make staff feel that he was a pleasant, personable and reasonable young man. And a female staff member who had been amiable, kindly and perhaps even a bit chummy might well have some difficulty managing her feelings and maintaining a clinical demeanor after this amiable fellow made her a target of a sexual assault. Nor was he always unable to rekindle the friendship with promises – promises of very questionable value – that he would "never do it again." He made people want to like him, want to be able to believe him, in spite of the fact that they knew – or should have known – better.

For his part, Mr. Gonzalez claimed to find the inevitable change in attitude toward him by the victim of an assault both dismaying and bewildering. As always, he was able to tell himself that he meant no harm, that he thought that she "might like it." Just as he was so frequently and bizarrely disappointed in the less-than-appreciative responses he received from his victims in the outside world, he was disappointed – perhaps even more bizarrely so – with the responses to his "seductions" in Kirby. As always, his impulse for coercive, rapacious sexual aggression was fully matched by his endless capacity for self-deception.

And so the pattern that had long been established in his years of freedom persisted in his life of incarceration. It was, by then, a pattern that had become deeply ingrained, a way of life that had become all of life, really, for Mr. Gonzalez. By the time of his arrest, it had long been a settled issue. Much as he may have craved approval, there was no longer any serious question of socially sanctioned accomplishment; no struggle to curb or contain the antisocial press that impelled him ever deeper into his dark and malevolent depravity. Drawing, relationships and attempts at earning a living had perhaps not been abandoned entirely, but they were a tissue-thin and emotionally-vapid facade behind which lay his more substantial existence. Any semblance of normality was a mere veneer over the world wherein he truly lived, the world in which he could feel excitement, the world in which he could feel alive, the world in which he could pursue the only activity which quenched his relentless thirst and scratched his deepest itch, the need to impose himself on young women, to reign supreme over them and their attentions, to possess them as helpless victims of his omnipotent control. Nothing, no thing, could compete with his need to forcibly dominate, render helpless and seize what he wished from the objects of his desire.

But I am forgetting, forgetting that Manolo Gonzalez was not a cruel rapist, but a romantic, a lover, an admirer of feminine beauty, a tender and affectionate suitor, ardently courting the pretty young things that struck his fancy. Just ask him.

Darkness and Depakote

THE KIRBY FORENSIC PSYCHIATRIC Center does not have the dark, foreboding appearance of many large prisons, institutions that often look like medieval castles. It is not a building that readily attracts attention. Most who see it while driving past, if they think about it at all, might assume that it is a hospital, an office building, or even an apartment building. It can be seen from Manhattan's F.D.R. Drive as well as from the Triborough Bridge – but the razor-wired fence surrounding it is visible from neither of those vantage points. And as drivers pass it on their daily commute, they have no way of knowing that the building houses many of the most mentally ill and dangerous individuals in all of New York State, in all of the country.

Within the walls of Kirby is a unique world, a world apart, a frightening and nightmarish world, a world of illness and incarceration which is neither hospital nor prison as those terms are generally understood, a world populated by individuals whose lives have gone grotesquely wrong, a world which is, for many, a quagmire of stultifying stagnation and unending helplessness and futility.

The hospital stands on Wards Island, a small bit of land in the East River, midway between Queens and Manhattan, and can outwardly be distinguished from its two neighboring buildings only by the fence that stands guard around it. The other buildings comprise the Manhattan Psychiatric Center which, as well, houses people with severe psychiatric problems; however, its residents do not share the violent and destructive tendencies of Kirby's inhabitants. All in all, the island, which also features a homeless shelter, is a drab and dreary affair, contrasting sharply with the wealth and excitement of Manhattan, so very close by.

Kirby is in many ways a universe unto itself. An eleven-story, sandstone-colored building, the views from the various vantage points within the building tend to accentuate the contrasts with its surroundings. From the lower floors, one is eye-level with the Triborough bridge and can watch the endless flow of traffic moving in both directions across the bridge, each of the numberless cars and trucks driving home the point that the surrounding world is free, active and mobile while Kirby, to its residents, is the essence of stagnation and constraint. From the upper floors, there are breath-taking panoramic views of the flowing river and of Manhattan, showing off by day the beautiful architecture of its individual buildings, the vast collection of towers seeming to compete with each other for space, majesty and prominence, and the whole bursting with a feeling of energy, life, industry, ambition and possibility. By night, the countless points of light transform Manhattan into a cosmopolitan cornucopia of glamour and excitement with the promise of entertainment and enjoyment, luxury and comfort. For a staff member, surveying the scene can easily evoke a feeling of apartness, of being segregated and sequestered. Imagine, then, the feelings of a patient, locked in this oppressively grim hospital-prison, as he looks out over a city overflowing with freedom, life and opportunity. Locked in, that is, with the inherent degradation of the situation and the hopelessness and helplessness born of knowing that, although he could be released much sooner, he just might be held there until death. Even a patient free of the fierce paranoia of many of Kirby's occupants could well find himself feeling that the setting was effectively and sadistically designed for his torment. Perhaps it is fortunate that most residents are dulled by chemical means, as well as by psychiatric conditions, that take at least some of the sting out of such musings.

The hospital is closed to all who do not have official business there. The many staff members come and go every day, always through a guarded entryway complete with metal detector, but the residents are incarcerated as if in a maximum-security prison. Kirby is, in fact, a maximum-security forensic psychiatric hospital, one of only three in New York State, and it houses a very select group of individuals. Such facilities, in the past, were known as hospitals for the "criminally insane." Now, in what seems a particularly ineffective bit of political correctness, its residents are referred to as the "dangerously mentally ill," as if this term had less awful meanings. Kirby opened in 1985 and brought together patients who had been housed in a number of hospitals that had before that time comprised New York State's forensic psychiatric system.

No patients are admitted to Kirby voluntarily; all are committed by the courts. Numbering approximately 160 in total, the patients are housed on seven wards, six for males and one for females, each with a census of 20 to 25. The patient population is composed of three groups, groups that are quite distinct in terms of the circumstances of their commitments, the problems they present, and the treatment goals that are attempted. The mainstay of the hospital – in the sense that they are generally those who will remain there for the longest period – are people who have been charged with a crime and found not guilty by reason of insanity – or not guilty by reason of mental disease or defect, as the statute actually reads. Contrary to popular belief, such individuals do not "get away with murder." In fact, they often serve longer periods of incarceration than they would if convicted and sentenced to prison. Furthermore, even if they should ultimately serve less time than they would if convicted, they are faced with the hellish situation of being retained indefinitely, their release depending on a vague, imprecisely-defined set of conditions. When first committed to Kirby as an insanity acquittee, one might theoretically be released in six months. But this is a rare occurrence and, as happens more often, one might be held for decade after decade. I will discuss the experience of these individuals in greater depth and detail after introducing the reader to the two other groups that occupy Kirby's beds.

The group that has the shortest average stay are the "fitness" patients, patients who have been committed after being found incompetent to stand trial or "unfit to proceed." Before discussing their experience in Kirby, however, it might be helpful to clarify an issue that is often confusing to the public, that of the difference between incompetence to stand trial and acquittal on the grounds of insanity. The two legal designations are alike only in that they both involve mental illness; they are radically different in terms of both their meanings and consequences. Essentially, the difference centers on the question of when the individual is or was incompetent. If, as a result of mental illness, an individual is found to have been unable to have the state of mind – the "mens rea" or "guilty mind" – that is an essential part of legal guilt, at the time that he committed the offense, then according to the laws of New York State, he will be deemed not guilty by reason of insanity. The individual's state of mind during the legal proceedings is irrelevant to his guilt; the only issue of concern is his mental status at the time of the offense.

In contrast, an individual may be found incompetent to stand trial if, due to mental illness, he is unable to participate meaningfully in his defense. His mental state at the time of committing the offense is irrelevant to whether he may be tried; what matters is his state of mind, his mental competence, during the legal proceedings against him. The law takes the stance that to prosecute an incompetent individual is tantamount to trying someone in absentia – something generally antithetical to American jurisprudence. An individual may be found incompetent to stand trial if he is unable to understand the proceedings or charges against him, or to rationally consider his options, or to work cooperatively and productively with his attorney. But in any event, the proceedings are delayed until the defendant is restored to competence. The incompetent individual, however, is not released from custody; he is committed to a facility such as Kirby to be restored to competence.

It is Kirby's task to render these individuals competent and return them to Rikers Island, the local jail, and the custody of the Department of Corrections. Fitness patients are given psychotherapy and legal education, but the most essential part of their treatment is psychopharmacological - the administration of today's potent and effective antipsychotic medications. In the simplest cases, it is often a matter of only a few months before the patient can be sufficiently cleared of psychosis to be found competent and returned to jail to await trial.

Interestingly, it is generally the more severe, florid symptoms of psychosis that respond quickly to medication. Patients with intrusive, distracting hallucinations that leave them unable to engage in rational conversation, or whose thought processes themselves are so disturbed that they are unable to think or speak in a coherent, linear manner often improve dramatically within a few weeks, sometimes within a few days. On the other hand, patients who are free of hallucinations and able to think and speak coherently, but who are under the influence of long-held delusional beliefs that impair their decision-making capacities, may be far more resistant to treatment. Or, even more difficult to treat, are patients who may not have a clear-cut delusional belief, but may be so inflexible in their thinking as to insist - in the face of all that they are being told by their attorneys - that they cannot be found guilty of their charges. Such rigidity of thought may be highly resistant to change, whether treated by medication, psychotherapy, education, or all three. One of the more difficult fitness decisions faced by both clinicians and courts is whether such patients should be thought of as mentally ill – or simply foolish and stubborn.

This particular problem brings me to another peculiarity of the forensic system, one in which reality, in a manner of speaking, flies in the face of what the law actually intends. One of the purposes of the competency requirement is to protect the defendant from pleading guilty in cases in which such a plea is inappropriate or unnecessary. Some states, in fact, have a more stringent standard for competence when an individual pleads guilty, as opposed to when he pleads not guilty. In actuality, however, at least in New York, there is a de facto higher standard for pleading not guilty. In the vast majority of cases which involve mentally ill defendants, the defendant has actually committed the offense, and the defense attorney strongly believes that the defendant would be convicted and suffer a more severe sentence were he to insist on a trial rather than accept a plea bargain. The defendant's competence may be questioned by any of the parties involved in the case – the defense, the prosecution or the court. Most often, however, the issue is raised by the defense, and it is very frequently raised by the defense if the defendant insists upon pleading not guilty, against the advice of his attorney who feels certain of an unfavorable outcome at trial. Thus, a defense attorney whose client is of doubtful competence but willing to follow his attorney's advice that he plead guilty is less likely to request a competency evaluation than the attorney of a defendant with similarly doubtful competence but who is unwilling to plead guilty. There is, therefore, in practice, a higher standard for competence to plead not guilty than to plead guilty.

Another difficulty is more a result of the correctional system than of Kirby or the courts and leads to what was sometimes referred to as the Kirby-Rikers shuttle. It is a very common occurrence for a fitness patient to be shuttled back and forth between Kirby and Rikers Island – or between any forensic psychiatric hospital and the jail in its jurisdiction. The patient is rendered fit at Kirby and shipped back to jail where, within a matter of weeks, his lawyer finds him to be incompetent, another competency evaluation is requested, the defendant is again found to be incompetent and is again committed to Kirby. Although there may be various reasons for this pattern – such as the stress that the defendant feels in jail – the most common problem is that the patient, medicated and stabilized at Kirby, promptly stops taking his medication once back in jail and, before long, has regressed to his full-blown psychotic state. The problem of noncompliance with medical treatment is an enormous one in the treatment of severe mental illness in general, and is dramatically demonstrated in the pointless and wasteful Kirby-Rikers shuttle.

An additional thorny problem for the legal system is that of the incompetent individual who refuses to be medicated – whether in jail or in Kirby. The courts have struggled to decide whether they have the right to force an individual to take medication so that he may become competent to be tried on criminal charges. (Thorny though it may be, this question is certainly less emotionally-charged than that raised by the fact that individuals sentenced to death must be deemed competent before the sentence can be carried out; courts have been faced with deciding whether a condemned person should be forced to take medication so that he may become competent to be executed.)

To round out the discussion of fitness patients, it should be noted that there are cases in which it becomes clear that the patient is unlikely ever to be restored to fitness. The law states that a defendant can be held as a competency patient for only two-thirds of the maximum sentence to which he would be subject if convicted of the charges against him. However, there are provisions in the law, in such cases, which allow the patient to be converted to civil status; that is, the criminal charges against him are dropped, but he is involuntarily committed to a psychiatric facility as a civil patient. Although there might be legitimate civil rights concerns about such situations, it should be recognized that patients who are handled in this manner are generally among the most psychiatrically compromised and are frequently clearly dangerous to themselves, or to others, or both.

All these difficulties notwithstanding, as a group, the fitness patients are nevertheless the ones who spend the least time in Kirby, the average length of stay for such patients being only a matter of months.

Before turning to the fate of insanity acquittees in Kirby, I will discuss the only group of patients who arrive at Kirby by a route other than the criminal justice system. They are committed to Kirby by the court system, but in civil, not criminal proceedings. They are, for that reason, known as "civil" patients, or "Part 57" patients, based on the relevant statute in New York's mental health law. Somewhat paradoxically, these patients, although the only ones at Kirby not charged with crimes, are generally the most violent, the most difficult to manage of all of Kirby's residents. They are often patients who have been committed to other state psychiatric facilities for years – often from a very young age – and who have been unmanageably violent in such facilities. They are deemed to require the more stringent security measures employed at Kirby in order to prevent them from perpetrating their mayhem on themselves and others. Actually, in the more severe cases, even Kirby's security procedures are inadequate to the task, and it is these patients who are generally the most demanding of attention and contribute the most to making day-to-day life at Kirby as trying as it often is. They tend to be relatively young – often in their late teens, twenties or thirties – as their violent behaviors, if not their psychoses, tend to diminish with age and become more manageable, thus allowing them to be housed in less secure facilities.

It is mostly for these patients that Kirby's more extreme security measures are utilized. They tend to be the patients placed in seclusion and who need to be controlled by means of the various restraining devices. PADS, preventive aggression devices, are the least restrictive of these devices. They consist of a heavy leather belt, worn around the waist, to which the patient's wrists are bound, preventing him from moving his arms. Should this prove insufficient, the patient is placed in 4-point restraints, laid on a gurney with straps immobilizing both the arms and legs. A fifth point – a strap over the chest, holding the body down to the gurney – is added if necessary. Of course, "chemical restraints," injections of sedatives, are also part of the armamentarium.

I have worked in quite a few psychiatric settings, including hospitals with severely ill, deeply regressed psychotic patients.

Nowhere, though, have I encountered individuals who seemed so profoundly tortured, psychologically crippled and completely incapable of living among their fellows as do Kirby's civil patients. Many of these individuals, although never legally committed for more than a period of months at a time, have been hospitalized for decades. Many of them are unremittingly hostile and evoke little empathy from clinicians. Others, however, seem more like helpless infants than anything else; they can be endearing in their quieter moments and they thirstily drink in attention from clinicians like a hungry infant at the breast. But even if emotionally infantile, they are physically mature, and rather than scream in helpless rage when frustrated, they attack – wildly, uncontrollably, savagely, with unrestrained ferocity. They are human powderkegs, coiled springs of rage that might be sprung by the most trivial of events, the slightest of frustrations.

Some, in fact, seem to need no observable external stimulus of any kind to prod them to violence. There was one young man of my acquaintance, one David Garrett, who, for a period of many months, assaulted at least one person every day. No provocation was necessary; the victim might be walking down the hall or sitting on a chair when Mr. Garrett, for reasons known only to himself, might launch an attack, flailing away at the victim with his fists until the poor unfortunate could be rescued by aides who would quickly bring Mr. Garrett to the ground. He would then be restrained and either placed in seclusion, put in 4-point restraint and/or given a sedative. This became such a routinized part of the Kirby day that the question would sometimes be asked by an aide coming on duty for his shift, "Has Garrett done his thing yet?" as if to know whether he need be on the alert for a

115

coming assault. An interesting aspect of Mr. Garrett's brutality was that it was, at least in part, an iatrogenic effect; that is, it was caused by the medical treatment he received. When first admitted, he was one of Kirby's living dead; he spent all day, every day, sleeping in a chair in the day room, rousing himself from his slumber only when coerced into action by hospital staff in order that he might go to the dining room, where he would eat, or to some treatment or activity, where, if possible, he would promptly go back to sleep. This behavior pattern, common though it was at Kirby, was particularly disturbing in Mr. Garrett's case. It is often the more elderly, long-term patients – the not guilty by reason of insanity (NGRI) patients – who fall into such semi-comatose states of existence. Mr. Garrett was all of nineteen years of age and it was particularly disturbing to see someone of that age live in such a manner.

The reasons for Mr. Garrett's somnolence were never clarified. Certainly, he was a severely psychiatrically ill young man, but he had been sent to Kirby as a result of unrelenting violence in a civil hospital. What there was about the transfer to Kirby that put out the fire of his aggression and lulled him into a state of somnolence is unknown. Also unknown is what might have occurred at Kirby over a longer period of time if the staff had not elected to intervene. But intervene they did and, after failures of all manner of psychotropic medications, it was finally decided that shock therapy would be administered. Shock therapy – electroconvulsive therapy, or ECT, a series of electric shocks which cause convulsions – is used mostly as a treatment of last resort in cases of intractable depression. Although it has sometimes been decried as something akin to witchcraft; it is not. There appears to be a connection between serious mood disorders and convulsions, whether or not this connection is well understood. Several anticonvulsant medications – Depakote and Neurontin, for example – are often used to good effect in controlling bipolar mood disorders. In any event, shock therapy is often effective when nothing else has been. And it most certainly had an effect on Mr. Garrett.

A change occurred in the type of depression that Mr. Garrett was experiencing. As I've said, his state in Kirby at first was one of extreme inactivity, lack of energy, and a wish to sleep at all times. How he felt, the nature of his subjective, inner experience can only be guessed; he was most certainly not given to sharing his thoughts and feelings with others, and most likely would not have had the verbal ability to do so even if he had the desire. Judging by his behavior, however, it would seem that he felt some terrible sense of deadness and inertia; he showed no overt indication of sadness or guilt or other common emotions involved in depression. After shock therapy, however, his stagnant, vegetative depression changed into one of great agitation. In fact, depression might not be as accurate a term for his condition as acute dysphoria, a state of feeling bad, uncomfortable, distressed, irritable and, in Mr. Garrett's case, prone to violence. It was as if the treatment awakened him, shaking him out of his lifeless and lethargic existence into what was apparently his only other mode of behavior – that of being unendingly assaultive.

Mr. Garrett's predicament illustrated some of the ironies of life at Kirby, some of the absurdities that perhaps resulted from directives being issued from too high up and too far away, directives which prevented the use of methods that might have circumvented Mr. Garret's need to assault. Certain such directives prevented staff from holding a patient in seclusion for more than a brief period of time, or from using other forms of restraint – physical or chemical – without following strict and exacting rules and procedures. Mr. Garrett requested seclusion. His disinclination to communicate prevented any real understanding of his motivations, but he apparently wished to be away from other human beings and, perhaps, did not enjoy the daily ritual of being pulled to the ground and placed in restraints such as PADS or 4-points. Regulations, however, directives issued by the Office of Mental Health in Albany, the state capital, prevented him from being kept in seclusion for more than brief periods of time – whether he wished to be or not, whether his fellow patients wished him to be or not, whether the clinical staff felt it appropriate or not. People who didn't know Mr. Garrett and did not have to cope with his behavior, people who may never have spent time dealing with anyone remotely like Mr. Garrett, issued rules and policies. And those who were given the task of handling him, of living with him, so to speak, were prevented from dealing with him in a manner that might have made him feel more comfortable and might have spared both staff and patients considerable insult and injury.

In fact, especially in Mr. Garrett's case, absurdity was piled upon absurdity. As the ward psychologist, I was tasked with developing a behavior modification program that would render Mr. Garrett less aggressive. Behavior modification is based on a few seemingly very simple principles: individuals tend to behave in ways that maximize reward and minimize punishment.

If undesirable behaviors are punished and mutually-exclusive desirable behaviors are rewarded, one would expect the latter to win out over the former. That is, in Mr. Garrett's case, for example, if assault were punished and peaceable behavior rewarded, it might be expected that his assaults would come to an end. The administration hoped that we could find rewards of some kind that would motivate Mr. Garrett to stop his aggression. There were two closely related factors, however, that made this pleasant notion fall on its face. The first was that any external reward had to compete with the potent internal motivation that compelled Mr. Garrett to attack; any punishment had to compete with the tension and discomfort he evidently felt if he restrained himself. The second was that the administration, bound by Albany's directives as well as its own self-imposed restrictions, could allow no punishments and only the most trivial, meaningless "rewards." Some in the administration actually seemed surprised and disappointed when they found that offering Mr. Garrett the opportunity to wear his favorite sneakers more often or to have an extra candy bar each day were not sufficiently potent motivators to prevent this profoundly psychotic individual, an individual who had been locked in hospitals for approximately thirteen of his nineteen years, from giving vent to the bottomless destructive urges in his tormented soul.

People closer to the action could not help but eventually develop a more realistic appreciation of the difficulty of the task of trying to becalm and pacify individuals such as Mr. Garrett. The difficulty persists even in the face of the advent of potent mood-stabilizing medications such as Lithium, Depakene and

Depakote. I recall, for example, the psychiatrist who, during a staff meeting about Mr. Garrett, seemed to capture the situation very eloquently and succinctly. We were discussing the possibility of increasing the dosage of his medication when this gentleman, given to pointed and pithy comments opined, "You could dip him in Depakene and it wouldn't help."

While discussing policies that almost seem designed to promote danger, I would like to digress for a moment from civil patients and refer to the case of a fitness patient whose story illustrates well some of these policies. Kirby's population, in and of itself, insures that it will be an institution which holds some degree of danger to both patients and staff. But some of this danger could be ameliorated were it not for the fact that the institution strives to be more hospital than prison. The attempt is necessary, noble, and, for the most part, appropriate. There are times, however when it seems to involve a willful refusal to face reality.

Among staff, those most at risk are the SHTAs – Secure Hospital Therapy Aides – the men and women who watch over the patients as they eat, sleep, sit in the day room or have recreation in the yard. There are generally three aides per ward per shift, three aides to watch over twenty to twenty-five patients. Yes, some of the aides are large, burly men, but others may be petite women, seemingly half the size of some of the patients.

Many of the patients present little or no risk of violence. They may be individuals with limited propensity for violence but who are being held at Kirby because they are psychotic and unable to proceed with their cases. Others are more prone to violence, but because they are medicated – sometimes heavily so

– their ferocity is under constant chemical restraint. But on every ward there are those whose truculence is such that it cannot be dampened by medications within the limits to which they can be prescribed. SHTAs are vulnerable to such patients, other patients even more so. There are assaults – "incidents," as they are called – every day at Kirby.

Both SHTAs and the more vulnerable patients are acutely aware of the danger and often decry the lack of adequate security. Kirby is a hospital, and the powers that be strive to make it safe. But there are many precautions and safety measures that they are unwilling to impose in the attempt to make it more of a hospital and less of a prison. The administration strives to find the proper balance between security and an atmosphere of humane psychiatric treatment. There are rules and policies affecting almost every aspect of life in Kirby, and in no area are the rules more restrictive and rigidly enforced than in the domain of patient restraint. Certainly, considerable thought has been put into the development of these rules, but there are nevertheless occasions when they are blatantly unsuitable and their imprudence is glaring and frustrating; there are times when they seem to be the product of a willfully blind, Pollyana-like ignorance.

I can recall no better example of such a situation than when Cheyango Umboka was admitted to the facility, a day that will long be remembered by at least a few of Kirby's staff. Mr. Umboka had been arrested after a vicious assault, and in jail had shown himself to be not only incompetent to stand trial, but so unremittingly brutal that he was brought to Kirby late one afternoon under very special conditions – conditions which included the use of not only handcuffs, but of leg irons and a genuine Hannibal Lechter-type anti-bite and anti-spit mask, as well. Furthermore, the usual contingent of two corrections officers was apparently deemed insufficient, and he was accompanied by four armed officers, all almost as large as the 6 foot, 4 inch, 275 pound prisoner.

Prisoner, that is, until he crossed the threshold of Kirby – whereupon he was transformed from prisoner to patient, from fiercely dangerous criminal to a psychiatric patient in need of care. Off came the handcuffs, off came the leg irons, off came the anti-bite mask and away went the four armed officers, leaving Mr. Umboka free and unfettered among the 25 patients and 3 SHTAs on the ward. As I left the hospital that afternoon along with the other clinical staff, I was certainly not the only one wondering and fearing what might happen. What did happen was that before he had been on the ward for an hour, Mr. Umboka came within seconds of strangling an SHTA to death. It was only the sheerest of luck that another aide happened upon his greatly overmatched colleague as he was struggling desperately and unsuccessfully to free himself from Mr. Umboka's grip.

This incident was often invoked by those who argued that being conferred with the status of patient, rather than prisoner, does not change the nature or lethality of Kirby's charges. But no rules were changed.

There are many moments of fear and horror at Kirby, but there are also moments of poignant sadness. And before leaving civil patients to turn to the fate of insanity acquittees, I would like to briefly relate a story involving a civil patient, a story which, yes, involved violence, but which for me, brought home the weighty sadness of the place; it was a Kirby moment which I will remember always.

Mark Millinder was a young man, about twenty-seven at the time, who shared with Mr. Garrett a great propensity for violence. In contrast to Mr. Garrett, however, he was relatively articulate and quite willing, often anxious, to speak with clinical staff. Usually, what he wanted to discuss was the unfairness of his retention at Kirby and how his altercations were the fault of others. He, like Mr. Garrett, had spent the great majority of his years in hospitals due to his chronic violence. His assaults were somewhat less regular and frequent than Mr. Garrett's, but often considerably more harmful. His most recent admission to Kirby, for example, was occasioned by his slamming a blood pressure machine across the back of a doctor in a civil hospital. It took little to trigger an assault by Mr. Millinder, but there was always an identifiable cause – however trifling it might seem to another. Like many other violent young men, both in and out of hospitals, Mr. Millinder was exquisitely sensitive to any slight, insult or sign of "disrespect," especially any that might impugn his masculinity. That tendency, along with his ever vigilant paranoia and his young, healthy, well-muscled physique, combined to make a potent and dangerous cocktail. On one occasion, for example, I saw him launch himself at another patient, seemingly without provocation, knocking the unfortunate to the ground and kicking him viciously until he could be stopped. He later explained to me, in his signature fashion, that he could not be blamed, that it was the other man's fault. The man had walked past Mr. Millinder with what he judged to be a feminine gait, implying that Mr. Millinder was "a faggot," leaving him no alternative but to attack. This incident was absolutely characteristic for Mr. Millinder – both in the provocation and in the utter refutation of any responsibility.

Sometime thereafter came the incident which stands out in my mind as an illustration of the bleak futility that is often felt at Kirby – at least sometimes by staff as well as by patients. Mr. Millinder asked to see me and, once in my office, spoke to me about his great frustration. Speaking earnestly and with sadness, he poured out his despair, lamenting the fact that he had already spent so many years in hospitals, institutions for boys or locked facilities of one kind or another and wondering if he would ever have a semblance of a normal life. At least for a moment, he acknowledged that he had a hand in creating his own fate and that his release, were it ever to occur, would depend on his exercising self-control, restraining himself even when feeling provoked. Appealing for my help and support, he vowed to start anew. He said he realized that he would have to have patience, that his freedom would have to be earned over a period of time, but that he would "take it one day at a time," and declared that today would be Day One. Our conversation ended when Mr. Millinder, along with the rest of the patients, lined up to go out to the yard for recreation. After musing over his situation for a while, and wondering about his capacity to curb his anger, I turned to other work. Not twenty minutes after he left my office, I heard a commotion in the hall outside the locked door to the ward. I walked out of my office in time to see three security guards dragging a shackled but still cursing and snarling Mark Millinder into the ward, heading toward the nursing station where he would be strapped to a gurney and sedated.

"Mr. Millinder!" I said, "What happened?"

"I punched that motherfucker in the face!" he spat out, adding the name of his victim.

"*Why*, for God's sake?"

"The way he looked at me, that fucking punk! What else could I do?"

So much for Day One.

* * *

My first few years at Kirby were spent on wards that housed mostly civil patients and fitness patients. Then, in a re-shuffling of staff, I was transferred to ward Two West, a ward of individuals who had been found not guilty by reason of insanity. I was disappointed to learn of my new placement. Six West, the ward where I had been, was where the "action" was. The fitness patients had relatively short stays, and there was a constant turnover of patients, meaning that I had the opportunity to meet many people, learning something new from each. The civil patients were the most violent, affording me the opportunity to observe the eruption of aggressive urges and behaviors in "real time." The joint was jumping. I was afraid that my stay on a ward housing insanity acquittees, the "330" ward, so named for the statute in New York law pertaining to such cases, would be far less exciting. After all, it housed a group of patients that rarely changed; most had been there for many years, and new admissions were relatively rare. The patients, as a group, were considerably older than the fitness and civil patients and much less active. The ward, in fact, was sometimes known as "the dustbin."

The executive director of the hospital, however, a woman whom I respected and trusted, assured me that I would find Two West to be fascinating, even if slower-paced. She did not deceive me, except, perhaps, by understatement. In fact, I soon came to realize that I had been given a wonderful opportunity – an opportunity to visit a world that may be the closest approximation of purgatory that Earth has to offer.

No one was tortured on Two West. Patients were fed three meals a day, could associate freely with each other, were offered a wide variety of treatments and activities and could be visited by friends and family on a weekly basis. They went outside daily, weather permitting, and were never locked in cells or small rooms of any kind. They were never punished and they were never restrained unless they became violent. The ward was warm in the winter and reasonably cool in the summer; the furnishings and decor were comfortable and pleasant, if not luxurious. Patients were treated humanely by staff, if not always by each other. The surroundings and conditions were a vast improvement over any jail or prison I have ever seen or heard described.

Yet a darker, more oppressive atmosphere would be hard to find; a collection of individuals more tragic, more wretched, more lost, more woeful, difficult to imagine.

In the thick, pervasive sadness that seemed to spread itself into every corner of the ward, one could discern two general modes of feeling, two modes of adaptation that characterized the inhabitants; I always had trouble deciding which of the two was the more awful. There were those who had fallen into a somnambulist, zombie-like existence. Medicated halfway to oblivion, they were the living dead. They moved like automatons, did what they were told and seemed to have no concerns beyond the vegetative needs of human existence. They ate and they slept, and one could see in their faces a glimmer of interest in having the opportunity to do so. Other activities were approached with the animation and vitality of a corpse. They went through the motions of recreational activities and "therapy" groups with a demeanor of sluggish lethargy, following the program only because it was easier than resisting.

Then there were those who were alive and alert – painfully, frustratingly, agonizingly alive and alert. Alive and alert almost as one might be when caught in quicksand, fearing that, struggle as he might, the muck was slowly sucking him under.

The men who fit into either of these groups, as well as the many who fell somewhere along the continuum between the two poles, are the people who have escaped legal responsibility for their crimes by virtue of having been found not guilty by reason of mental disease or defect – people who have been found insane. They have escaped legal responsibility – they have been acquitted; but they have most certainly not escaped the awful consequences of their actions. They are remanded to the custody of the Commissioner of Mental Health of the state of New York under whose auspices they are incarcerated in Kirby. When they enter, they do not know, they cannot know when, or if, they will leave.

Imagine. Imagine yourself one who has been found "insane." Imagine yourself nevertheless having a relatively good grasp of reality. These people often do. You have been in jail or out on bail for many months, wondering what will be your fate. You have now had your final court appearance and learned that you

127

have been acquitted on grounds of insanity. You will be returned to your jail cell – or taken to one if you've been out on bail – but you know that your stay in jail is temporary. You will very shortly be brought to the Kirby Forensic Psychiatric Center on Wards Island. You know that you have been committed there for 60 days for a psychiatric examination, but you also know that it is almost a certainty that you will be re-committed for a longer period of time, and that you may be re-committed repeatedly over a period of decades. You have no idea when or if you will ever leave the confines of this building on a small island in the East River.

Let us assume that you are reasonably knowledgeable about your destination. You know that it is not a prison, that it is a hospital. But you know that it is a hospital unlike any other. You know that the professional staff, no matter their determination to be humane, will regard you as criminally insane. But they are not your primary concern. You know that your peers, your ward-mates, your roommates will be others who have been found insane, or incompetent to stand trial, or so uncontrollably psychotic and violent that they can be managed in no other facility. These will be your compatriots, your fellows, your peers, the only people with whom you will socialize as equals – for years. Or for the rest of your life. You will eat with them. You will sleep with them. You will be surrounded by them at all times. Imagine.

Perhaps you are one of those who has been spared this anticipatory hell by virtue of having been misled by your attorney. You believe that you will be spending only 60 days at Kirby because your lawyer, owing to his incompetence, his indifference, or both, has informed you that that is the period of your commitment – without informing you that, in all probability, you will be re-committed. Many times. Or perhaps he has told you in an offhand manner that you will probably spend a year or two in Kirby. So you have not had to endure the anxiety of the more knowledgeable patient-to-be. But then, over the initial days, weeks or months of your stay, the reality of your situation gradually dawns on you. You might first hear from one of your ward-mates that your lawyer's promise of a limited stay is unreliable. You might dismiss it either as the wild idea of a madman or as a sadistic attempt to frighten you, but you are likely to dismiss it. But then you hear the same warning from another patient and another. Then a staff member, perhaps an aide, echoes the statement. Then, a professional, a psychiatrist or social worker or psychologist whom you have started to trust reiterates the idea, telling you that, yes, it is conceivable that you might get out in a year or two, but far more likely that you'll be here for much, much longer. Imagine how you feel as the reality sinks in. As you settle in and get to know your fellow patients, you hear from one after another that they've been held for five years, or ten years, or twenty years or more. You can no longer doubt the truth of what you've been hearing.

A man who has committed murder and would otherwise have spent many years in prison might still feel that he is better off for his decision to plead insanity. But imagine the case – the not at all uncommon case – of the Kirby patient who, having committed a lesser offense, ultimately realizes that he has traded off a year or two in prison for decades in Kirby. Imagine as the years pass and he realizes that the past five or ten or twenty years that he has been incarcerated, he could have been a free man – if not for the incredibly foolish decision that he made, often at the urging of a well-meaning but ignorant attorney.

The decision to plead insanity is strictly at the discretion of the defendant. No judge, prosecutor, or defense attorney, regardless of how convinced he may feel that the defendant warrants an insanity acquittal, can force such a decision upon a defendant. Jury trials resulting in insanity acquittals are rare, but insanity plea agreements much less so. And if the defense attorney, who is guiding the defendant and the only party responsible for safeguarding his welfare, is ignorant about the actual workings of the insanity defense, his client may pay dearly for that ignorance.

The reader must understand that there are two different standards involved in an insanity commitment to Kirby – one is applied in order to be admitted and a very different one to be discharged. The law states that an individual should be found not guilty by reason of insanity if, due to mental disease or defect, he was, at the time of the offense, unable to understand the nature and consequences or the wrongfulness of his actions. The statute pertaining to discharge states that he must be held in a forensic hospital until he is deemed to no longer have a "dangerous mental illness." The illegal actions that were committed by the patient, the actions that led to his incarceration, are only one of the factors that must be considered in assessing whether the individual is dangerously mentally ill. Theoretically, an individual might have been arrested for spitting on the sidewalk and, once found legally insane and committed to Kirby, if judged to be dangerously mentally ill, he could spend the remainder of his life there.

While I knew of no patients committed for such a trivial offense, I was acquainted with several whose potential prison terms were far exceeded by their sojourns at Kirby. But one should beware leaping to the conclusion that such individuals were being held unjustly.

John Mirelli had been in Kirby for ten years when I arrived. Despite desperate and repeated attempts to be released, with the aid of the publicly-paid lawyers assigned to work on his behalf in that regard, he was there when I left. I last heard of him several years ago, at which time he was still in Kirby, having been there for close to twenty years. He had been charged with reckless endangerment after entering a bar with a shotgun and firing it wildly around the room. No one was killed, no one was injured. At the time he had a criminal record for minor offenses, and lawyers I've asked have estimated that he might have spent two or three years in prison had he pleaded guilty. He was not psychotic; he had never been psychotic. Nor did he ever meet the standard for legal insanity; he was angry, moody, impulsive, self-destructive and almost entirely lacking in judgment, but at no time did he fail to fully understand the nature, consequences and illegality of his actions. But he and his lawyer "outsmarted" the criminal justice system and somehow managed to negotiate an NGRI plea. He may never leave Kirby.

Surely, in some sense, this is not fair. It is, however, entirely legal. Mr. Mirelli must be held in a secure facility as long as he has a "dangerous mental illness," defined by the laws of the State of New York as a "mental disease or mental condition which is manifested by a disorder or disturbance in behavior, feeling, thinking or judgment to such an extent that the person afflicted requires care, treatment and rehabilitation." Mr. Mirelli most certainly had such a "disturbance in behavior, feeling, thinking or judgment." In fact, the disturbance in his behavior was such that he had been able to maintain himself outside of institutions – jails, prisons and hospitals – for a total of only about three years in the thirty or more years since he reached adolescence. Assaults, drug possession, robberies and petty thefts would lead to his arrest. More often than not, he would end up in a hospital or drug treatment facility, rather than a prison. Once hospitalized, his aggressive, belligerent behavior would lead to his being held longer than he might otherwise have been.

Mr. Mirelli could not help but sink himself. He was given trials of virtually every possible medication and combination of medications, and would sometimes appear to be making gains. But then, inevitably, he would revert to form and would commit some act of violence which was, by all normal standards, unnecessary and astoundingly foolish. He had several advocates among the clinical staff, often those who were recent arrivals. They felt that he surely could refrain from senseless violence, at least long enough to earn his transfer to a civil facility. They tried many approaches to helping him including self-understanding, moral support, "tough love," etc. All to no avail. He would sometimes seem to be on the brink of accomplishing his great goal and would then snatch defeat from the jaws of victory by committing some foolish act such as groping a female staffer. On one occasion, the one on which he came closest to being discharged, he made it past every hurdle except the final one – the judge who would have to sign the order of transfer. He sat patiently through his hearing until, almost at its end, he had a fit of rage in the courtroom, yelling at – and perhaps frightening – the judge who, unsurprisingly, refused to release him.

There is an irony to Mr. Mirelli's situation. An irony that he, in his rage and desperation to be discharged, appreciated not at all. He did not meet the standard for insanity, but "gamed" his way into Kirby, where he most certainly did meet the standard for retention. He may spend the rest of his life there when he might well have been out of prison in a few years.

Unfair? Perhaps. Yet in a larger sense, in an almost cosmic sense, it may be that it was profoundly right. If we look at the bigger picture of Mr. Mirelli's life – his "arc," as it has sometimes been called – it is not difficult to feel that he, somehow, engineered his way into the most appropriate place for himself. He had been in juvenile detention centers, drug treatment centers, jails and hospitals. Released, he never managed to retain his freedom for more than a period of a few months. It seems almost undeniable, in spite of his great rage against his "unfair" incarceration, that there was a drive within him to have himself confined and constrained. His actions, beginning in adolescence, if not childhood, all tended toward that end. It was as if he would not relent, would not be deterred; he would not cease his antisocial behavior until he forced society to wall him in, for his own safety as well as that of others. It strikes me as being much like the screaming of an infant, a screaming that will not abate until the distressed infant is held, comforted and made to feel safe.

133

Surely the prisons hold many with a similar "arc." But if we look at Mr. Mirelli's situation as being guided by a relentless and, in some way knowing, inner pressure – or, for that matter, some sort of cosmic justice – then we must account for the fact that he found himself not in a prison, but in Kirby. Kirby, where incarceration has the added feature of the uncertainty of the length of stay. Kirby, where a soul such as Mr. Mirelli, who consciously felt an overwhelming need for freedom, would be doomed to a constant but fruitless quest to obtain his release. He is a Sisyphus who must roll his boulder not up a mountain, but out of a pit.

For that matter, out of a dark pit, an ink-dark pit. For neither Mr. Mirelli nor most of his ward-mates had an adequate understanding of what they had to do to earn their release. For some, it was a matter of complete indifference; others wanted nothing more than to know that they could remain in Kirby for life, assured of warmth in the winter, three meals a day and a bed at night. Anything outside of Kirby was not only physically closed off to them, but mentally, as well. They had no interest in knowing or thinking of anything beyond Kirby's walls. But there were many who awoke in the morning and went to bed at night thinking of little else. It is for these individuals that Kirby is a quagmire through which they must endlessly wade, hoping to find their way out of the morass. But many have no idea in what direction to head; they lack any compass by which to navigate. Others have a sense of the general direction they must take and make serious efforts to cleave to what seems the correct path; but they find themselves perpetually frustrated because, try as they might to stay the course, they inevitably take a wrong turn and fail to reach their goal, the firm ground at the far end of the bog, the exit door from Kirby. The living dead who have no wish to leave and no apparent interest in much of anything else, the somnambulists who are either hopelessly engulfed in their own autistic revery or are lacking even a fantasy life and exist in some form of incomprehensible mental vacuum are certainly pitiable beings, but I often wondered if their anesthetized, semi-comatose wretchedness was not preferable to the acute frustration of being perpetually thwarted, seemingly doomed to strive interminably for that which seems both absolutely imperative and hopelessly unattainable: release.

To be released, the patient must make the ward clinicians feel that he is no longer "dangerously mentally ill." Many of those who wish release and hope to be seen as meeting the qualifications are unable to get past the first hurdle: refraining from violence. Unsurprisingly, these are often the same people who complain the most vociferously about the unfairness of being retained. Their lack of ability to tolerate frustration leads to both their angry complaints and their acts of violence. There are many, however, who are able to avoid violence and yet are unsuited for release, and they often have great difficulty in understanding what more is being asked of them. The reader, in fact, may share that sentiment. But the reader, and certainly the Kirby inmate, would do well to understand that violence tends to erupt under particular conditions and that the clinicians at Kirby, as well as the judges who make the ultimate decisions, are being asked not simply to affirm that the patient has been non-violent in Kirby, but to assert with some degree of assurance that the patient will be non-violent under very different circumstances. The hospital is obviously meant to be and most certainly is a sheltered, protective, controlled environment. It is an environment meant to contain and render peaceful people who have committed egregious and utterly irrational crimes – pushing a complete stranger in front of a subway train, or mutilating a family member who is believed to be an agent of the devil, or beating to death a man in the street because, based on the man's facial expression or the color of his clothing, the patient believes that the man is casting aspersions on his manhood, thinking that he is homosexual. Can non-violent behavior of such a man in Kirby's controlled environment – where he is fed, clothed, kept warm, watched over 24 hours a day, carefully medicated and prevented from using or abusing alcohol or illicit drugs – be enough to assure that this man, having committed some horrible offense in the past, will not revert to such behavior when all the restraints and controls have been removed?

I was always profoundly grateful that the final decision about a patient's release was made not by myself, nor by any other clinician, but by a judge of the Supreme Court of New York State. Those judges, however, burdened by a great responsibility, understandably turn to the clinicians who work with the patients for thorough and thoughtful information and opinions. The fact that what they actually get from the clinicians may fall far short of this goal is a topic that cannot here be addressed at any length. Suffice it to say that most clinicians take this responsibility seriously. They understand well that they may have a great influence on a judge's decision and they wish neither to be party to the victimization of some poor innocent by a released patient nor to unnecessarily deprive a human being, often one aching for freedom, of his liberty. Even the most careful of clinicians, armed with both clinical acumen and a familiarity with the considerable scientific literature on the prediction of violence, are faced with a daunting task. Those with good intentions are often troubled by doubts about their written reports or court testimony. They should be.

The list of factors to be considered is not terribly lengthy; rather, the difficulty is that most of them are vaguely defined and open to widely varying interpretation. The patient's insight into his mental illness, his understanding of his need for medication and of his potential danger, his capacity for frustration tolerance, and his remorse for his past crimes are all key. But these are not traits that yield to simplistic measurement, especially when one realizes that nothing the patient says should be accepted at face value. Any patient even close to being ready for discharge will emphatically state that he knows he needs his medication and that he understands the nature and extent of his illness. He will be able to list the symptoms to which he is subject and speak reassuringly about his wish to avoid violence. He will tell of his great remorse for the harm he has done in the past. The clinician's task is to listen carefully, to listen "with the third ear," as it has been described, to understand what the patient truly feels, not simply what he says. Clinicians vary in how they approach the work. To some, it is an obligation to be taken seriously, and their curiosity about the mind, their enjoyment in their work, enable them to listen patiently and to devote appropriate time and thought to the job. They know, for example, that a savvy patient, one who may have spent many years in this or other psychiatric wards, understands that he must forswear the delusional beliefs that led

137

to his past offenses. They therefore let the patient speak freely and at length, giving him a chance to inadvertently reveal the denied but lingering belief that, for example, he is an emissary from God. Unfortunately, there are those clinicians who have grown tired of their work or who perhaps were never truly interested in it, whose only thought is to bring the interview to the swiftest possible conclusion. Never will I forget the psychiatrist whom I watched conduct a dangerousness evaluation by asking one question: "So, do you still believe all that nonsense about being in the F.B.I.?" No? O.K. Good to go. He won't live in the good doctor's neighborhood, anyway.

Such carelessness, perhaps rationalized and supported by a belief that the Kirby "has no right to hold people forever" – a sentiment sometimes expressed by clinicians – certainly meets with counterbalancing forces. For example, another incident unlikely to ever escape my memory was when, along with a psychiatric resident and a senior clinician, I conducted a group examination of a patient seeking release. The senior clinician, who seemed to harbor intense animosity toward some patients, requested of me and the third clinician – no, demanded – that we flatly lie about the patient's behavior in the meeting, sabotaging his attempt at release by saying that he became hostile and belligerent.

These experiences, very fortunately, are extreme examples, outliers, and depart greatly from the norm in terms of the responsibility usually shown by those involved in conducting risk assessments, as the evaluations of N.G.R.I. patients seeking release are known.

In the end, is the system fair? Not if you ask the patients yearning for freedom. Is the system fair? Not if you ask the victims or the families of victims; not if you ask the relatives of patients who will again be faced with feeling endangered by newly-freed kinfolk with a frightening history. Is the system fair? Some clinicians say that we have no "right" to try to predict future behavior, no "right" to hold someone indefinitely. Others say that no one should support a patient's release unless willing to have that patient live next door; he will, after all, live next door to someone. Is the system fair? My guess is that Kirby's executive director would shrug, as if to say that fairness is not the issue, that societal pressures are the factors of weight. This very capable and down-to-Earth woman once told me, with a sigh, that her job consisted mostly of managing mutually contradictory directives from the state capital, the opposing directives generally representing the two sentiments of the elected officials – that is to say, of the voters. She lived under a constant pressure to minimize cost by reducing the census of the hospital, and to maintain public safety by not releasing anyone dangerous. If the census rose too high, her position might be in jeopardy. If a released patient were to commit a publicized crime, her position might be in jeopardy. I was glad not to be the executive director.

I was glad not to be the executive director, I was glad not to be a judge, but mostly I was glad not to be a patient. Spending considerable time with patients fosters a certain tendency to in some ways identify with them. And in my years at Kirby, I don't think I ever let myself out of the locked ward at the end of the day without having the fleeting but discomforting feeling that

139

I was somehow getting away with something. I was always able to dismiss the "ridiculous" thought that staffers might grab me and take me down, medicate me and restrain me, telling me I'm not allowed to leave. But I always marvelled at the fact that my place in the scheme of things could be so radically different from that of the people with whom I shared Kirby's wards for eight hours a day. How did I come to be someone who not only could live in freedom, but could earn a living by having the joy and satisfaction of studying and trying to understand the aberrations and deformities of the human mind and soul, rather than a tortured wretch, condemned to a prison-hospital of steel doors and stupefying dreariness, of regulation and regimentation, of tedium and torment, and, worst of all, of my own private, psychotic hell.

What a place.

Ivy League Insanity

RONALD WALENSKY WAS AN UNUSUAL Kirby patient. Before psychosis robbed him of his future, he had already, as a very young man, accomplished something remarkable in his world, the world of science. Before finishing his undergraduate degree, he had published several articles in prestigious scientific journals and was well-known within his field before earning his Ph.D. When schizophrenia struck, it robbed him of the success, prestige and accomplishment that seemed his for the taking. When it led him to murder, it robbed another of his life and Mr. Walensky of his freedom. Instead of enjoying professional accomplishment and personal fulfillment, Mr. Walensky has spent the past decades among Kirby's living dead. By the time that I made his acquaintance, he had apparently forsaken all thought of any other life, and consistently resisted any effort to help him earn his way towards freedom. Most of his time was spent sitting in the day room in animated conversation – with hallucinated others. He asked nothing of and offered nothing to corporeal others; he wished only to be left to his own, private, sealed-off world. He took his place in line with his ward-mates for meals and ate what he was given; he walked with them to various activities, never protesting and never participating. He could reliably be seen either staring straight ahead or gesticulating with his arms and making facial expressions as if deeply absorbed in conversation – but always with phantoms of his own making. Should another individual address him, he would answer politely, but make no attempt at maintaining a conversation.

He was willing to engage with certain few members of the professional staff, but placed strict limits on even these relationships, refusing to discuss all but the few topics which he deemed suitable. These relationships, nevertheless, were unfailingly polite and cordial unless, that is, the clinician expressed an interest in having his patient transferred to a less secure hospital – the first step towards eventual freedom. Mr. Walensky would have none of it. His preference, he clearly showed, was to simply avoid ever having to address the issue. When it was forced upon him, as occasionally happened, he was willing to demonstrate the imprudence of the idea by refusing to take his medication, or, if need be, assaulting another patient. His attitude seemed: "This is my home. I want nothing more. Leave me alone to my fantasy world and I will not bother anyone. Try to make me leave, and I will prove to all concerned that I am unfit to live beyond these walls."

His fear of being evicted, as he evidently saw it, from his solitary but apparently comfortable universe, seemed to be the only thought which troubled him – that is, when he was properly medicated. He generally offered no resistance to taking his medication which, fortunately, seemed to forestall a regression to the state of mind which led this seemingly mildest of men to murder. His offense was decades in the past, and, by all accounts, his background and general appearance – that of a physically underdeveloped, meek, gentle academic, wholly absorbed in his intellectual pursuits and preoccupied with his own musings – made him seem the unlikeliest of murderers at the time. And the passing of many years, the effects of stultifying institutionalization, an aging process unadulterated by exercise or physical activity and compounded by isolation, emotional numbness, and the cumulative effects of years of powerful antipsychotic medications, certainly did nothing to make him appear more fearsome.

But now that we've glimpsed the end, let us return to the beginning in an attempt to understand. There are a number of reasons why that understanding will be, at best, partial. Our understanding of psychopathology such as Mr. Walensky's is far from complete, and Mr. Walensky's reticence places very strict limits on what I or others can know of him. The statements he made to the police, along with some stories told by his mother and a few others after the incident – now many years ago – are all that we know of him beyond what he, himself, is willing to tell. And he tells little.

* * *

Ronald Martin Walensky was born and raised in the heartland of America. The small family farm in northern Iowa, in his family for generations, was the only home he ever knew until he left for college. His quiet and distant father had only two interests, both of which he pursued with zeal. By day he worked the farm; by night, the bottle. Ronald remembered his mother once telling him - well before he was old enough to take her meaning - that she was not sure if his father knew that anyone else lived in the home. His mother seemed well aware of the presence of others, and worked endlessly to keep house and feed and clothe the family, in between the cow-milking, egg-collecting, butter-churning and countless other chores that helped to exact a marginal living from the tiny farm. His mother was a steady and loving presence, but Ronald was later to say - perhaps hyperbolically, perhaps not - that he was not sure if his father ever addressed him in his life.

Young Ronald showed himself to be different from other Iowa boys at a relatively early age. His older brother, Andrew, for example, sat impatiently through school, watching the clock and awaiting the 3:00 p.m. bell that would free him to play baseball with his friends. He understood, however, that he had to help on the farm and, apparently thinking that he might one day have his own farm, he showed an interest in learning how to operate one. He particularly wanted to learn to drive his father's tractor and use other equipment, but he also enjoyed tending to the animals and wanted to know how to maximize the farm's output. Ronald had no such concerns. He enjoyed neither sports nor farm work, so he avoided the former and tolerated the latter in silent but unhappy obedience.

It would be hard to know whether the cold distance between Ronald and his father was cause or result of Ronald's utter disinterest in his father's work - very likely it was both. Whatever originally set the course of their relationship, long

144

before Ronald was a teenager, he and his father showed a mutual disappointment in each other. Ronald, always a curious child, saw that his father showed no interest in learning or understanding things, and the elder Walensky seemed to see his son, his small, skinny, bespectacled and unathletic son, as a poor specimen of a male. This did not seem to concern him much, but in assigning the chores, he made sure that if he had to work alongside one of his sons, it would be the older boy, although he did not seem overly interested in him, either.

Ronald's only concern about doing his chores was to put them to an end as quickly as possible so that he could do what he wanted to do. What Ronald wanted to do was to read, to read about science. And read he did. He read about biology, chemistry, astronomy, about virtually any field of physical science. His only interest in the farm was in the functioning and repair of the farm machinery and he liked to watch when his father had to effect some repair to the tractor or other equipment. His father in no way encouraged his interest in the inner workings of the machinery, and viewed the breakdown of equipment as a grievous annoyance, mumbling and cursing to himself as he tried to reverse the problem in the most expeditious way possible.

Others, however, offered more encouragement. Although his teachers might have wished that Ronald showed a comparable interest in English, history and civics, they were pleased to have a student who had a great interest in mathematics and science and whose ability was fully on par with his interest. His most ardent supporter, however, was his mother, whose involvement in and enthusiasm for her son's scientific inclinations stemmed from more than motherhood. She had been denied the fulfillment of her own wish to attend college and become a teacher; her parents would not tolerate such ambitions. Her father, a widely respected and intellectually accomplished minister, felt that such attainments were for men, and that women should devote themselves to marriage and family, and the sooner the better, once having reached adulthood. When his daughter found herself in a relationship with a young man with solid roots in their community, she apparently felt unable to resist the pressure exerted by her father and abandoned her own goals in favor of her father's. She probably found little outlet for her academic inclinations in her roles as mother and farm-wife and seemingly diverted all such ambitions into her son, whose abilities and academic propensities became of great importance to her.

Ronald was a quiet child, a strange child, an isolated and lonely child. He was not unlikeable; he was too diffident and unassuming to garner resentment from anyone. One might have thought that he'd be a perfect target for the school bullies; small, frail, unassertive, an A student "egghead." But somehow, the bullies showed little taste for tormenting him, easy as it might have been. It was as if they could sense that he was so involved in his own world, and so uninclined to compete with others or in any way claim anything for himself, that they had no interest in him. Perhaps they felt that they were unable to elevate themselves by abusing or demeaning him, as if they couldn't set themselves above him since he was not lower in the schoolyard social hierarchy, he was entirely apart from it. Always modest, always polite, he was loved by his mother and – possibly – even by his father, in his own cold way. He was liked by teachers, tolerated by his brother, ignored by his fellow students, and close to or open with no one on Earth. Whether he was unhappy or not, no one could say. He did not complain and he did not appear depressed.

He awoke each morning, went to school, eager to soak up all that he could in class. However, by the time he reached junior high school, there was little for him to learn in the lessons taught his classmates. His teachers understood this and the ones who were interested enough to do so gave him special assignments and put aside a bit of time to discuss them with him. But by the time he reached high school, he had surpassed not only his classmates, but his teachers, as well. They could suggest readings to him, but could not discuss them with him on his level. There was one teacher, however, the physics instructor and chairman of the science department for the school district, Dr. Josef Schuster, who was advanced well beyond the level of most of the science and math teachers and he, and only he, was able to engage young Ronald in discussions of his readings. He was more than happy to do so, as he also lacked for anyone else with whom he could have conversations which challenged and stimulated him. In fact, both he and Ronald reveled in the time they shared and seemed to feel very grateful for having found each other. As Ronald's mother explained years later, she had gotten the impression that it was as if her son and Dr. Schuster were two isolated souls, trapped in a universe of dissimilar others – people who were not like them, who could not share their interests, who seemed to see and experience the world in ways which they didn't, people who didn't understand them and whom they could not understand. Then, they found each other.

They were truly kindred souls, regardless of the fact that one's love of science bloomed in the academies of Europe and the other's in the cornfields of Iowa; regardless of the fact that one was at home in the heart of Vienna and the European capitals, and the other was awed by his one visit to Dubuque. Nor did it matter that the elder man – elder by more than thirty years – had lived through World War II, the war which claimed the lives of his entire family, and the younger had never lost more than a pet calf. Though the differences in their backgrounds were vast, their common love made any dissimilarity between them utterly irrelevant. They lived in a world together, the world of physics; they were fellow explorers, and the differences in who they were or how they got there would no more interfere with their journey together than would such differences between two astronauts sharing a voyage into the realms that young Ronald and old Josef explored in their minds.

They sought each other's company at every opportunity. Ronald would complete his classwork as quickly as possible and then, with the blessings of both his teachers and the principal, who well understood that he had educational needs that could not be met in the ordinary ways, he would join "Dr. S," his mentor and companion, in his office. They discussed math, they discussed chemistry, they discussed many things, but, most of all, they discussed physics. This was Dr. Schuster's love, and he imparted his endless fascination with the topic to Ronald, who, having been headed in the same direction himself, eagerly followed his mentor into the realms of physics' endless theoretical possibilities. Together they explored the infinite universe and infinitesimal particle.

Their time together was not limited to school hours. Dr. S lived alone and, at least in certain ways, so did Ronald. Each wanted to spend time with the other more than either wanted to be with anyone else. Both preferred talking about science above all else. After school, they took long walks together when weather permitted, or sat in Dr. S's office when it didn't. Then Dr. S would drive his young protégée to the farm before continuing on to his own small home. Often, Dr. S would be invited to have dinner with Ronald and his family. He would engage in polite conversation with Ronald's mother, brother and, occasionally, his father, but they were excluded from the conversation between Ronald and Dr. S by virtue of their near total inability to understand it. Neither Andrew nor the elder Walensky seemed troubled by their exclusion, but Mrs. Walensky later acknowledged that she felt a pang of jealousy, jealousy of both the obvious delight that her son and his mentor took in their flights into scientific discourse as well as of her son's evident attachment to Dr. Schuster.

Sophia Walensky appreciated that her Ronald was a well-mannered and respectful son who unfailingly treated her with deference and courtesy, and she knew that he loved her. She knew also, however, that he was an emotionally-guarded child who kept himself to himself and was disinclined to share his thoughts or feelings with anyone. As he passed the age of 6 or 7, and more so as he approached his teens, she watched him gradually become more reticent, more averse to displaying or speaking of his feelings, and she felt the loss. It was not that he was not affectionate; he was. He enjoyed talking with his mother and never objected when she kissed or hugged him. But she knew that he was reachable only to a point. She knew that she had in some way lost contact with him, and, having an older son with whom things were different, she knew that it was not merely a matter of age; Ronald was removed from her – and seemingly all others – in a way that Andrew was not. She was often conscious, when with him, of a sense that he was simply not available to her.

She therefore took immediate notice, with great interest, with surprise, and with a mixture of pleasure, relief and envy, when she first saw Ronald engrossed in conversation with Schuster. She felt that she was seeing him come to life, that she was seeing a reprise of the bright-eyed, animated excitement that her little boy had shown years ago. She knew that although the subject matter was as impersonal as it could be, that her son and his teacher had established a profound connection, as if the very impersonality of the topic allowed Ronald to forget or forego his customary self-imposed restraint, permitting him to feel and show an aliveness and an enthusiasm usually forbidden him by his caution. And she knew that she could not elicit this from him.

So while his mother stood by on the sideline struggling to amalgamate her joy and her envy, while his brother farmed and played baseball, while his father farmed and drank, young Ronald progressed through high school, immersing himself in physics, the world in which he felt at home, the universe in which, accompanied by his great and good friend, he could soar, unfettered. Alone, he read, he studied, he thought, he imagined. With Schuster, he discussed, he questioned, he listened, he absorbed. In the early years of their relationship, he listened far more than he spoke, bowing appreciatively to his teacher's greater knowledge and comprehension. But as time passed, the balance gradually, almost imperceptibly, shifted.

Ronald slowly began to feel more sure of his reasoning and grew progressively emboldened. Feeling both less reticent and more in need of validating his own ideas, he interrupted his friend more, as if the power of his ideas impelled him to speak, as if the ideas, themselves, insisted on being heard. Schuster took notice of the change long before Ronald did, and encouraged his independence of thought at every opportunity. More, like the best of teachers and parents, he gladly sacrificed his own need for affirmation in favor of his pupil's need for growth, silently allowing Ronald to struggle with an idea on his own rather than too hastily leaping to his aid.

Thus, slowly but inexorably, Ronald grew from a youngster who hungrily devoured and rapidly assimilated scientific information, to one who had full command of it and was able to critically evaluate the importance and worthiness of the new ideas he encountered. And he advanced from that point to being able to think innovatively and creatively, not only having a solid grasp of the body of knowledge, but being able to add to it his own original notions. Schuster carefully observed this progression, doing all within his power to nurture it, to nudge Ronald further in both his understanding and his self-confidence. So when, as happened early in Ronald's junior year, our remarkable young man happened upon an idea for a new way of understanding and describing the movement and relationship of particles, his teacher seized upon the opportunity to urge him to nurse and develop his idea. This Ronald did. And, to shorten a rather lengthy story, by the next fall, Ronald had accomplished the astounding feat, for a high school student, of having a paper published in one of the most prestigious peer-reviewed scientific journals. Published, that is, under his own name; Schuster had steadfastly refused to accept co-authorship.

There are occasionally accomplishments which, all of their own, can "make" an individual, opening carefully guarded doors, smoothing bumpy roads and paving the way for one's success in a given field. Ronald's journal article was such an accomplishment. Although both he and his mentor recognized that it was the culmination of years of disciplined study, to the world outside of his high school, it was as if he had sprung suddenly into existence - abruptly, out of nowhere, and fully-formed. One day, a high school student; the next, the subject of newspaper articles and a prized target for Ivy League academic departments and administrators. He needed only sit back and make his choice among the offers made by the nation's most prestigious universities.

After considering all the offers - the scholarships covering all tuition and expenses - and discussing them with both his mother and, of course, Dr. Schuster, Ronald chose. And the following fall, he left the farm, his home town, and, for the first time in his life, the state of Iowa, for the east coast and one of the nation's premier universities. Ronald being Ronald, and maintaining his ever-present phlegmatic demeanor, none could know just how he felt about this transition, how he felt about leaving everyone and everything he had ever known to relocate in a strange and - in a very real sense - foreign world. There must have been some strain; surely there must have been. But none showed. Not in his phone calls, not in his letters, not in his grades. He struggled a bit, at first, in his liberal arts courses; he had no great love for literature, language or social science, but he never earned a grade below B+. In his math and science courses, it was almost as if he hadn't left high school. He earned a straight 4.0 without much effort, and usually found himself treating the course material as nothing more than a starting point for his own more advanced studies.

If the reader finds himself wondering about Ronald's college social life, I'm afraid he must be disappointed; no one who knew him earlier was able to provide much information in that regard. What can be said, based on several phone calls that came to Ronald at the family home during Christmas vacation, is that Ronald apparently did have some male friends or, at least, friendly acquaintances at school. The nature and extent of these relationships Ronald did not share with his family. His mother, certainly, made an attempt to draw him out, asking him about the phone calls to the home and his life on campus, but his persistent – although always polite – refusals to satisfy her curiosity soon discouraged her. She knew better than to even ask about what she discovered – to her great and happy surprise – at the bottom of his suitcase. Tucked neatly away in a zippered compartment, she found a perfumed hair ribbon and a small, black and white photograph of a fairly plain, but very sweet-looking young girl. Almost desperate to know something about the girl and her relationship with Ronald, she turned to Dr. Schuster in the hope – foolish as she thought it was – that he might be able and willing to shed some light.

Dr. Schuster told her that he could offer no information about the girl, but did speak openly about his own relationship with Ronald, helping her to better understand that greatly important part of his life. He confessed that he always had a great

153

deal of curiosity about Ronald, that he had often wished that he could know him more fully, but early on in their relationship had realized that Ronald's personal life was off limits to him. He had noticed that Ronald, during his high school days, did have friendships of a kind with some other students; some of the more quiet, serious-minded, high-achieving students sought him out at lunch time or after school. In observing the situation, and in occasionally being told something by one of these students, Schuster came to the conclusion that Ronald did not shut them out so much as passively go along with their attempts to befriend him while taking absolutely no initiative in developing or even maintaining the relationships. Schuster, himself, never felt that he knew whether Ronald was truly indifferent to the relationships or perhaps cared about them but somehow felt too shy or inhibited to show any interest. He recalled with a smile an incident that occurred in Ronald's senior year, an incident which one of Ronald's "friends" had told him about in an after-hours tutoring session, the boy still laughing to himself about what he'd seen earlier that day. In the lunch room, a girl known to her classmates as smart and nice-looking, but so quiet and "mousy" as to be almost non-existent, approached Ronald and, blushing furiously, asked him if he would accompany her to the upcoming school dance. Ronald, according to his friend, did not respond in kind, showing no embarrassment whatever. But it was his friend's perception that Ronald was unembarrassed only because he was unable either to understand or believe what had happened. He stared at the girl, mouth hanging open, unable to speak until the poor young girl turned and ran. The professor added that, although neither Ronald nor his admirer came to the dance, he saw Ronald, months later, sitting on the school's back stoop with the girl, looking like he was not thinking of physics.

In college, however, Ronald's mind was very much on his work, and he continued to develop the ideas he had presented in his published paper. He received considerable support and encouragement from the faculty and, during his undergraduate years, published several more papers – two on his own and one in co-authorship with a faculty member. He was, by the time he was a junior, a well known and highly respected voice in the world of physics and, as such, had incurred more than a bit of resentment from some of his instructors, people who had labored for decades without achieving any of the recognition that Ronald had garnered before earning his undergraduate degree. He appeared not to notice, however, and went on with his work in a single-minded manner, a manner which earned the respect of those faculty members who did not suffer from an excess of envy. And when graduation approached, he was again besieged by offers, this time for admission to graduate programs from the country's most prestigious institutions, all of which were anxious to have an affiliation with him and evidenced their eagerness with offers of cost-free Ph.D. programs and coveted teaching assistantships. After due consideration, and, of course, consultation with Dr. Schuster, he chose his program, another east coast university where he was offered a chance to help in creating the courses he would teach and to freely pursue his research. It was, in fact, Dr. Schuster's good counsel, that was the deciding factor. Ronald had wanted to return to the mid-west, to be closer to home, but his old friend and mentor had urged him to put his career first, saying that once he had earned his doctorate and had the credentials he'd need, he could then return home or, indeed, join the faculty of any university of his choosing and settle anywhere he desired. Ronald's mother, while respecting his decision, later suggested that this was an unfortunate choice, and laid to it partial blame for the events which were to follow, events with such tragic consequences for Ronald, his family, and Dr. Schuster.

Ronald settled into a new university, a new home where, at first, all went well. He was, in important ways, where he belonged. No longer the outsider, the odd and aberrant egghead that he'd been in high school and even in college, he was now amongst his own. Here, in the somewhat insulated world comprising the physics department of this most excellent of universities, although he still kept his distance, he found others who showed more understanding of him, more interest in him, who, indeed, were more like him and seemed fully at ease with his head-in-the-clouds manner. It all seemed to work; Ronald learned and taught, excelling in both. It was no surprise that he was an outstanding student; that he had been for many years. How he would fare as an instructor was much less of a certainty. One might well have wondered whether his shyness, his reticence, would be enough to make him a less-than-stellar instructor, his command of his subject matter notwithstanding. Whether Ronald, himself, entertained such doubts was, unsurprisingly, evident to no one. But Dr. Schuster, if no one else, was concerned. He knew Ronald well enough to have doubts, and loved him well enough to be frightened for him. When, after delivering his first lecture, Ronald called him, bubbling – Ronald didn't bubble much – about how he had loved it, how much he had enjoyed the attention and how comfortable he felt, it was a relief and a comfort to Dr. Schuster.

To his own surprise, Ronald did love it. A neighbor from his Iowa home town might have felt hard-pressed to realize that the confident and articulate young instructor standing before a room full of underclassmen and holding forth on the wonders and mysteries of physics was actually the same Ronald Walensky of years past. It could be hard to comprehend that this was the same young man who might be seen wandering through the hallways of his school, looking as if he were an inhabitant of another world who had little connection with the affairs of this one. For that young man to have to face a room full of students could have been terrifying and, as Dr. Schuster learned after the fact, it had been. Once the class was over, in the midst of his bubbling, Ronald confided to his mentor that he had been so filled with dread at the prospect of holding the class that he spent most of the previous evening vomiting and considering the possibility of leaving school. What he hadn't realized was the tremendous opportunity it afforded him.

As a shy and intensely private young man, Ronald had known little comfort in interacting with people. He had always felt distant from others, self-conscious in most circumstances and unnerved and threatened in some. The chronic tension and distress that he experienced in the presence of others often made itself felt even when he talked physics with fellow students or faculty members; he was rarely free from a sense of dread that the conversation might turn from physics to more personal, casual topics and that he would be faced with making small-talk, an arduous task that made him long for the comfort of his books.

But there was no such risk in front of a class. Here, he was the instructor and would be seen and respected as such by all his students. Here, he had an inviolable shield, the shield of his role and the protection of his title – Instructor Walensky. He knew that he could impress his classes with his understanding of physics, and he knew that they would respect his authority and not attempt personal relationships with him – at least not without a clear signal from him that he was open to such relationships. He found, in this role, a greater comfort than he had ever known in a group of people and, like many a show business performer, felt more alive in front of his audience, his class, than in any other setting. He loved it.

For the first time in many years, for the first time since he discovered his love of science, he considered the possibility of devoting himself to something other than scientific thought and research. He had never thought that there could be any pleasure to compare with discovery, with the thrill of struggling and wrestling with ideas, with facts and figures that seemed ungovernable, unconquerable, and, in a moment of triumph, grasping what had previously been hidden. Now he had discovered a new pleasure – the pleasure of teaching, of imparting his knowledge to others. The gratification he felt in being able to convey complex ideas to students, the sense of self-worth he felt when he looked at their openly admiring faces, and, above all else, the feeling of accomplishment when he saw an expression of frustration and confusion transform into one of enlightenment and satisfaction – these were new and wonderful experiences for him.

They were new not only because he had never taught before; they were not merely a new pleasure, but an entirely new class of experience. This was the first time that Ronald had ever felt comfortable in a group of people, the first time that he had any sense that people, as a group, in a group, could offer anything to him other than feelings of anxiety, apprehension and dread.

And it was seemingly only these precise circumstances that could have allowed the young teaching assistant to have this experience, to feel this pleasure and to see himself in relation to others in a way radically different way than he ever had before. Given Ronald's shyness and strangeness, it is unlikely that he could have tolerated being in front of an audience in any capacity other than as a teacher. And, it is very likely that had it not been for his renown in the academic world, which he carried with him into his first classroom experience, he would have had great difficulty, perhaps insurmountable difficulty, in establishing himself as a teacher, in commanding the respect of a class. His ability as a teacher might never have had a chance to reveal itself – to him or to others – if he had stood before a class as an unknown instructor, feeling the terror that he would have felt. Being faced with a class of uninterested, unimpressed, bored young students would likely have been more than he could have tolerated, and his teaching career might well have ended before it really began. His name and accomplishments spared him the need to face such a class or such a test.

Had Ronald considered all these issues it might have deepened the enjoyment he felt as he became more at home in this new world, with his new source of enjoyment and the new way of experiencing himself that he had discovered. And, had he had more time to dwell in this new world, perhaps he might have more fully absorbed this new, confident way of seeing himself; perhaps it would have become more a part of him, in a deeper and broader way, so that it could have generalized to other parts of his life. Perhaps he might have become more comfortable with himself as a human being, instead of only as scholar. But what could have developed can never be more than speculation, just as what he actually felt as a graduate student and instructor can only be surmised. What I have said of it is conjecture, based on third-hand reports, reports from his mother, based on reports to her from Dr. Schuster, based on his own speculations and extrapolations, based on his conversations with Ronald. The events that followed made any more direct knowledge of Ronald's actual feelings forever unknowable; the psychic devastation that befell him has sealed within him all such memories. Whether they are available to him is a matter of speculation, but that they were not spoken of by him is a matter of history. Dr. Schuster would be the next best source of insight into Ronald's inner world, but Dr. Schuster, Ronald's great and good friend, the closest thing he had ever had to a confidante, his teacher, adviser, supporter, counselor and all-around booster, was also silenced by the events of the ensuing months. Silenced by Ronald's hand.

Two momentous events – one great, one terrible – happened almost simultaneously in Ronald's life. First, at the age of twenty-two, our young scientist found that he was in contention – one of the finalists – for one of the most prestigious prizes, including honors and grants, in the world of physics. An award that represented success achieved by only a select few was within his reach. Few things could dim the luster of such an accomplishment, but the second momentous change in Ronald's life was more than equal to the task. Only a few months before learning that he was being considered for this great honor, Ronald had begun the descent into schizophrenia.

The first noticeable indications were some rather strange things that Ronald was heard to say, strange comments that led to whisperings among students, and a change in his demeanor, a change that some found difficult to understand.

Later, his colleagues looked back over this period, trying to understand what had happened, and trying to construct a chronology. They struggled to recall the earliest signs of his illness. Although the whole horrendous affair was history by that time, it was almost as if they felt that if they could recognize where he first veered off from the world of shared experience, from the everyday world of the university into the realm of his private nightmares, they might somehow go back in time and hold him back, build a roadblock, forcing him back into the world they still inhabited. They were frightened as they witnessed his appalling and grotesque transformation and horrified at the ultimate outcome. Be it all over or not, they strove to find some way that it could have been understood and prevented, perhaps only to diminish the sense of helplessness felt by all those who were fond of him.

The first incident they could recall seemed trivial at the time, strange and inexplicable perhaps, but surely nothing to cause great concern. The students reacted with nothing more than humorous puzzlement. Even the person most directly involved, a student named Glenn Harley, laughed it off. This young man had

161

been an excellent student in Ronald's class; he sat in the front row, often asked intelligent questions and frequently offered insightful thoughts. It had always appeared that Ronald thought well of young Mr. Harley. But Mr. Harley's midterm exam – on which he achieved his usual excellent grade – was returned to him with more than the large A at the top of the front page. In the upper right-hand corner of the page, in black, block letters, his instructor had written "CAVE FORNICATIONE." Mr. Harley was curious, indeed. But he decided to try to decipher the note before asking his teacher about it. He wondered, he said, if it had something to do with fornicating in a cave, but could not believe that Mr. Walensky could possibly be broaching such a subject. But he found it equally difficult to comprehend when a classmate who knew Latin told him the note's actual meaning: "Beware immorality."

He hardly knew what to think. Did Mr. Walensky know or think he knew something about his personal life? Was he, perhaps, implying that Mr. Harley might be somehow cheating in the course? Or was the straight-laced teacher merely imparting some words of wisdom to a favored student? In the end, despite the urgings of his classmates, Mr. Harley decided against asking Mr. Walensky about the note. Too bad, perhaps.

Was it that the note had sparked an increased focus on Mr. Walensky's demeanor and behavior, or was it that he had begun to feel more ill-at-ease in the classroom? Hard to know. But the students, in the following weeks, noted to each other that Mr. Walensky seemed tense in front of the class. A few thought they noticed an occasional glance at Mr. Harley with a troubled or even angry expression on the teacher's face. And more than a few noticed that Mr. Walensky had begun to sweat in class – despite the comfortable room temperature.

Nor did the changes in Mr. Walensky's demeanor and behavior go unnoticed by his fellow doctoral candidates or by the faculty. His discomfort in social situations, especially with his peers, had never left him. Walensky's fellow students saw him as aloof, and assumed, incorrectly, that he believed himself to be above them. They did not know him well. But certain shifts in attitude nevertheless became clearly observable. Aloofness is one matter, frank rudeness another. He was seen in a different light after an incident in the library when two of his fellow graduate students approached him for casual conversation. They looked at each other in confusion when, without saying a word, Walensky pointedly turned his back on them and walked away. This, his first display of open animosity towards his fellows, later seemed to have been an announcement of his new but increasingly evident antipathy toward those who might have been his friends. It was actually, in its own way, an announcement of something far more sinister.

The students in his classes might have been more concerned had they been aware of what was happening outside the classroom; and the faculty members and his fellow Ph.D. candidates might have been more alarmed had they known of the changes in his classroom demeanor. But apparently, such communication never occurred. Too bad, perhaps. But Mr. Walensky's new and peculiar behavior was, at first, sufficiently subtle that none of his colleagues – the faculty and his fellow doctoral candidates – thought to sound out the students on his comportment in class. They thought it might be the strain of being so young and the object of the envy of so many, that made him become a bit more quarrelsome when he had previously been so docile. And, in meetings of faculty and teaching assistants, they were surprised when Mr. Walensky, always the first to side with the students, always the first to defend them in discussions of their work, began to show a different attitude, an attitude of irritation, of disapproval or even of anger. What made it all the more strange was that none could discern from his comments what, precisely, was the nature of his complaints. He did not seem to be saying that they were lacking in either ability or motivation as students – concerns often raised by his colleagues; such complaints they would have understood. Instead, it sounded as if he had some other less defined but darker complaint about the character of some of his students – particularly males, it seemed.

The discussions among faculty about this change in his temperament were casual, at first. They conjectured, much as did the students, that there was something about the strain of his situation that might be weighing on him. They thought, perhaps, that some students who, after all, were no younger than Mr. Walensky, might have given him cause to feel that they resented him. But, like the students, the faculty too shrugged it off at first. Too bad, perhaps.

Their concern was kicked up to another level, however, when Mr. Walensky was openly disrespectful to the department chair, Dr. Robert Stephens. Dr. Stephens was taken aback, shocked, in fact, when the incident occurred.

Mr. Walensky, perhaps appropriately so due to his age, was the most deferential of the instructors in the physics department.

Respectful of all his elders and particularly of the faculty, his attitude toward the chairman was almost reverential, and Dr. Stephens had developed a genuine fondness for the young man over the course of the months of working with him. The younger man had always been somewhat shy in his presence; diffident and unassuming, that is, but at ease, as if in the presence of a slightly distant but protective parent. The chairman, of course, expected nothing but Mr. Walensky's consistently mild and modest, courteous and respectful demeanor when he summoned him to discuss the unsatisfactory progress of a physics major who was approaching graduation. He knew almost immediately that something was wrong.

As he sat down in front of Dr. Stephens desk, instead of smiling pleasantly, Ronald looked harried, tense, almost frightened. His eyes darted back and forth across the room, as if looking to see who or what was lurking in the corners, as if Stephens might spring some unpleasant surprise upon him.

Noticing this, but not quite knowing how or whether to address it, Stephens simply asked Walensky how he'd been.

"Fine," was the curt reply, offered – to Stephens' great surprise – without reciprocation of the question.

"Er, I've asked you in to discuss the Morris situation. I'm concerned."

"What did he tell you?" asked Walensky, sounding both angry and frightened.

After pausing and giving his young friend a concerned and inquisitive look, a look that was met only by a tightening of Walensky's face, a clenching of his jaws, Stephens said: "He didn't tell me anything. I'm concerned about his work. It's unclear that he'll be able to complete his graduation requirements in a timely manner."

"You're telling me that that's the only reason you called me here?"

"Why, yes, of course. What were you thinking?"

"I was thinking that he was talking, going around saying things, going around saying things that he has no damned right to say, or even to think, for that matter. I know the things they're saying, even if they think I don't! WHAT DID HE TELL YOU?!"

"Mr. Walensky!" Stephens said, stunned at what he was hearing. Then, softening, "Mr. Walensky... Ron... something's troubling you. Please tell me what's wrong."

"They get ideas about people and they start spreading rumors! I'D LIKE TO..."

"Who? What ideas, what rumors?... Ron, listen to me; please tell me what's bothering you.... I hate to see you so disturbed, I'd really like to help if I possibly can. *Please* tell me what's wrong."

The evident sincerity and unquestionable concern and kindness in Stephens's manner touched the younger man, soothing him. The anger seeped from his body like air escaping from a balloon, leaving him deflated, shriveled, less vigilant and threatening, but deeply distressed and confused. He sat quietly for a long moment, seeming to become more thoughtful and looking at the elder man with a questioning and pleading look, as if deciding whether he could trust him and hoping he could. Sounding as though he might cry, he quietly asked, "Dr. Stephens, are you having me watched? Are you... is the administration having people report to them about me?"

"Of *course* not, Ron. Why *would* I? Why would *they*? We're all so proud of you here, and so pleased with how you've handled yourself. *Why* would we do that?"

Walensky's attention seemed to turn to somewhere inside himself, his suspicion now directed within. Frowning and perplexed, his voice seeming to grow smaller, he said, "It just seems... I'm not sure... I can't... I'm not sure." He sat hunched over, his eyes apparently directed toward Stephens' desk, but his gaze turned inward, his head shaking slightly and slowly from side to side.

They sat in silence for several minutes, Stephens looking at Walensky with curiosity and concern, considering various options about how to deal with this clearly troubled young man. Walensky sat, seeing nothing, shaking his head, struggling to understand something that he couldn't or wouldn't openly address.

After a few moments, he seemed to pull himself upward, took a deep breath and, in a business-like manner, said, "Let's discuss Mr. Morris. I share your concern. He has been sloppy in his work and I've been wondering what sort of grade I'll be able to give him. I understand that his GPA is very borderline even now."

Now it was Stephens who had to struggle to compose himself, to concentrate on the ostensible topic of conversation.

One afternoon shortly thereafter, a young man who had been a Walensky admirer said to a classmate, "What on Earth was he saying this afternoon? Did you get that comment about the government?"

"Yeah, I heard it, but I thought I must not have understood it. Did he say that the government is observing his classes?"

"I don't know if he really meant it, but it sounded pretty weird."

"He's always been sort of unusual, that's for sure. Maybe that goes along with being as brilliant as he is. But this was some weird stuff."

"Yeah, and besides that, he just hasn't looked the same recently. It's almost as if he's on some kind of drug or something. One minute he's talking calmly and lecturing, the next, he looks like he's a million miles away, and he's wild-eyed."

"Well, who knows. A guy like that, so brilliant, having done so much at that age." Laughing, he added, "He can't be normal, that's for sure."

But as the semester wore on, the change seemed to take greater hold and was increasingly difficult to dismiss. Ronald was less his usual self, more a distracted, troubled man, a man who seemed to have to struggle to concentrate on his lectures, as if something – something that none of his students understood – was pulling him away into an unknown world, slowly but steadily and insistently. One young woman, shy and awkward with people, her perception perhaps sharpened by her emotional attunement to those similar to herself, said that she saw him as a man adrift in an oarless rowboat, a boat slowly drifting further from the shore, its occupant looking on in helpless panic as the tide pulled him slowly out to sea.

The timing couldn't have been worse. If it had gone on for much longer, the reality would have been unavoidable. The brilliant young scientist would have been recognized as ill and would have gotten the medical attention he desperately needed. Had he become more emotionally erratic, had he become more undeniably paranoid, had his thinking become blatantly bizarre, something would have been done. In all probability, he would have been placed on a medication regimen which might have made all the difference in the world. If he had received treatment, it is entirely possible that the medication could have been effective and tolerable – as modern medications often are – and that the whole awful turn of events could have been averted. No such luck.

Just at the time that Ronald's students and colleagues were becoming increasingly concerned, Dr. Schuster had occasion to travel to the east coast and he could not conceive of doing so without including a visit to his young friend. After all, they had been in regular contact throughout the time that Walensky had been away; their relationship had not been diminished by the distance or the time apart from each other. Schuster was even more anxious to see his protégée after calling him to arrange the visit. On the telephone, young Ronald at first seemed pleased – in fact, unusually so – to hear from him. But as the conversation went on, Schuster found that there were moments when Ronald seemed to have tuned him out. He asked a question and got no response. Then, a moment later, as if returning from some distracting preoccupation, Ronald said: "Oh! Yes, my classes are going very well." The response was not reassuring, however, as he seemed quickly to drift away again: "Yes, they're going well... one section is not... some students..." Then, silence. But Ronald would say nothing of anything troubling him, giving no hint other than telling Schuster that, when he saw him, he might like to ask his advice about handling certain classroom situations. The older man, recognizing that he was unlikely to get Ronald to say more on the phone, decided he'd simply see for himself what the situation was when he arrived for the visit. He did think that he heard a note of uncertainty in Ronald's voice when he invited him to stay in his campus apartment, but he dismissed that as Ronald's characteristic tension about interpersonal situations, and Ronald's insistence on the plan convinced Schuster that it was his sincere wish.

It was Ronald's wish – sort of. He knew that he must extend the invitation, and he knew that at other times he would have been glad to be able to offer the hospitality. Such was his fondness and respect for Dr. S that, the dread that he now felt at the idea of having him as house guest notwithstanding, he could not bring himself to be so insulting as not to make the offer.

In fact, it may well have been the prospect of sharing his living quarters with another man that pushed Ronald over a line that he had been for some time able to draw for himself. Uncertain about what he felt and thought, Ronald had decided to refrain from making accusations, accusations that at times felt as though they might fly out of his mouth involuntarily. There was a part of him that felt absolutely certain about the abuse he had been experiencing, absolutely certain that people were targeting him with unfair taunts and insinuations. But they wouldn't come out and say what they were thinking, and Ronald did not want to show his hand first. He had decided that they were trying to drive him out of the school; they didn't want him as a doctoral candidate, they didn't want him as a teacher. He was uncertain when and how they had all come to this decision, but faculty, fellow doctoral candidates and undergraduates all seemed to turn against him at the same time. They wanted him to do something foolish, they wanted him to show his hand, they wanted him to give vent to his rage in a display of aggression that would give them license to say that he had proven himself to be an uncivilized, deviant homosexual, a pervert who could not be trusted around college students.

He had thus far outsmarted them. In spite of their insinuations, in spite of the leering looks that Glenn Harley had been giving him on a regular basis, the invitation to engage in filthy homosexual acts, he had held his tongue. Even when a female classmate in his doctoral program came to class wearing that awful shirt, the one with pictures of apples, pears and oranges, he swallowed the insult rather than confront her for her villainous suggestion that he was a "fruit." He did not know what he would do, how he would handle it. How could he endure the years of torment until he could complete his Ph.D. and relocate? But he felt that he could not allow these people, however determined they may be, to drive him away. Even when he found that the townspeople had been enlisted in the task – men in the street trying to get him to look at their crotches, women making faces, moving their lips in ways to mock how they thought he might look in the act of fellatio – he held firm. He would not voice his complaints; he would not let them defeat and destroy him.

But then he could resist no longer. The tragedy that ultimately unfolded would certainly imply that it was the prospect of Schuster's presence as a house guest that pushed him over the edge, but, be that as it may, he now struck back openly. Harley was his first target, Harley who had taken him in by making him think that he was a promising and admiring student, a protégée, perhaps. Harley had made it almost impossible for Ronald not to like him – as a student, as a mind that he could encourage, as a fertile field where the seeds of wonder about the world of physics could be planted.

But no, Harley had other ideas in mind. Ronald wanted to befriend him, to teach him; Harley wanted only to seduce and humiliate his teacher. In spite of Ronald's utter lack of sexual interest in Harley, or any other man for that matter, Harley aimed to force him to make a move of sexual intent whereupon Harley would not only reject him but would advertise the incident to all who would listen. Ronald had not allowed himself to fall for it. But one day after class, weeks after the "cave fornicacione" incident and hours before Schuster's scheduled arrival, Ronald confronted his tormentor. He called to him outside the building, and began berating Harley for his deviousness, his duplicity and his disgusting sexual proclivities. He believed them to be alone, out of hearing range of all others, and at first they were. But as Ronald's outburst gathered steam, as his ire rose to a crescendo, his voice did likewise and, before he realized it, a crowd of students stood open-mouthed, listening to their skinny, bespectacled teacher, their brilliant and mild-mannered instructor, screaming at the top of his lungs at a student who appeared frozen in place, as unmoving as a mannequin, but with a look of uncomprehending horror on his face.

Had this not been the very eve of Schuster's arrival, perhaps something could have been done. As soon as he recovered himself, Harley and a group of his classmates went to the university counseling center. The counseling center's outreach program had made them aware that the aberrant behavior of anyone on campus should be brought to their attention as soon as possible. What the counseling center personnel would have done, how effective they could have been at helping Ronald, will never be known. Events stunningly short-circuited any plans they might have had.

When Schuster arrived, he must have known immediately that his young friend was not the person he had known for so many years. By this time, having had a few hours to consider what he had done in full view of dozens of undergraduates, Ronald was in a whirlwind of emotions – a turbulence that exceeded even the confusion, despair and terror that he had experienced in recent weeks. His feelings covered quite a range, but none were anything resembling contentment or peace. He wanted to run away, feeling that he had humiliated himself in front of his students; he was enraged at himself for falling into their trap; he wanted to resign from both his teaching assistantship and his doctoral candidacy; he wanted to find Harley and not only continue his blast of rage at him but perhaps, just perhaps, actually assault him. He was enraged. He wanted to buy a weapon. He wanted to humbly apologize to Harley and the others. He wanted to scream. He wanted to cry. He wanted to kill, but he didn't know whom to kill. He wanted to die. He wanted to die.

Schuster must have been shocked. His reactions can only be surmised; he never had a chance to share them. He might have considered taking his friend to the school infirmary or the counseling center or even to a local hospital emergency room. Surely many possibilities crossed his mind. But he had arrived relatively late at night and, much to his misfortune, apparently elected to delay any attempt to get help for his friend until the next day. For Dr. Schuster, Ronald's great and good friend, the next day never came.

* * *

What sickness of the soul, what internal demon could have made Ronald repeatedly stab his mentor with a steak knife? What power could make a young man do such a thing to his beloved teacher and friend? What force can so twist, so distort, so contort the working of the human mind as to turn one's love, admiration and devotion into the brutal, animalistic state of mind that allowed – or compelled – Ronald to do this? And how, how on Earth, having killed this man – the meaning and importance of whose relation to him I can find no words to further convey – could he approach the lifeless man, pull his clothes off and castrate him?

A mild, reticent, introverted man, a man of great curiosity about the secrets of the universe, about the nature of nature, a man who until recent days had literally never raised his voice or uttered a word to any human being in anger, kills someone – kills him and finds his bloodlust still raging, raging and pushing him to commit an act beyond his murder, an act of grotesque and horrific mutilation. A young man of accomplishments far beyond his years, a man who might have added to mankind's store of knowledge and technological capability in ways no one can guess, never again engages in productive activity. A brilliant and promising physicist, a man who had already earned great respect and might have won honors attained by few, becomes a

174

reviled murderer, an outcast, a miscreant, an inmate in an asylum for the criminally insane.

Can there be an explanation? There are those, those who seem desperately to want to reduce mind to brain, who might say, "Well, he had an excess of dopamine and serotonin," or "He lacked sufficient norepinephrine," or some similar statement, as if such an assertion in any way spoke to the feelings and motivations involved in the act. For all I know, Ronald might have had too much serotonin or not enough norepinephrine, or both, or any other possible chemical or physical disorder of his brain. But what did he *feel*? What did he *think*? What motivations, overwhelming as they must have been, drove him to his act of madness? Surely, he didn't think to himself, "Well, I have too much serotonin, so I'll murder and mutilate my beloved mentor."

Ronald had become schizophrenic – schizophrenic and acutely psychotic. Yet this fact, in and of itself, does not explain Ronald's motivations any more than would an assertion of a chemical imbalance or other pathology of the brain. What motivated Ronald was his paranoia, a cognitive/emotional condition that is often a component of schizophrenia. The word paranoia is frequently used, not only in popular literature, but in everyday life, as well. Its usage is often both apt and correct, but the phenomenon is nevertheless not well understood – much as people often speak of thunder or lightning, accurately referring to the phenomenon but having no comprehension of its cause or its underlying nature.

Paranoia, when present, is often such a central and predominant feature of schizophrenia that one specific subtype of the disorder is termed paranoid schizophrenia. As is well known, paranoia involves a feeling that one is being persecuted, that one is being singled out and targeted for abuse by others – often, though not always, by a broad community of others. What might create such a feeling? Why should it occur with such frequency? There is no end to the variation of form that delusions might assume, yet perhaps forty percent of cases of schizophrenia are of the paranoid type. What accounts for its ubiquity?

The answer to the question can be found in the nature of paranoia, in an understanding of the psychological mechanism which underlies it. This mechanism is known as projection, a term originated by Freud which, like the term paranoia, has seeped into common usage. Projection is a process of externalization, a process whereby an inner feeling, attribute or experience is perceived as existing in the external environment. Externalization is a universal aspect of human experience and, as so much else in the realm of the mind, exists in a wide spectrum, ranging from everyday, more-or-less normal functioning to the profoundly pathological.

At the more normal end of the spectrum of externalization, is the ordinary human tendency to interpret the world in terms of our own inner experience. Thus, we attribute human feelings and attitudes to non-human entities of all kinds. Anthropomorphism – the attribution of human traits to non-human entities – is as old as history and extends to our perception of creatures low and high, from the pests and beasts that we loathe or fear to our beloved pets. And who has used a computer and can honestly say that he never had the feeling, even while knowing better, that the lifeless machine was intentionally thwarting him?

Interpreting the world based on one's own view of oneself accounts for the fact that people often have difficulty understanding those who act differently from themselves – or, indeed, simply recognizing the reality that others might not feel things or see the world as they do. I recall a young woman, a fellow doctoral candidate who, as we began to study psychopathology and psychotherapy, often said that she thought she would feel a strong urge to grab some patients by the collar and shake them. What she apparently was saying was that she assumed that others were or should be like she was, and if they could only be shaken out of their false or somehow invalid feeling of being different, they would surely be just like her and all would be well.

As projection moves in the direction of psychopathology, it takes on a different character; it becomes less casual, more exigent and acquires a more insistent tone. Its purpose and nature change. It ceases to be simply a means of helping the individual to comprehend his world, of using his own inner life to help organize experience, and becomes a means of protecting oneself from unpleasant thoughts and feelings. In other words, it takes on a defensive function. The essential aim of externalization or projection now becomes to get rid of something from within, to expel it, to spit it out, so to speak, into the external world, freeing oneself of its noxious influence. And, in the process, projection becomes more costly to the individual. The price exacted by this more rigid and urgent, ardent form of projection is a loss of self-awareness and a corresponding loss of a full appreciation of reality. It has an almost arithmetic quality; one's self-perception is changed by the subtraction of some trait or tendency, and the perception of the external world is changed by the addition to it of that very feature.

The more mildly pathological versions of projection are less troubling to the individual and less distorting of reality – but they may cause a great deal of mischief, nonetheless. The reader almost certainly has known someone who tends to be overly suspicious of people, attributing their every act to ill intentions, yet manages to function relatively well. Such a person, if the problem is sufficiently pronounced, will be known to his associates as paranoid – but surely in a less severe form than Walensky.

In everyday life, people employ a wide variety of means of psychological self-protection or, perhaps more accurately, self-preservation. In fact, it sometimes seems that the more attempts we make to catalog the "defense mechanisms," the more the futility of the task becomes apparent; the human mind is inexhaustibly inventive. But it appears that the more severe forms of psychopathology are somewhat limited in their variety. There is no end to the subtle differences between personalities, even within a given "personality type." But as psychopathology becomes more severe, the pathological aspects of the personality assume such importance and such rigidity and gain such sway over the person as a whole that it is as if the personality, with all of its idiosyncratic individuality, is swallowed up in the pathology, much as a face, if sufficiently swollen or bloated, would become very similar to all other equally swollen or bloated faces and would suffer the loss of its own unique and distinctive features. Thus, projection, one of an endless variety of defense mechanisms in the healthy, becomes one of the limited number of profound distorters of the mind, corrupters of the soul, destroyers of the self in the severely ill.

It would be unfortunate both for his general understanding of paranoia and projection and his appreciation of Mr. Walensky's predicament if the reader failed to understand that projection is most certainly not an intellectual exercise; the paranoid individual does not consciously decide to pretend not to see his own unacceptable feelings – his aggression or homoeroticism or other unwanted traits – and to attribute them to others. To understand the importance of such pathological projection to the individual, to understand its capacity to preserve, as well as possible, the individual's psychological integrity, it must be understood that the paranoid individual is not simply trying to disavow something about himself; he is ridding himself of the unwanted feelings or perception, he is expelling the experience from his conscious awareness. An appropriate metaphor, perhaps, is the case of an individual choking on a piece of food. It would help not in the least for the sufferer to imagine the piece of food to be gone. He may imagine to his heart's content, but if the food is not dislodged, he will suffer a non-imaginary death. As the offending piece of food must be expelled from the windpipe to save the bodily functioning of the unfortunate diner, the offending awareness must be expelled from the mind to preserve the remaining psychological integrity of the unfortunate psychotic.

Projection is an attempt to preserve psychic integrity, much as the coughing up of a piece of food on which one is choking is an attempt to preserve physical integrity. But the analogy holds only to a point. The diner, once he has expelled the offending piece of food, is well; he can go on with his meal, even if he might think to eat a bit more slowly. Things do not end so well for the person who engages in wholesale projection; it does not serve its employer well; he has not restored himself to a state of well-being; he cannot simply go on with his meal; he cannot eat in peace. The paranoid individual may rid himself of his unacceptable feelings and his self-hatred, but he trades these for a different torment; he is perhaps escaping the frying pan for the fire. The end result of his psychological acrobatics is that he has the experience of being hated and persecuted, the object of villainous, malevolent treachery. It may be hard to say whether or not he has made a good bargain – although, again, I don't mean to say that the paranoid person has made a conscious, rational decision; much to the contrary. But he is perhaps escaping the fire for the frying pan; one must consider that it may be preferable to be pursued and hated from without rather than from within; one has at least some theoretical chance for escape! Unfortunately, in the process, the extremely paranoid individual undergoes the disastrous loss of reality. He becomes psychotic.

Any unwanted trait can be projected; one may excise his own greed or arrogance or vanity and implant it in those around him, that is, in his perception of those around him. This, by the way, is certainly not to say that those others may not actually be greedy or arrogant or vain or whatever; it is only that their actual traits are overlaid with projected material. In fact, one generally picks targets for projection that are, in one way or another, fitting. Paranoid people, incessantly on the alert for the malevolence of persecutors, actually can be very perceptive of people's hidden tendencies. They exchange an awareness of their own unacceptable tendencies for a capacity to sense them in others. Of course, when the psychopathology is deeper and more pervasive, when the need is more dire and reality-testing closer to obliteration, the individual becomes less discriminating and the projections become more outlandish and distorted.

Why, one might ask, when all indications are that Mr. Walensky was predominantly heterosexual, did he focus on homosexuality as the "crime" for which he was to be hounded and persecuted. A fair question. Of course, it is possible that, predominantly heterosexual or not, he did experience especially strong homosexual urges that troubled him and called forth feelings of shame or guilt. But that need not be the case. Although many believe that all human beings feel, on some level within or without their awareness, a panorama of sexual appetites and inclinations, we have no particular reason to believe that Mr. Walensky's homosexual urges were anything beyond the ordinary. "They think I am gay" is a statement that one often hears as the culmination of a paranoid individual's explanation for his persecution. But it seems, actually, that it is not the fact of being gay that is associated with paranoia, but, rather, a preoccupation with the possibility of being gay – the fear that one will be seen as gay. That this is so is a clinical reality; why it is so is open to conjecture. And a fair amount of conjecture has been offered. But one of the more uncomplicated and appealing explanations may be subject to empirical verification in the coming years. It has been suggested that, to the extent that a system of paranoid belief is logical or coherent, it must have as its basis an offense

– an action or a trait – that will be found repugnant or offensive by one's community. And homosexuality has, until recently, been among the more egregious "crimes" in the eyes of our society. If homosexuality continues to gain general acceptance, beyond the level of superficial political correctness, it may at some point lose its utility as an explanation for the paranoid individual's persecution and may be replaced by some other trait that confers pariah status.

Regardless of the explanations he offers to himself or others for his persecution, the paranoid individual feels that others wish to exert some form of malicious power over him. If they do not wish to kill him, they wish to control, dominate, humiliate, subjugate and oppress him. The paranoid person is on the alert for such tendencies in others; he fears allowing himself to be the weaker party in any interaction; he fears allowing anyone to wield power over him in any way.

Power is the coin of the realm in the world of paranoia; the paranoid person must never allow another to have the upper hand; if he feels himself slipping into a one-down position, he must right himself by taking action against the offender. To allow another to have undue – or any – influence over him is intolerable. Thus, paranoid people often have very difficult relationships with those who have some form of realistic power over them. Relationships with authority figures, for example, often present a great challenge. The paranoid individual may either be unable to submit to appropriate authority, or he may compensate for his rage by being obsequious, or he may fluctuate between these two polarities of behavior. This is certainly not to say that paranoid individuals do not often perceive strangers –

people who not only have no power over them but with whom they have virtually no involvement whatever – as threats. Possibly the most common cause of someone pushing a complete stranger in front of a subway train is a paranoid delusion in which the innocent stranger is believed to be thinking derisively of, or plotting against, or otherwise offending the paranoid individual, leaving the "victimized" paranoid "no choice" but to take such retaliatory – or pre-emptive – action.

But the individual who actually holds some form of power over a paranoid person – by virtue of his authority or of his personal importance to the paranoid individual – is particularly likely to be seen as a threat. This, incidentally, presents a great challenge for the psychotherapist working with a paranoid patient, something I learned, much to my chagrin, very early in my career. In a training position in an outpatient clinic during my days in graduate school, I worked with an intelligent but fragile and rather paranoid woman, Monica, a nurse of about thirty-five years of age. Recognizing that she was hypersensitive to anything she perceived as criticism and quick to feel ill-treated or offended, I was cautious, gentle and affable – perhaps too much so. I may have failed to appreciate that coming too close to her, not taking care to respect her need for distance, and allowing her to feel dependent upon me might, in itself, evoke a paranoid reaction.

In her sessions, she would frequently lament the treatment she was receiving at work, imagining herself to be the target of her supervisor's animosity and abuse. She felt herself lucky to find the position she had and was pleased with her remuneration, but she felt that she was being given more than her share of unpleasant assignments, that her talents and work ethic were never adequately appreciated, and that the supervisor even encouraged her co-workers to demean her in subtle ways. In this, her supervisor seemed to be a latter-day version of her mother, who was also a frequent object of Monica's complaints. She spoke painfully of how, as she viewed the relationship, she had always and forever been unable to please her mother or to wrest from her the approval or affirmation which she sorely lacked. Her sisters, she maintained, were favored over her at every turn. I was accustomed to hearing the complaints about both mother and supervisor but was taken aback when she informed me one day that she now knew that I had been in contact with her supervisor and had encouraged the woman to make all manner of unreasonable demands upon Monica in order to test her mettle and force her to learn to "toughen up and take it." She informed me of this in an almost casual manner and did not seem to expect or be demanding any defense or denial from me. In fact, her tone implied that she was not accusing me of being against her; she seemed to have concluded that this was a well-intentioned feature of the therapy. In a session shortly thereafter, however, I was again rudely surprised when, as I sat quietly, listening to her train of thought, she suddenly and utterly without warning loudly erupted, this time with clear wrath and condemnation.

"WHAT ARE YOU DOING? STOP IT! STOP IT! HOW AM I SUPPOSED TO TALK TO YOU WHILE YOU'RE DOING THAT TO ME ? STOP IT! STOP IT!"

"What am I doing to you?"

"AS IF YOU DIDN'T KNOW! YOU'RE HYPNOTIZING ME! THE WAY YOU'RE STROKING YOUR BEARD! I KNOW WHAT YOU'RE DOING! YOU'RE TRYING TO HYPNOTIZE ME AND MAKE ME DO THE THINGS YOU THINK I SHOULD DO TO GET BETTER! BUT ALL YOU'RE DOING IS UPSETTING ME! STOP IT! STOP IT!"

Although she soon regained her composure – while I struggled internally to maintain mine – this was but a harbinger of the profound illness which soon overtook her; and our work was brought to an abrupt halt when she was hospitalized with a paranoid psychosis.

I never learned what ultimately became of the unfortunate woman, nor have I ever known with certainty my role, if any, in her breakdown. Did allowing herself to feel susceptible to influence in therapy hasten her psychic disintegration? Perhaps; perhaps not. But it is a certainty that, at the very least, I became incorporated into her delusional system, assuming an integral role. And it would further seem that her wish to have my approval and her vulnerability to being affected by me catalyzed my incorporation into her delusional system.

This poor woman may have left me a bit shaken, but her response to her paranoid fears was surely far more benign than that of Mr. Walensky and I emerged from the experience alive and physically intact. Yet there are clear similarities and parallels between her personal tragedy and Walensky's. In fact, the woman's experience actually mirrored Walensky's in important respects. Both focused their paranoid delusions on individuals whom they perceived as having power over them. In

Monica's case, it is true, her main tormentor may have been her supervisor, a woman who wielded some degree of financially-based power over her, but she also drew me into her circle of persecutors based, apparently, on her emotional connection to me. Furthermore, it was not her supervisor's power over her career that tormented Monica; she rarely referred to such issues. It was the woman's refusal to offer up to Monica the praise and recognition which she so ardently craved. Mr. Walensky did, at some point, include Professor Stephens – an individual with some degree of power over him – in his world of persecutors, but Stephens was not his main tormentor; that distinction was reserved for Glenn Harley and, ultimately, Dr. Schuster. These were not individuals who held authority over Mr. Walensky, nor were they strangers to him. Their importance lay in their emotional connections to him or, rather, his to them.

Young Mr. Harley was a male student who assumed an important place in Walensky's life. He recognized that Harley respected and admired him and wished to be respected, in return, by his instructor. He was Walensky's star pupil who not only paid rapt attention in class, but sought out Walensky before or after class to ask questions; Walensky began to see him as a protégée. He was, of course, familiar with the mentor-mentee relationship, but only from the mentee's perspective. For him to find someone admiring him in anything like the way he admired Dr. Schuster was an emotionally powerful experience. Harley began to assume a great importance to Walensky. For his part, Dr. Schuster had long occupied a place of special importance in Mr. Walensky's emotional ecology.

What I am suggesting is that both Ronald Walensky and Monica were tripped up, so to speak, by their own needs, needs which they had been more or less successful in fending off until circumstances undermined their defensive attempts. Monica had moved out of her mother's home at an early age and had supported herself with a variety of short-term jobs. She had also avoided enduring relationships with men, generally finding that they were "too critical," and terminating the relationship. When she entered nursing school, she struggled with instructors who were, from her perspective, too demanding and "critical," but these, too, were short-term relationships and she managed to successfully complete her training. Now, however, she seemed to feel locked into a relationship with a woman who was the second coming of her mother. The more desperately she needed this woman's approval – and my help and support – the more endangered she became.

A very similar situation pertained in Mr. Walensky's case. Throughout his life, as we have seen, he maintained a distance from others, keeping himself to himself and, probably without ever articulating such a thought to himself, fearing involvement with other people. Dr. Schuster was of great importance to him, but he maintained his distance in that relationship by limiting it to the discussion of science; he kept the relationship, in a manner of speaking, on a business or professional level. Now, at school, he felt the tug of needs that had long been kept in abeyance. His involvement with his classmates and colleagues, and his enjoyment of being admired and respected as a teacher created a vulnerability that seemed to overwhelm him. He could not tolerate his own needs for closeness to and affection from other males. It must be remembered, after all, that as small child, in the formative years of his personality, he was virtually ignored by his father, who was physically present, but distant from and largely uninterested in his children. Children have a profound need for emotional sustenance from their parents – they are hard-wired in that way – and the very young Walensky must have unknowingly, unthinkingly, unconsciously found ways of warding off, denying or negating his needs for affection and attention from his father. His situation at school may well have reanimated the needs for such relationships with male figures and he was unprepared to accommodate or assimilate such feelings. In his torment, he may well have misinterpreted his own needs for male-to-male relationships as homosexual strivings; that is to say, not that he misunderstood his feelings but that they were actually transformed into such homoerotic urges. And his paranoia – his expulsion of his own feelings and urges into his external environment – created for him the delusion that he was surrounded by people trying to seduce him into forbidden behavior. Was it forbidden to him because of societal attitudes? Perhaps. Was it forbidden to him because it represented a need that, in very early childhood, he had learned was dangerous and could not be given free rein? Almost certainly.

I must make it clear that I am surely not suggesting that every woman who grows up with a hypercritical mother or every man who has lived with an emotionally-absent father becomes paranoid and psychotic; what I am suggesting, however, is that such profound emotional conflicts can be part – along with whatever other factors, as yet unknown to us – of what pushes an unfortunate individual into psychosis and will, almost certainly, play an important role in shaping the particular form that his or her psychosis assumes.

Monica's and Mr. Walensky's experiences lend support to these ideas in similar ways. In both cases, their ambivalence, their contradictory and confused feelings toward the objects of their paranoia, were manifest. With Monica, it was remarkable – and, at the time, startling – to hear her tell me, in effect, that I was exerting a manipulative, insidious and malevolent influence over her – but with only the best of intentions. As she perceived the situation, I was surreptitiously "hypnotizing" her, making her feel that I was usurping control of her mind, but only in the service of helping her.

And if we now return to our point of departure from Mr. Walensky's tragic tale, we may come to see how it was his affection for Dr. Schuster, and his hope of gaining some sense of security from his presence, that led him to viciously murder this kindly, helpful, tormenting villain.

* * *

There may be little that can be said with certainty of the experience of our wretched, ill-fated protagonist, of the days and weeks of his torment and its crescendo during that awful night that destroyed the lives of his mentor and himself. Perhaps the best we can do is to surmise, to construct a credible narrative – one that, if not provable by objective means – is at least coherent and suggests itself as the most plausible explanation. We are, of course, trying to make sense of the seemingly insensible, trying to impose rationality – of a kind – on horrendous, almost unimaginable behavior. What horrendous, almost unimaginable feelings must Ronald have had? What could have made him feel a need to kill a man whom he loved? Was it, in fact, as I am suggesting, the very affection that he had for his friend and mentor that made him kill him?

There was, in a way, a profound injustice to Ronald's illness. His life was in ascent. He not only had years of brilliant productivity in front of him, but he had begun to enjoy life in a new way; he had reached an accommodation – or so it had seemed – with his isolative needs. He could enjoy not only the life of his mind but a life with at least some degree of fellowship with his colleagues and students. He may never have known the joys of life and the kinds of relationship that are open to many; he may or may not have been able to marry and have a family, but he had, for the first time, found a place for himself.

But then, so tragically, everything changed. From our perspective, he changed – his sanity, his psychic solidity crumbled. From his perspective, the change, the corruption, occurred all around him. At first, he felt a vague sense of discomfort, as if someone was thinking that he had done something wrong, as if perhaps the administration or his colleagues were for some reason unhappy with him. But then he saw that it was nothing specific that he had done and that the hostility came from more than a few individuals. He began to realize that people were looking at him in a new and disturbing way. He noticed it more and more. They looked at him, they stared at him, and there was no doubt what they were thinking. Their vile accusations! They had decided that he was homosexual and the word had quickly spread. And Harley! Looking at him, seducing him, trying everything in his power to expose him! Yes, there were moments, such as happened in Dr. Stephens' office, when he felt uncertain – less threatened by his environment perhaps, but more confused, more frightened by himself than by others, more horribly frightened – terrified, in fact, that he was facing some incomprehensible form of inner disintegration. But as he later thought about Stephens' behavior, he realized that it was perhaps the most reprehensible thing of all, to try to weaken him, to lull him into a sense of safety only to get him to betray himself. No one was to be trusted! Not his favorite student, Harley, nor his kindly superior, Stephens. Their treachery was all the worse for the way they had induced him to like them. All of them! They all wanted to trap him and destroy him, to force him into disgusting homosexual acts only to expose him, humiliate him, degrade him, ruin him – to make him a public spectacle and drive him from their midst.

And then, the visit from Schuster. Maybe he could trust him. After all, they knew each other since long before all this began happening, and Schuster had been thousands of miles away. Surely he had nothing to do with all this. What a great relief it would be!

And at first it was. He felt good when he saw him at the airport, a feeling of familiarity and safety. But as they made their way back to Ronald's apartment, he thought he'd wait, wait and see. At first, it felt a balm to be able to try to reveal the chaos swirling within, and if he could confide in anyone, it was Dr. Schuster. But warning bells sounded. He would start to tell his friend about a recent experience, but the feeling of relief would quickly give way to doubt. A question from his friend was a welcome opportunity to unburden himself, but the gratitude he felt could not endure in the face of the misgivings and suspicion that intruded. Every feeling of affection seemed countered by a feeling of apprehension - and the stronger the affection the more insistent and ominous the foreboding that followed. He began to regret inviting Dr. Schuster to be his guest for the night. But perhaps it would be alright; he would wait and see.

He would wait and see if he really could trust him, if he really was a friend. But the see-sawing of his ambivalent feelings became ever more weighted on the side of distrust, and as the ride continued, he felt trapped in the car with Schuster. His friend's questions - was he his friend? - felt more intrusive, more like accusations than questions. For a while, he just didn't know what to think. But in a short time he had his answer. He saw that look, that same look that he saw in the faces of all around him, the look of contempt, of disgust, of hatred. He really didn't want Schuster in his apartment with him. Why did he ever think it would be alright to have someone stay in his apartment? How foolish. But he decided that the best course would be to act as if nothing were wrong, not to let Schuster know that he knew. He would take him home, leave him in the living room and close himself in his bedroom for the rest of the night. He'd make it through the night and Schuster would leave tomorrow. He cursed himself for being so gullible, for not realizing immediately when Schuster had telephoned him that he had been enlisted by his enemies. They knew, of course, that Schuster would be the one who could ensnare him. Maybe they would even be spying on them, waiting to see if he actually was disgusting enough to spend the night in his apartment with another man.

Well, he had his plan. He would show Schuster his coldness toward him; he would make it entirely clear that he had no wish to be near him. He felt frenzied and terrified; sweating and trembling, he decided he would lock the door to his bedroom, and he would place objects in front of the door so that the noise would arouse him should Schuster try to break in during the night and violate him. The plan would work!

At home, pacing in his room, he wondered what else they might try. The bastards! He almost panicked when he realized he needed to use the bathroom. He looked around the room for something – a glass, a bottle, anything into which he could urinate, but he found nothing. More pacing. Then, his discomfort growing, he thought he'd take the chance; he'd walk straight to the bathroom, close the door and lock it, and then return quickly to his room. But when he opened his door and saw Schuster, standing there, standing there in his underwear, looking at him with that look, it was just too much. There was no option, no choice. It was a matter of saving his life. There was no choice. They'd arranged for him to be cornered, trapped in his own apartment! They'd found a way to invade his private sanctuary. There was no choice! He knew they'd never stop. He'd either have to allow them to turn him into a homosexual or kill to stop them. They deserved it! Schuster, above all, deserved it! They all deserved it! There was no choice.

And so Ronald Walensky did what had to be done.

He took the measures required by the situation. He fought to protect himself against Schuster's evil intentions. And who could

193

say that Schuster's death was sufficient? Perhaps by ordinary standards it would suffice, but there is little of the ordinary in a feverish moment of psychotic paranoia. No. All possibility of male assault must be eliminated. Dead or alive, Schuster could not be allowed to keep his genitalia.

* * *

When, within a very short time, the campus police broke down the door to his apartment, they found Ronald sitting on a chair, holding the knife, blood splattered everywhere. He was sitting, staring at the floor and mumbling to himself.

And he sits and mumbles yet. The police could not hear what he was saying. And when he now holds private conversations with unseen others, no one can hear the words he speaks. But speak he does, and if his words are not audible, his gestures and facial expressions are certainly visible. His conversations are lively, important to him; he is deeply involved in them – and in little else. He occasionally watches TV, or at least looks in the direction of the TV. He occasionally reads – cheap mysteries and romance novels. He has no books on science and will not discuss physics or anything remotely related to his work. When I once tried to engage him in a conversation about physics, he quietly and firmly said, "I have no interest." Attempts at conversation about other aspects of his past are similarly unrewarding. My bid to elicit his view of what led to his incarceration yielded, "They say I killed someone, but I did not." Nothing more. When I asked him about his refusal to attempt to leave Kirby's confines, he would say, "It's alright here." Nothing more.

His life is his conversations, his animated, engrossing conversations. When I asked about these conversations, he told me, pleasantly and matter-of-factly, that his conversations are with women, not hallucinated women, but women whom he is imagining. He imagines them, he told me, to keep himself feeling alive, to keep himself feeling like a man. They are lovely women, engaging women, women with whom he has lively and enjoyable conversation.

Psychotic individuals relate to their hallucinations in many different ways and invest in them varying degrees of reality. It may well be that Mr. Walensky is hallucinating, but chooses to say that he is not. I don't know. In Kirby, there is nothing unusual about a patient hallucinating. And there is nothing unusual in Kirby about someone who is reluctant to leave; institutionalization exerts a powerful force upon many. The emotional lives of Kirby's inhabitants are studies in complexity, conflict and chaos. The very air seems suffused with sickness, rage and desperation. Denial, psychotic denial, is rampant. But simple human remorse is not foreign to Kirby, although it may be unknown to many among its residents. Severely disturbed individuals are capable of remorse, even if that remorse is psychotically tinged and strangely amalgamated with denial.

There is a great deal I don't know about Mr. Walensky, about his past experiences and his present inner life. And behaviors may have many simultaneous and concurrent motivations and meanings; they are, to use a clinical term, "multiply determined." But I find it almost impossible not to interpret Mr. Walensky's behavior as his way of saying this:

195

"I must not leave Kirby. I must be punished and I cannot be trusted outside such a setting. I do not deserve to enjoy my love of science. I must be punished. I am dangerous and I must be punished. But I am not homosexual; I am a lover of women, not men, and I will prove it. I am not homosexual, and I would not, I could not, I had no reason to, and I *did* not kill and mutilate Josef Schuster, my beloved friend and mentor."

A Psychopath

ON THE LAST MORNING OF HER LIFE, Merill Baskow awoke in a sweat. The New York summer had been brutal, almost unbearably hot and humid for a young woman who had lived her entire life in northern Wisconsin. But the heat was not responsible for her sweat; that was the product of a very disagreeable dream. Nor did her apprehension diminish as the dream-world fell away to the day. In fact, the unpleasant thought with which she awoke did not so much return to her as simply continue, unabated, from the night before. The dream was of a piece with the anxiety that had been growing, slowly growing, steadily building in her over the past several days, the same dread, the same awful foreboding, merely translated into the alien and obscure language of the netherworld of nightmare; familiar melody, strange lyrics. She knew it was an unpleasant situation; that, she knew. But what it was that gave it the aura of true terror eluded her. Was it all really just that one moment of looking into his eyes?

She would call her parents; that's what was needed. Not that she was eager to do that. They had told her she wasn't ready, that twenty-two might mean adulthood, but that she hadn't had the experience, the exposure to people, the self-protective hardness that would be required of an attractive girl struggling to become a professional dancer in the cold and callous concrete of New York City. They never doubted her talent; no one did. There was something about her gracefulness, the flawless fluidity of her motion, whether in ballet or jazz or rock, that moved anyone who saw her dance. She doubted her talent; she was too innocent not to. She wasn't sure if she could dance well enough, but she wasn't frightened of New York. Her parents were. Her parents knew best, but when they flew to New York to claim their precious and beautiful young daughter's body, or what was left of it, they knew nothing, blinded by grief.

David Reardon, thinking about it, had a good laugh.

Many years earlier, in Miss Harper's second grade class, in an elementary school in Garfield, Nevada, sat Laurie Ann Raskin, an ordinary student. She was not the smartest girl in the class or the most athletic or the most popular. Although her parents thought she was the prettiest seven-year-old on Earth, most of her fellow students would have said she wasn't even the prettiest girl in the class. Not even close. But what they would have said was that she had the prettiest hair. Even the boys who hated girls said so. It was not exactly yellow, not exactly blonde, not exactly gold, but whatever the exact color, it was beautiful. It shone like the sun and draped over her shoulders like silk, falling from there almost to her waist. Her mother always said that nobody, but nobody, ever saw her little girl without commenting on her magnificent hair. Laurie Ann knew this and, although as sweet a little girl as one could ask for, she was terribly proud of her lovely hair.

But it was Laurie Ann's misfortune that Miss Harper always arranged the students in her class in alphabetical order. So on a Friday morning in December, having brought the necessary implement into school that day, the tall, nice-looking boy in the seat behind her, suddenly pulled her hair together, yanked her head back, and using the largest scissors he had been able to find, cut her hair off in an intentionally diagonal line about two inches from her scalp. He then held her hair high in the air – in a gesture of great triumph – before dropping it in front of Laurie Ann on her desk.

When she realized what had happened, Laurie Ann began sobbing hysterically and she continued sobbing for days to come. Her mother cried with her and her father had to be physically restrained from assaulting a seven year-old boy.

David Reardon, thinking about it, had a good laugh.

About five years later, in Clayton, Idaho, Helen Jenkins, an 89 year-old woman, returned home from church on a Sunday morning. Her small but comfortable home was situated on a dead end street next door to a similar house, the only other home on the block. A thick wood abutted the back yards of the two houses. Mrs. Jenkins' husband had passed away six years earlier, and she had become accustomed to living alone – alone, that is, except for her beloved cocker spaniel, Duke. The dog, a well-trained and loving companion, was devoted to Mrs. Jenkins. His love was fully reciprocated by her, especially so, perhaps, because Mr. Jenkins had brought Duke to their home only a month before he died and was tremendously fond of him. Duke roamed the neighborhood freely, eagerly running home whenever Mrs. Jenkins opened the door and called his name.

Mrs. Jenkins and her neighbor minded their own business, but there was no fence separating their lots. The elderly lady enjoyed looking out into her backyard at the wild flowers that grew near the woods and, on occasion, she would see her neighbor's tall, nice-looking twelve-year-old boy in his back yard. It disturbed her to see the boy throwing rocks at birds, but she consoled herself with the thought that it was very unlikely that he could ever hit one. It was far more disturbing to her when she saw him shooting a rifle, a B.B. gun, she assumed, in his backyard. She wondered if his parents knew that he was shooting at live targets and fretted about whether to inform them. She came to regret her hesitation.

On this Sunday morning, she was sitting at her kitchen table having an early lunch when she heard her front doorbell ring. She had few visitors and was curious to see who was calling, but she moved slowly and it took her a few moments to get to her front door, time enough for a healthy twelve-year-old boy to run away. There was no one on the doorstep when she opened the door. But when she happened to glance down and saw her beloved Duke lying there obviously dead, with blood dripping from his head, she passed out.

Later came the ambulance, the screaming neighbors, the police, the court. When it was over, the Reardon family had to move. Again.

David Reardon, thinking about it, had a good laugh.

Stan Reardon had very marketable skills. He didn't earn a great deal of money, but he was always able to find a job. Fortunately. Emma Reardon said she'd lost count of how many times the family had to move, always as a result of some piece of outrageous behavior by their son, but Stan had always been able to find work. Speaking of her husband, who had died a few years earlier, she said that, had he lived to see the day that David was committed to Kirby, he would have been greatly relieved to know that their son would now be off his hands for an extended period of time, and would feel none the worse for the realization. As she spoke with the doctors involved in the evaluations while the case was being settled, as well as with Kirby personnel once David was ensconced therein, she said Stan would also have felt relieved that this time he would not be the target of people's rage. Yes, their son had committed a grievous crime, but this time David, not Stan or Emma, would feel the brunt of the consequences; David would not talk his way out of this one, he would not whistle while his parents wept. This time, Stan would have been glad that he and his wife were not being held responsible; no one was threatening them, no one was suing them. Stan would have to cope only with his sadness.

Emma Reardon, for her part, was distraught. But that was nothing new; she had been distraught almost incessantly since her beloved son was very small. She might have been better able to withstand the past several decades had she been capable of somehow distancing herself from her son. When he was small, she found ways of believing that he might change. When he was older, if she had been capable of somehow achieving some slight measure of detachment, or of simply facing full-on the reality of what her son was, she would have been better armed to cope with what he had to offer her. But she couldn't; her love was her burden, her hope was her downfall. When felt for a child such as David Reardon, she later said, a mother's love is a curse.

If one holds a tiger by the tail, the horror will soon end; if a woman of decency holds such a son with her love, the anguish is interminable. Consider the clash of her wishes with the realities: on one hand, she wanted nothing in life as much as to feel that her son was a "good boy," that he would behave decently, that he would treat people well, that he would be a man with a strong conscience, a man of integrity, a son of whom she could be proud. On the other, it seemed to be David's mission in life to wreak havoc in whatever way possible, to cause as much pain and unhappiness to others as he could find means of accomplishing. And at no time did he ever give a sign of feeling even the faintest trace of remorse.

The realization of what their son was came upon them only very slowly. Slowly, because a person takes on his shape only slowly. Slowly, because a person comes to recognize realities of such unpleasantness, of such grotesque disappointment, of such overwhelming unhappiness only grudgingly, and only in the increments that are demanded at the moment. Slowly, because we forestall comprehension and acknowledgment of the full horror of such realities until the picture presents itself in a manner and with a force that cannot be denied.

Emma Reardon could not have been happier with her newborn son. A good size, pink-faced and robustly healthy, he was the fulfillment of everything she'd wished for ever since first feeling her own powerful maternal drive. Certainly it is not unusual for a little girl to play with dolls, but Emma's wish for a child was perhaps outsized. Not only did she care for her dolls in a way that amply demonstrated her motherly instincts, but should the family be in a home of friends or relatives with a real baby, she had to be torn away almost forcibly. Now, she had her own precious, darling baby to love. And what a lovable child he was. Beautiful in not only her eyes, but in all, and as easy a child as one could want. Calm, placid, contented. He slept well, fed well and, within a few weeks, smiled at his mother in a way that melted her heart. When she held him, he molded to her body in a way that gave her a feeling she had neither before nor since. She had said many times that the first two years of his life were the happiest of hers.

Her happiest times were before long occasionally interrupted by moments of disquiet. Not too often, at first, and not by anything that could readily be detected by others. But she knew her son, and even though he was her first child and she had little basis for comparison, she sensed that there was something... something. It wasn't that he became disobedient or that he had a particularly bad case of the "terrible twos," he wasn't especially stubborn; he didn't insist on having his way. It was just that, strangely, if his mother became angry at him, if she frowned at him, he didn't quite respond the way one might expect. He would do what his mother told him to do, but Emma somehow had the feeling that – curiously – he just didn't seem upset if she was angry at him.

Within a few years, her feeling had been painfully confirmed; she noted it time and again and it never failed to make her uneasy. And in the aftermath of his butchering of Laurie Ann's hair, the tendency which she found so disconcerting made itself plain to school personnel. In the meeting in the office of Mr. Pringle, the principal, David sat with Mr. Pringle, Miss Harper and his parents, as each had their say about what he'd done earlier in the day. He listened politely, as his legs, too short for the adult chair, swung back and forth. He didn't argue or protest or explain, he simply listened. And he showed not a trace of discomfort.

"David," began Mr. Pringle, "do you realize how Laurie Ann felt?"

"Oh, yes. She was unhappy. She cried."

Then why did you do it?

David shrugged.

"But you must have had a reason."

"Well, sometimes her hair gets on my book and I don't like it."

"But David, that's no reason. You could just ask Laurie Ann to pull her hair away."

David shrugged, his legs swinging, his face unperturbed.

"David!" his father almost yelled, "that was a terrible thing to do!"

"Okay," he replied, legs swinging.

"What do you mean, 'Okay'," said his father. "What's wrong with you?"

With another shrug, David stated quite matter-of-factly, "I don't like her hair," and seemed to feel that no further comment was needed. "Can we get some ice cream on the way home?"

"NO!" exploded his father. As David swung his legs, the adults exchanged looks of wonderment and despair.

Later that night, when she heard David giggling in his bedroom, Emma Reardon could not bring herself to ask him why he was laughing. She cried herself to sleep that night and, years later, said that she knew then that there was something terribly wrong with her son.

In the morning, however, there was a reality to be faced. What she and her husband had been trying to deny, minimize or rationalize away for the past few years could no longer be avoided. Both saw quite clearly that David had done something cruel – vicious, really – with no comprehensible motivation, and not only showed no remorse, but seemed utterly oblivious to the fact that he had done anything wrong. The couple's breakfast was a quiet one, but the few words that passed between them and, perhaps even more so the looks they exchanged, spoke volumes. Something must be done.

It is tempting to wonder what they might have decided had they been able to look five years into the future and see, despite all the their attempts to change David's behavior, the outrage that he was to perpetrate in their backyard – against a defenseless dog owned and treasured by a sweet, pleasant old lady. Or if they could have had foreknowledge of the horrendous crime that would land David in Kirby – or the countless other acts, inconceivable to them, that David would commit in the years in between. Of course, they had no such prescience. My guess, though, is that they would have marched ahead with their attempts – with the rewards, the punishments, the counseling from priests, the counseling from social workers, the psychiatric medications, the psychotherapy, the residential treatment programs, the hospitalizations, the turning their son in to the police, the cajoling, the screaming, the occasional beating – even knowing, with certainty, that they were doomed to failure. He was their son. What were they to do? He was their son.

First, came counseling. The Reardons were church-going people and their priest seemed the obvious person to turn to.

Although the priest had already been troubled by what he'd been told by the church's religion instructor about David's behavior in class, he was clearly disturbed by what he was now hearing about the hair-cutting incident. He quickly agreed to meet with David. David resisted, but not too strenuously. It was not that he was in any way afraid of what the priest would do, or even that he would feel uncomfortable at being lectured, it was simply that he'd prefer to spend the time doing something else. And David didn't like being unable to do what he felt like doing.

It may have been at this time, and may have been for that reason, that David came to understand more fully the value of telling people what they wanted to hear, a skill at which he ultimately excelled and which he employed often and to his great advantage. It was a skill of great value to him as one whose mission in life was to get away with doing exactly what he wished. He met only twice with the priest but was able to make an impression on him such that the priest informed his parents that there was no need for further counseling. David, he assured them, had learned the error of his ways.

It was in their second meeting that David told the priest that he himself felt confused at why he had wanted to do such a thing to Laurie Ann. He wondered, with a maturity and thoughtfulness beyond his years, if he had perhaps felt jealous of the attention that Laurie Ann received from their teacher, a woman whom he admired and whose approval he'd felt unable to win. He said, with clearly evident remorse, that he had, in an act of desperation, lashed out in the only way he could find.

"But my child," asked the priest, "how did you come to such a realization? I am impressed that you have been able to see this on your own, but you have taken me by surprise. When did you begin to see your behavior in this new light? After all, it is only within the last few weeks that you did this cruel thing."

"I know, Father," said David, "I guess it does seem like a sudden change. I guess, yes, it was kind of sudden. I don't know. But it just seems like last Sunday I started to feel different about it. I remember that Sunday night I felt like I wanted to pray for forgiveness."

"Was there anything that happened that made you feel that way? Your parents have told me that you never seem anxious to pray, not even in church."

"Well, I don't know. I guess it seems strange, but … "

"But what, son? Please say what you have on your mind."

"Well, I don't really understand it, but somehow on Sunday during your sermon, I just seemed to get it that what I had done was really bad." He continued, head hanging onto his chest, "I could see that it was … sort of like a sin … I guess really it wasn't only something I did to Laurie Ann … I guess it was really what you sometimes call an 'offense to God,' and to my parents, too."

When the priest reported to the Reardons that David had shown true repentance and that he expected no further problems from him, they were grateful indeed. But both their gratitude and their opinion of the priest would have diminished considerably had they understood how he'd been beguiled. As for the priest, the inflation of his vanity as well as his new-found fondness for the boy might have abruptly collapsed had he known that, on his way out of his office, David had helped himself to the shiny silver crucifix he'd noticed on the priest's desk.

All in all, quite a triumph for David.

David had many such triumphs. It was remarkable, in fact, how often he managed to talk his way out of the trouble he brought upon himself. His parents, while growing more desperate and more enraged, would occasionally marvel to each other – with perhaps a tinge of admiration on his father's part, if not his mother's – how their son's silver tongue and seemingly innate acting skill, his seductive charm and limitless capacity to convincingly feign remorse and repentance, enabled him to extricate himself from one scrape after another. In school, another who was as consistently truant as was David might expect himself to be expelled, suspended, or, at the very least, a frequent companion of the after-school detention monitor. Not David. Calling upon every manner of excuse that the mind might manufacture, playing upon the sympathy and gullibility of teachers and administrators, and making himself almost irresistibly likeable, his gift for manipulation would free him of punishment or discipline. His father, seeing the inevitable, would say that when David finally does find himself in jail, he will probably just talk the cell lock into opening. And every time David succeeded in liberating himself from the seemingly imminent consequences of his actions, he would laugh to himself with contempt at those whose good will and compassion he'd turned to his advantage.

Had he limited himself to more pardonable infractions of law and morality, he might have been seen as a lovable rogue; but such a romanticized view of him could not withstand a recognition of his appalling viciousness and utterly gratuitous cruelty. He spared no one, not the most innocent of people nor their even more helpless pets. Animals, in fact, were a favored target; it must be understood that poor Mrs. Jenkins' dog was but one member of a of an abounding list of such victims and neither the first nor the last. As we've seen, neither an animal's ownership nor its harmlessness and domesticity served to protect it from David's malice. But he was not partial. Many a furry or feathered wild inhabitant of his environs fell prey to him. The variety of methods devised by David to inflict pain on these poor creatures – squirrels, opossums, and birds, among others – were too great and perhaps too gruesome to be catalogued in our limited space; they will be left to the reader's imagination. Suffice it to say that his inventiveness was remarkable.

Nor did an animal's status as David's own pet mean it would be spared his cruelty. His mother later told a story of one particular incident, an incident which the passage of many years had not stripped of its horror in her mind, as evidenced in the telling by her patent abhorrence of her son's actions and her own credulity in their wake. Of the many aspects of the tale that might engender shock or wonderment, what seemed to be the most difficult for her to comprehend was the fact that the pet in question, a hamster, had been David's pet, a pet of which he'd seemed fond, for more than a year.

Emma Reardon had never really liked the animal. Earlier in her life she'd had her own pets – a cat, a canary and some tropical fish, but she had an intense dislike of rodents. Yet knowing their son's cruelty to animals, she and her husband decided to take a chance when David, at the age of fourteen, asked them for a hamster. They hoped that taking care of his own pet might help him to understand that animals were living, feeling beings. It didn't work.

Certainly his parents were disturbed when they witnessed some of the "games" that David played with his pet. He would set out a dish of food, then repeatedly prevent the hamster – at the last second – from getting to it; and they found his delighted laughter during this pastime unsettling. More troubling, however, were the sudden and unusually loud squeals which they occasionally heard from the hamster or the fact that he began to limp for no apparent reason. But they would sometimes see David hold and stroke the animal and this small act, insignificant as it might be in other circumstances, filled them with hope – hope that was suddenly and cruelly dashed.

On a quiet Saturday afternoon, Mrs. Reardon heard David moving around in the kitchen and thought she'd go see if he wanted something to eat. She found her son sitting quietly at the kitchen table, smiling to himself. When she asked, he told her that he was thinking of a funny TV show that he'd recently seen and asked her if she'd make him a sandwich. Without hesitating, she went to the refrigerator and opened the door. David's father, dozing on the couch, heard the scream and ran to the kitchen to find his wife bent over the sink, retching and crying as David was laughing. She couldn't speak, but David pointed to the refrigerator where his father, upon opening the door, was greeted by the sight – front and center on the eye-level shelf – of his son's hamster's severed head impaled on a steel paper spike.

When Stan realized what David had perpetrated on his mother – and on his own helpless pet – he became so enraged that he further exacerbated his wife's distress by beating their son with a fury that terrified her. She was able to get him to restrain himself only by pleading with him and repeatedly crying,

210

"Stop! Stop! We'll punish him! We'll punish him! Stop! " And when all was calm, they applied themselves determinedly and with inventiveness born of desperation to the task of devising consequences of appropriate severity.

After they informed David of the many and strict punishments he was to endure, Stan Reardon wondered to himself what, if anything, might be accomplished. He later said that, by this time, he knew that no punishment would awaken normal human sentiment in his son, but that he'd hoped that he might convince him to concern himself, in a practical, self-serving manner, with the consequences of his actions. But it was not to be; it served merely as another opportunity for David to hone his manipulative skills. First, he told his parents that he had done it because he knew that his mother did not like the hamster. Emma seemed about to accept this explanation when her husband so forcefully ridiculed the idea that she began to feel foolish. Yet David was not stymied. David was never stymied. Within a matter of days, his mother dolefully recalled, he asked his parents if he could see a psychotherapist and made a commitment to regular sessions to "find out why he liked to do such things." Although his father was somewhat less sanguine about this turn of events than was his mother, they ultimately agreed that they could not deny his request for help nor could they continue to punish him given his wish to better himself, and his privations were therefore terminated. Within a matter of weeks, he had convinced the therapist that the insights he'd gained from therapy allowed him to see himself and his relationships with others in a new light and that there was no need for further treatment or further concern.

Actually, one might have been tempted to give some credence to David's claim of enlightenment; after all, it was at around this time that he seemed to lose interest in tormenting animals. However, while the small birds and mammals in David's vicinity might have acquired a degree of safety and relief from this change in his inclinations, their gain came at very great cost to another class of creature, the new object of his attention, his new prey: the female human being.

I must not allow the reader to labor under the false notion that David, to this point, had shown no interest in girls. Much to the contrary. As a matter of fact, almost from the time that he had butchered Laurie Ann Raskin's hair - along with God knows what else inside her - he had begun showing a somewhat precocious interest in girls, an interest that revealed itself in some rather grotesque ways. It's a reasonable guess, in fact, that his great triumph over Laurie Ann and the anguish he saw her suffer served to awaken in him a realization of the wealth of vulnerable victims all around him and the abounding pleasure he could derive from their pain.

At first, his cruelty toward girls was simply that - cruelty, devoid of any overt sexual behavior or feeling - but it encompassed a wide assortment of relatively minor torments such as locking a girl in the closet of an empty classroom, tearing up a girl's homework before she could turn it in, putting a dead mouse in a girl's desk or pushing a girl dressed for a school dance into a mud puddle, to more serious outrages such as he inflicted on Laurie Ann. His mother, in recounting these incidents, mused that memory mercifully fades, and said, with the heaviness of one who had long been numbed from repeated emotional batterings, that she could recall only a small sample of the seemingly endless string of offenses perpetrated by her energetic and imaginative son.

"But what got me," she sighed, shaking her head, "was how he always seemed to get away with it. It was unbelievable. He would do some awful thing and somehow, somehow talk his way out of it. Lord, how he could talk. Sometimes I would think that these teachers and principals must not be so smart after all... I don't know. But then, we must have been even stupider. These people, they didn't know him like we did and half the time he talked us into thinking that he, you know, didn't really do it, or that it was a mistake or an accident or something. I tell you, he just had my head spinning. We'd find out about something awful that he did and make up our minds to really give him what for, you know, to punish him 'til the Lord cried for mercy. Then, the next thing you know, he'd have us believing he didn't do anything, that we were being mean to him and we'd be just about apologizing *to him*. Then, after he stopped talking and went away, Stan and me would sit there and I'd say to him, 'What just happened?'"

At first, David's sexual attraction to girls and women showed itself in outlandish ways. Some incidents were outlandish and frightening, such as his attempt, as a ten-year-old, to force a girl into sex in a wooded lot near the school. Others were outlandish and almost comical, such as his adventure, the following year, when he sought the services of a prostitute. How he had obtained the money was anyone's guess, although his thefts of objects and cash from both family and others were a matter of course. Likewise, one might wonder about his means of locating and

213

transporting himself to the seedier section of town, far from home; but his unexplained and sometimes lengthy absences from home and school were also becoming routine. No one can know what would have happened if the young girl he'd induced to come with him to the wooded area hadn't been able to fight him off – or at least make the struggle too difficult for him to persist beyond a certain point. Nor is it clear what would have developed with the prostitute if he hadn't, by the merest of chance, found himself caught up in an anti-vice operation by the local police – who likely had themselves quite a laugh.

What other activities David pursued without detection during those years is also unknown. As far as anyone knew, he seemed to content himself for a while with looking, not doing. He was caught numerous times attempting to catch glimpses of undressed girls in the bathroom and the girls' locker room in school and of his mother at home. And his thefts of pornographic magazines resulted in scrapes with the law on more than one occasion.

But when he reached dating age, a whole new world of mischief opened to him. Not for David was the adolescent angst, the sweaty anxiety, the intense self-consciousness, the secretive and shameful-feeling longings for attention from and fears of rejection by the opposite sex. To David, in fact, such feelings were not only foreign but utterly beyond his comprehension. In matters of boy-girl relationships, as with all other areas of social interaction, he neither knew nor understood such distress. Of course, he could feign an endearing shyness, should the situation call for it, but his imperviousness to self-doubt was remarkable. As we have seen, it showed itself early on and was

214

not a byproduct of his physical attractiveness; but attractive he was – much to the ultimate chagrin of many a young girl. Tall and well-built, with thick, coal-black hair, he had clear skin, pleasing and perfectly symmetrical features, baby-blue eyes and a Hollywood smile. With his effortless charm, his mesmerizing glibness and his endless self-assuredness, attracting girls required nothing more than being in their presence.

David did as many an adolescent boy blessed with his attractiveness might; his list of seductive conquests was long. And the apparent lack of concern that he showed for these girls' feelings would certainly not be confined to adolescents of his particular character; such self-absorption sometimes seems endemic to teenaged males. But there was a difference. For David, in fact, it was not that he was actually unconcerned with the girls' feelings, nor was his pleasure the more expectable narcissistic gratification of knowing that he had such powers of attraction. No, for David, the greatest pleasure was the knowing infliction of pain.

And inflict he did, with determination and expertise. He particularly relished inflicting emotional pain; humiliating girls was his preferred pastime, peerless in its promise of pleasure. David took his satisfaction where and how he could find it; if the chance to inflict physical pain should present itself, he was not one to overlook the opportunity. But embarrassing girls was his forte – at least in his high school years. Public humiliation, above all, was seemingly irresistible. His mother offered some particulars of his escapades as she spoke of the many times that she found herself on the receiving end of hysterical calls from teenaged girls or irate outbursts from their parents.

The luncheonette near the school was the scene of some of his early triumphs. There was the time, for example, when a sweet young girl, greatly enamored of our young man, was contentedly sitting on his lap in the midst of the swarming after-school crowd. Perhaps tiring of her, perhaps seeing someone more attractive, or perhaps simply recognizing an opportunity too good to pass up, David quickly and unceremoniously stood up, dumping the young lady on the floor and, pushing her out of the way with his foot, before walking over to talk to another girl. The girl who found herself on the floor, who had actually believed herself to be David's girlfriend, ran from the luncheonette in tears and didn't return to school for over a week. In the interim, Emma Reardon endured a heartbreaking conversation with her and a threatening one with her father.

Simply impregnating two girls during his high school years and knowing that they, in the high school world of that time, had to go to "an out-of-town school" for a year or so was insufficient mischief for David. Not only did he make certain to publicize the facts of the situation to all his classmates, but a letter sent to him by one of these girls, avowing her eternal love and promising to indulge his every desire when she returned home, regardless of possible consequence, just happened somehow to fall out of David's notebook onto a table in the school cafeteria, to be passed around the school for days.

But his crowning achievement in humiliation came a few years after his graduation from high school, when he had rented a small apartment for himself with money he scraped together from odd jobs, petty thefts, and the money given him by the many girls whom he so delighted in hurting.

216

Sitting in a local park one afternoon, he saw several girls walking together in their Catholic school uniforms. One of them in particular caught his eye, just as he caught hers. He recognized the look on her face, the look of infatuation that he had seen so many times. He approached the girls and, in his effortless manner, struck up a conversation. Two of the girls kept walking, but the one whose attention he had captured slowed down. As he tried to engage her, he could read her reactions. Her friends slowed a bit, waiting for her, and she looked back and forth between them and David, knowing that she should ignore him and stay with her friends, but unable to take her eyes off him and blushing furiously. Before long, she pulled herself away from him, but not before telling him that, yes, she walked home this way every day after school. David was generally not one to tackle long-term projects, always preferring the quick and easy. But, he later explained as he boasted of this experience to a Kirby clinician, aside from finding the young girl very attractive, he somehow sensed that there was a great adventure to be had, that the girl had all the makings of a victim extraordinaire.

In the weeks that followed, David made a point of being in the park at the appropriate time on several occasions. He would catch up to the girls, the three of whom were always together, and coax them into conversation using all the charm and charisma at his command. Impeccably proper and courteous, he would walk with them, getting them to talk about the their school – they were all seniors, looking forward to graduation and college – as well as their families and friends. Although he felt utter contempt for what he saw as their comically naive world-view, he listened with evident interest to whatever any of them said, paying particular attention, of course, to Mary Alice McDougall, the girl of his fancy. Again and again, he would catch her looking at him, and again and again she would blush when caught in the act. The other girls, in spite of David's charm, seemed to maintain a certain Catholic school aloofness, but this was more difficult for Mary Alice, and it was clear to all concerned that she was the object of his interest and that the feeling was reciprocated. Nevertheless, whether it was her religious upbringing or her inherent shyness, she was not about to throw herself at David as had so many others. But he persisted.

When he asked her, one day, to sit with him in the park for a while, she blushed even more than usual.

"Oh, I couldn't do that. My mother is expecting me home."

"Well, it would be just for a few minutes, you'll just be a few minutes later than usual. I was hoping you'd tell me more about your brother's experience at the seminary. I've been thinking of studying for the priesthood myself, you know, and what you've told me about your family's religious devotion is very moving. You'd be surprised to know how much I've been thinking about it and how I admire your family. Please come sit with me for just a few minutes."

Out of the corner of her eye, Mary Alice caught a look of skepticism on her friend's face, and thought to herself that she'd ask her about it later. But for now, she could not resist the request of this sweet young man, so earnest, so sincere, so attractive. So she sat with him for ten minutes and they talked. For that ten minutes, she felt herself lost in his charm, and that brief moment was all she needed to feel completely taken with him – which was exactly what David had intended her to feel.

As she walked away, she looked back at him and smiled and he thought to himself that she was now his. But he knew that he'd have to move slowly and cautiously.

Patience and caution certainly did not come easily for David, but as he and Mary Alice began to date, they were the order of the day. He found much of his time with her to be tedious and dull, but he was fully up to the task of concealing this from her; and he had help in the form of the many other amusements with which he distracted himself. Never without girls fighting for his attention, he enjoyed their company during this period as well. Some of them, in fact, unknowingly financed his attentions to Mary Alice, the small gifts that he bought her, the movies they saw and the meals they had together. As time and their relationship progressed, her feelings for him were evident and, before long, she told him that she was deeply in love with him. She wanted him to know this, she said, because she knew that he felt the same.

As a point of curiosity, one can only wonder what Mary Alice would have felt if she had seen her serious, studious and ever so faithful young man in one of his frequent drunken revelries with other girls of his acquaintance. But of course these affairs, whether involving one or a group of young women, took place not only outside of her sight but, in a very real sense, in a different universe, in a plane of existence which was as foreign to Mary Alice as her world was to David. David, however, was capable of a degree of deception that made him appear to be not only a denizen of her domain, a member in good standing of the community of the chaste and the upright, but a true exemplar of all the virtues she held dear. Such was his ability to appear, smoothly and convincingly, to be something akin to a different species of being, when he so desired.

There were times when he did slip; focusing on the long run – anything more than the next few hours, actually – was surely not David's cup of tea. Even a payoff as tantalizing as he had been formulating was not sufficient to hold his interest consistently. So it would occasionally happen that, unable to forego some more immediately rewarding bit of pleasure, David would fail to keep a date or disappear altogether for a short while. But his tongue was unfailingly equal to the task and he was always able to make Mary Alice feel ashamed of herself for ever doubting his constancy. He felt, actually, that the joy of hoodwinking her in this way was his compensation for the hours of boredom which his plan demanded of him. He gloried in doing things that he knew would horrify her, only to then make her feel guilty for even questioning him.

And so to Mary Alice, David was a fine young man, a sensitive, thoughtful, religious young man, currently majoring in political science, in preparation for law school, but considering studying for the priesthood, either after or in place of law school. While he was holding various menial jobs for a few days at a time, until he was caught stealing, came to work drunk or didn't bother to show up at all, he would have deep, meaningful conversations with Mary Alice about his vocational conundrum. What would be more worthwhile, he wondered, a career in the law helping to protect the rights of the downtrodden or a life devoted to the cloth? In either case, Mary Alice thought that her boyfriend surely must be the most earnest, good-hearted and contemplative young man she'd ever known.

When alone together, much of their time was spent in serious discussions of their current lives and hopes and dreams for the future. Mary Alice spoke lovingly of her family, her parents' dedication to the church, and her father's work as a deacon. She also rhapsodized over her wonderful teachers and her boundless admiration for Father William, the headmaster of her school. For quite a while, their physical contact was limited to holding hands and a quick peck on the cheek when they parted. But after a couple of months, David began to let Mary Alice know that he had a yearning for her that went beyond their deep spiritual connection. In time, she became unable to resist not only her fervent wish to please David, but her own physical desires as well, and what Mary Alice called "necking" became a regular part of their evenings together. But, though David began gently letting her know that he wanted more, she was steadfast in her refusal to allow him to even touch her body. Her parents, she said, would be so disappointed in her that she could not live with the realization of how they would feel, even if they never actually knew.

David knew instinctively when it was time to make his move. After an evening of cuddling through a movie, he sat silently in the car and Mary Alice knew that something was troubling him. At first he demurred, but she persisted in her questioning. She could not stand seeing her David be unhappy. So, hesitantly and with evident distress, he began telling her about how he felt, and as he did, she could see the tears forming in his eyes. He was, he told her, deeply, profoundly in love with her. He thought of her night and day. He had always thought, never doubted, that he would remain a virgin until married. But he was terribly troubled

221

by what he'd been feeling. At almost twenty-one years old, so many young men of his acquaintance were speaking of their girlfriends and how they were learning about the joys of intimacy. As he listened to them, he found himself feeling deprived of something very important. At first, he dismissed such feelings as the price one must pay for a life of virtue, but as time passed, he became tortured by a terrible doubt, a doubt about Mary Alice's feelings for him. About his feelings, he had no doubt. And yes, of course, he knew that Mary Alice was being truthful when she told him that she loved him, but – really – how could she know how she felt until they'd had more intimacy? And how could he feel sure of her love if she were unwilling to give herself to him in that way? After all, it was really the same for him as for her; hadn't he had saved himself for the one he loved just as she had? He was just so desperately in love with her; how could he live with this torturous doubt about her feelings for him?

After much crying and holding each other, Mary Alice told David that she would think about and pray on the matter during the coming week and that she would let him know her decision when they were next together. The evening ended with David agonizing aloud over his guilt about putting her in this situation. She stroked his hair, put her finger to his lips, and said, "Shhhh, my darling."

The following Saturday night, David was embarrassed, contrite, and said nothing more about the issue. But after they'd eaten dinner at Mary Alice's favorite Italian restaurant, as they got into the car, she put her hand on David's arm and said, "Let's go to your apartment for a little while. I've never seen it." David knew that his great triumph was at hand. But he was not surprised. Feeling rather sure of himself before the evening, he had carefully prepared his small studio apartment in anticipation. He had cleaned it and straightened it far beyond his ordinary efforts. And he'd made certain other preparations, as well.

At first they sat nervously on his bed, but soon began kissing. Then, Mary Alice whispered to David that she had made a decision. Smiling at him with the joy of knowing that she'd be able to prove her devotion, she told him that she could not possibly surrender her virginity, but that she'd heard of other ways, using her mouth, that a girl might please a boy and that she would love to so please her beloved. And this she did with feelings, in succession, of embarrassment, curiosity, excitement and ecstasy. When it was all over, they held each other tightly. Mary Alice was crying while, at the same time, smiling adoringly at her David.

The following Monday, bright and early, David visited the local post office. He mailed two small, neatly-wrapped packages: one to Mary Alice's father and one to Father William, the head of her school. Each contained a videotape – a videotape of Mary Alice McDougall, the deacon's daughter, performing fellatio.

If you, reader, have trouble comprehending and digesting the treachery, the utterly unprovoked cruelty of David Reardon's actions, imagine yourself to be Mary Alice.

To David, though, there was perhaps a provocation. At Kirby, almost a decade later, David was still laughing about it. Pausing momentarily from his mirth, he explained himself very succinctly:

"Oh, the stupid bitch, she thought she was such a fucking saint. She deserved it." To David, her crime was her innocence.

Before turning to David's auspicious move to New York City – auspicious, to me, because it resulted in his incarceration in Kirby and my opportunity to know him – it might be helpful to discuss another form of recreation that David discovered early in life and that seems never to have lost its charm for him. It was a diversion that may have assumed even greater importance to him once ensconced within Kirby's tightly controlled environment, an environment which deprived him of many of his sources of amusement.

Among its many virtues for David was its great simplicity. As opposed to the planning, patience and delay of gratification involved in enterprises such as he undertook with poor Mary Alice, its quick and easy nature added to its appeal to him and it became a sort of old standby, an oft-utilized weapon in his armamentarium of malice. I speak of the common, quick and easy lie, the uncomplicated but well-placed, suitably timed comment. He was barely past kindergarten when David recognized the power of the simple lie, not merely as a means of evading unpleasant consequences, but as a method of causing mischief and misery. The reader might ask how something as prosaic as the ordinary lie could hold such enchantment for one as accomplished and as deeply involved in the art of cruelty as our young man, but the reader would be underestimating David's creativity as well as his great joy in putting something over on someone.

Yes, it began with rather simple forms. Even DaVinci did not start with the Mona Lisa; the great artist's technique surely must have been developed gradually, its origins in naive and rudimentary dabblings; his eye for beauty long-cultivated, gaining in depth and sophistication over a period of apprenticeship. So it was with David. As Leonardo in childhood must have made casual scrawls with whatever implement of drawing was at hand, David chanced upon an idea while playing with some of his schoolmates in the schoolyard. Why not whisper to Johnny that Joey said he was a sissy? Why not tell Freddie that Mike said he was going to steal his lunch? Elementary, yes, but nevertheless worthwhile. The simple, effortless comment made, David could stand back and admire his handiwork, just as DaVinci was probably struck by the enjoyment of his doodling and the feeling that he had a flair for it. And there is an elegance to the simplicity of such lies, so David returned to them many times, especially during his years at Kirby where the nature of his fellows greatly magnified the potency of such offhand comments.

"You know, Esposito, Jones said that you're a piece of shit, white faggot motherfucker and that he's going to fuck you up."

"Hey, Smith, Thompson said that you're the stupidest nigger he ever saw."

Fists and feet would fly, Esposito or Jones or Smith or Thompson or all of them would end up in restraints, and David would sit nearby and have himself a good laugh. Aides, too, were drafted into the fun, and a word to one about a threat made by a patient known to be assaultive would lead to confusion for the patient and enjoyment for David. Although David seemed never to tire of this merriment, it was not long before staff came to understand what he was up to, and he thereafter had to confine himself to stirring up trouble between the more gullible or feeble-minded patients.

But between the schoolyard and Kirby's day room, David branched out, experimented and grew evermore inventive and sophisticated in his application of the tool. Variety, after all, is the spice of life and I believe that David would have felt embarrassed had he not been able to embellish and elaborate and raise the form to new heights of refinement. Adolescence and dating ,of course, opened up new fields of opportunity, and a simple rumor about a girl or boy being with someone other than the "steady" was always fun.

But a full catalog of David's devilment is far beyond the scope of this chapter and we must soon return to David's penchant for other forms of conniving and cruelty; so it may be best to leave aside many of his accomplishments in the fine art of malicious mendacity and leap to his coup de grace in this realm of endeavor. Surely the incident can not be neglected; it may convey something of his inhumanity that would otherwise be missed. His mother, at least, seemed to feel that way.

"Oh, my Lord." she moaned. "What would ever make a body come up with such an idea. I just can't even think of it without starting to shake and feel all... I don't know, sick and dirty inside. . . He came from me!... Oh, my Lord. Is this something that I gave him?" After staring into space for a moment, she continued, looking at the floor, her voice almost inaudible, "You know, I can't go to church anymore. I haven't been able to ever since I found out about poor Mary Alice. We didn't go to her church, it wasn't about not being able to face her family... It was just that I felt that if I could give birth to someone like him...

I must be... I must be evil myself... It just doesn't seem like I belong in a church." And she sobbed.

The incident had been of significance in a number of ways. Whether it was the cause or not, it was almost immediately followed by David's departure for New York and a long period when his mother heard not a word from him. It was also one of the very few times that David did not escape the consequences of his grotesquery, and his mother saw him in a state that would horrify any mother. Yet as deeply as she was affected by these aspects of the incident, what she seemed to feel most deeply in the telling was her incomprehension of her son's motives and her revulsion at the thought that she was somehow responsible for his actions. Then again, she had at this point in her story been talking for quite a while and it may well be that, after recounting much of the story of her son's life, she was simply no longer able to control her emotions and, overwhelmed, began sobbing yet more violently and repeating, almost screaming, "What's wrong with him? What's wrong with him?"

Whence came the idea I couldn't say, but it was actually fairly simple. It's just that the sheer monstrosity of it makes it seem to be something that could hardly spring from human imagination. There was a young boy, about thirteen years old, whom David had seen a few times in his neighborhood and with whom he'd had a few brief conversations. A nice enough boy. He'd seen the boy, by name of Michael Overman, in a local luncheonette where Michael and his friends apparently sometimes came for lunch at about 12:30 from their nearby junior high school. On the day in question, David placed a call to the Overman home at about 1:15 pm and asked for Mrs. Overman. He then identified himself as

Sergeant Kavanaugh of the local police precinct and gently told Mrs. Overman that there'd been a terrible traffic accident, that an ambulance had taken her son to the local hospital where he had just died of his injuries.

The horrific experience that Mrs. Overman endured for the next hour or so until she learned that her son was sitting in his classroom in perfect health need not be reported in full detail. I will add only that en route to the hospital, Mrs. Overman, unsurprisingly, caused an actual traffic accident in which she sustained a broken bone in her arm and that she ultimately was admitted to the hospital, secondarily for treatment of the injury, and primarily, for treatment of shock.

We will not know whether David's tongue could have spared him what was to follow; he was not given the chance.

The police were well aware of David's presence in the community and had had occasion to cross paths with him in consequence of some of his petty thefts, an assault, and, as one officer put it, his "unusual sense of humor." It was not long before it was determined to their satisfaction that David had been the perpetrator of this joke, a "joke" which did, needless to say, greatly amuse him. Perhaps unthinkingly – perhaps not – they shared their information with Mrs. Overman and the senior Mr. Overman, an ex-Marine. Mr. Overman did not share David's sense of humor and, at his first opportunity, tracked David down and unceremoniously beat him within an inch of his life.

When his mother first saw him in the hospital, she said, she would not have recognized him; his face, she said, looked like "a piece of torn up raw meat." And Mr. Overman had gone David one better, breaking both of his arms.

"Oh my God!" she moaned when thinking of it. "What was I supposed to do? What was I supposed to feel? How much can a body take? I was looking at him and I couldn't let myself think that he deserved it, but I knew he did! How can a mother think that about her son? How could I not think that about someone who did what he did? Oh, my God! Oh, my God!"

Others, evidently, felt less conflicted in response to the situation. The local District Attorney flatly refused to take any action whatsoever against Mr. Overman. He knew better, he said, than to present such a case to a jury. The reader can guess whether that was his only reason.

Mrs. Reardon, pulling herself together a bit and considering overall the price exacted from her son for his actions, said, in a whisper, "God help me... I was glad ."

Many animals seek camouflage as a means of being able to pursue their aims, stalking their prey under cover while minimizing their exposure to creatures that could endanger their survival. It is likely that such a motivation animated David Reardon when he decided to move to New York. After being so readily identified by his home-town police, he might have felt that he'd benefit from the anonymity possible in a big city. On the other hand, he may simply have drifted there, pushed or pulled by whatever whim took hold of him at a particular moment. With rare exception, aimless drifting was, after all, his preferred mode of existence. In any event, a few months after Mr. Overman conveyed his feelings to David, David - newly healed, primed and ready for action, and not in the least chastened - found himself on the streets of New York City. And, as do most creatures of the wild, he sought out and quickly found those with whom he would best fit in. This is not to say that he felt anything like a kinship to them; such was not his way. But life would be easier among the drifters, grifters, conmen and drug addicts of the streets. David might have felt that he could learn some profitable schemes and quick-money tips from his street-wise confederates, and it was a certainty that he'd have both sources and markets for the drugs which he found enjoyable to use and lucrative to sell. He probably felt – quite justifiably – that life in the big city could be very much his cup of tea. And the various sources of information – police, court and hospital records as well as his own and his mother's accounts of that period – seem to indicate that he did quite well, taking advantage of both acquaintance and stranger at every turn and enjoying the opportunities for cruelty and chicanery made available to one of his inclinations by the homeless, the hopeless, the hapless and the lost whom he encountered in the streets, alleys and parks of the city, as well as in its bars, strip joints and assorted disreputable establishments.

Runaways, predictably, were a prime target. Teenaged girls, lonely and troubled but naive, inexperienced and ripe for the picking satisfied his needs for sex. Homeless young drug abusers, out to score using money likely stolen from others found, at David's hands, that the tables were easily turned on them. All these were his daily fare, his bread and butter. Both more enjoyable and profitable were the slightly older women, out on the town with their friends, or the well-heeled drug buyers from the suburbs; these were his steak and potatoes. He found his champagne and caviar in the occasional opportunity to scam or simply rob the wealthy. Meals of all kinds were often flavored with generous helpings of gratuitous violence or cruelty.

David was generally not one to take on long-term projects; he took what he wanted from people and discarded them. However, if someone were to virtually insist on being fed upon at greater length, to be a freely flowing fount of victimhood, David was not one to refuse her the opportunity. Yet perhaps he actually felt some particular attraction to the young girl that led him to form what was, for him, an enduring relationship.

April Rain, as she called herself, or Dolores Kappenheim, as her parents preferred, was sixteen when she had the misfortune of meeting David. There was never any doubt that she would be abused and misused by someone; she would not permit it to be otherwise. Her demeanor, her facial expression, seemed to say, "Here I am. What are you going to do to me? Whatever it is, it's alright; as long as you like me." Looking back at her history, one might be justified in feeling that when she left her home in North Carolina to escape her parents and their oppressive "middle-class values," she was determined to be so ill-treated by people that she could then allow herself to see that her parents were not the villains she'd come to believe they were. She left in a burst of very uncharacteristic courage, telling herself she'd find a place where people are loving and sensitive and kind. It didn't quite work out that way. That was predictable; what was not was that she would cross paths with someone as fully lacking in those characteristics as our protagonist. The blind easily stumble; but as a blind person might either stumble into a shallow ditch or off the edge of a cliff, Dolores might well have been ill-treated, might have achieved her inevitable destiny, without necessarily having to endure David Reardon and the entertainment he provided for himself at her expense.

He knew what he'd found immediately upon meeting her. By the time she reached New York, she was already looking bedraggled, and it was clear that she was not burdened by wealth. But David saw in her both a reasonably attractive young girl and someone whom he could use and abuse in any way he chose. And so he took her to himself to have as a fallback source of amusement when nothing of greater interest was at hand.

"Hey there, honey, you're looking kind of lost. Can I help you out in any way?"

"Oh, thanks. I'm trying to find a cheap place to eat. I just got here and I don't have much money."

"Well, come with me, baby. I'm a lifelong New Yorker; I know every place in the city including a good restaurant nearby where I'd be happy to buy you a good meal. You look like you could use it!"

"I sure could. Boy am I lucky to meet you right away. You're so sweet!"

So lucky Dolores and sweet David shared a nice dinner, during which David regaled her with tales - all entirely untrue - of his travels, far and wide; his accomplishments, glorious and varied; and his wealth, considerable and waiting to be generously spent on his friends. Dolores thought him the most exciting and attractive young man she'd ever had the great good fortune of meeting.

Within four days she was turning tricks to support her magnanimous benefactor, believing, as he passed her around to his acquaintances, that he loved her.

Within two weeks she'd had her first of numerous emergency room visits, necessitated to treat injuries sustained during beatings which she felt were her own fault for not appreciating all that her White Knight was doing for her.

Much of what she endured she understood was for her own benefit. Chaining her to the radiator, for example, she knew to be David's way of protecting her, of stopping her from taking ill-advised walks through the neighborhood where many dangers lurked. She realized that he was right when he said that, because she hadn't been allowed to leave the apartment in weeks, she might feel a strong urge to venture out.

It is true that she felt humiliated the first time when, after he'd prevented her from using the bathroom for many hours, David videotaped her wetting her pants. But she was pleased that he cared enough about her to allow her to change her clothes. And she was almost upset the first time he had several acquaintances simultaneously urinate on her, but he assured her that it was her great feminine attractiveness that made him and his friends wish to engage is such erotic experimentation with her. So pleasant was it to hear him deviate from his usual practice of proclaiming her ugliness, that she accepted the explanation with happiness. It was her pleasure to crawl naked in front of the crowd in the apartment held on a collar and leash by David; she loved that he took pride in showing her off. Besides, when he wanted to sit down, she would be allowed to eat some of their dog's food out of his dish on the floor – a treat after being denied food for two or three days.

After some initial concern, she had accepted that she was becoming scarred all over her body, the results of cuts and burns.

If it made David happy, she felt she should understand. More troubling – in fact, it almost made her consider leaving – was when David amputated two of her fingers at the first knuckle with a steak knife. The pain was severe and she had trouble understanding this need of David's. But when she came to, he did help her bandage herself and even gave her some pain killers – after a few hours.

Who knows how long Dolores would have endured – or enjoyed – David's treatment if his wish to take full advantage of her hadn't led to the end of their "relationship." Although he tried to take precautions in the instructions he made Dolores give her parents about how and where to send money, they tracked down their daughter and not only removed her from harm's way but also reported the situation to the police. David, with Dolores' aid and cooperation, managed to avoid serious consequences and never stopped to look back. Nor did he seem perturbed in the slightest that his recently-widowed mother was drawn into the drama.

At this point in her narrative, Emma Reardon stared at the wall as she spoke, not looking at me. She may well have been intentionally avoiding eye contact, but the impression she created was more of a person drawn deep into her own private retreat, half hell and half refuge, a world in which agony and insensate emotional deadness competed for the upper hand.

"Of course it was awful what he did to her. But she never did catch on that he didn't care about her; she just seemed like she didn't even know that he was treating her like you wouldn't treat a dog. I never did see a one to beat her in asking to be stepped on. What was wrong with her I don't know. I thought about it

234

sometimes back then, maybe just 'cause I'd sooner do that then think about that... son... of mine. His father never did get to even realize what she was like. Maybe somehow it would've been easier on him, maybe he wouldn't have up and died when we were told about it all. Just two days later, before we even got to leave for New York. Oh, I know that he'd had heart troubles for a while, but I saw his face - I never did see him look quite like that before - when that man told us about that poor girl's fingers. I tried for a bit to say that David couldn't have done it. But he knew; he couldn't tell himself stories like I sometimes did. I really knew, too... I just... I just . . ."

And she just sat, staring at the wall and slowly shaking her head.

David, of course, continued to cherish the memory of the entire affair. He especially liked to laugh about how "stupid" Dolores was, much as he laughed about Mary Alice's "purity and goodness." It was not as if David needed any excuse or justification for any of his brutality, but he seemed to always see his victims as "asking for it," perhaps by virtue of being foolish enough to cross his path.

He particularly treasured thinking about how any man in Dolores' future might react to the two messages he'd find written on her body. Inch-high block letters on her abdomen, formed by scar tissue from the deep but careful scratchings and scrapings of a knife, spelled out "THIS BITCH IS THE PROPERTY OF DAVID REARDON." Further down on her abdomen, just above her pubic hair, he'd had a friend tattoo another inscription in ornate red and blue lettering: " RENTAL: $2 PER HOUR" He'd laugh himself silly talking about this, but usually concluded by

235

saying that "any bastard stupid enough to give a damn about her probably can't read anyway."

David enjoyed many a good laugh during his years of freedom, and every laugh was paid for, ounce for ounce, by the suffering of his prey. The reader would be mistaken – understandably mistaken, given that most of us do not give ourselves over to a preoccupation with devising methods of inflicting pain – in believing that we have covered the full spectrum of David's nefarious talents and depraved inclinations. But any attempt at a comprehensive anthology of his exploits would be prohibitively long and, in spite of his inventiveness and the breadth and diversity of his sadistic interests, might become tedious. His quarry were animal and human, male and female, old and young, weak and strong, stranger and acquaintance. Do not think that any group omitted from this account was overlooked by David, much less that some class of individuals might be, due to some moral compunction on his part, intentionally excluded from his career in cruelty. Not helplessness, infirmity, invalidism, mental deficiency, extreme youth or advanced age exempted one from consideration as a mark, as an object to be exploited for amusement or gain. Mrs. Reardon once mused, as much to herself as to me, that there was virtually nothing that she could do or see or think that did not stir some unpleasant – or horrifying – memory of something that her son had done. But I am limited here to a mere sampling of his oeuvre, and we must now move on to the incident that brought David into my acquaintance, the incident that – to the greater good of the populace – put an end to his freedom, the incident that created and then extinguished Merill Baskow's terror.

Merill had become popular with the crowd of young people who frequented Washington Square Park, a crowd which included David Reardon. She was not really one of them in that she neither used drugs nor was involved in any of their scams and petty crimes. She also fell far short in the amount of time spent loitering aimlessly in the park. But she could frequently be seen there, in those spring and summer days, either doing her stretching exercises on a blanket on the grass or practicing her dancing in the paved areas. She did not dance there to attract attention, but merely for her own enjoyment; it was as if her youthful exuberance and her love of dance could not always be contained, especially on a pleasant afternoon in the park. In any event, her dancing sometimes caught the eye of the park denizens. They enjoyed her impromptu and unrehearsed performances and, before long, in her gregarious and personable manner, she struck up conversations with them. Her appearance was fully as pleasant as her manner; an attractive young woman, she had a sweet and pretty face to go with her shapely and well-toned dancer's figure. And some of the crowd took an uncharacteristic interest in her simply as a charming and affable person, rather than as someone with whom to trade in drugs or from whom they might find some means of extorting cash. For all her affability, she did not have the air of an easy mark. But some of the young men found her very appealing and it may have been this that spurred David to work his charm on her; he would enjoy showing the others that he could, with little effort, win out over them in a competition to draw her attention.

He paired his unerring intuition, his ability to read people in a way that would be admired by the most adept salesman, with his finely-honed capacity for glib and facile conversation and made his move.

"Wow, Merill, it's such a pleasure to watch you dance. I've never seen anyone move with such grace, not even at the ballets that my parents took me to when I was small. Even then I loved watching people dance; I think it must be the purest form of artistic expression. And jazz dancing, in particular, is so beautiful. I've always sort of wanted to be able to dance, but I'm about the clumsiest person in the world. I couldn't even try it."

She smiled inwardly, thinking that he was quite a smooth-talker, but smiled outwardly in spite of herself because she nevertheless felt flattered by his praise and charmed by his modesty and his irresistible smile.

"Oh, sure you could. If you appreciate dance as much as all that, you must have some flair for it; you just need to allow yourself to loosen up and feel confident in the way you move. I bet I could teach you."

She knew that he would not really have sufficient interest to pursue the attempt, but she felt that she'd enjoy playing along with him in wherever he wanted to take the conversation. So dance lessons never materialized, but they did begin a friendship – of a sort.

Merill was a young woman in New York City, a woman who had a dream of success as a dancer and who wanted to enjoy her first great adventure away from home. But she also had what some might call an "old-fashioned" Midwestern prudence and practicality. Her fantasies of fame and artistic glory were well balanced by a down-to-Earth realism, her romantic fancies by a hard-headed, self-protective skepticism. She could enjoy flirting and playing with David, and might even feel some attraction to him, but she was simply not one readily to offer herself up as victim; she was afflicted by neither Mary Alice's naivete nor Dolores' masochism. But neither caution nor canniness served to win her immunity from our young man, a young man who knew no restraints and tolerated no limits. In fact, it may well have been her very wariness that led her astray, serving her ill because it was too sharp to overlook David's malevolence, thereby preventing him from carrying out whatever he might have intended for her, but not sufficiently penetrating to grasp its depth. She may have failed to appreciate how he might react to the frustration her reticence brought to him. But that is speculation.

What happened to Merill is largely unknown; why it happened, entirely so. Even were one to take David at his word, one would be left in a haze of confusion. She was killed by a group of men trying to rob or rape her; he attempted to rescue her against overwhelming odds and was himself injured in the process; he killed her because she attacked him; he killed her because he was annoyed at her for her refusal to have sex with him; he killed her because she pestered him for sex too much; he killed her because she wouldn't give him money; she killed herself and he merely tried to dispose of the body; he had nothing to do with the ghastly things that were done to her body; he killed her because he enjoyed killing attractive young girls; she was the seventh or eighth of his victims; he had no idea what happened to her.

Certain facts are known – or at least generally accepted by both the police and David and Merill's acquaintances. Several weeks before Merill's death, the date of which is uncertain, David had moved in to the apartment she was sharing with a friend. On what basis they were living together is unclear; some said they were merely friends and that Merill was helping him out. Others insisted they were more than friends. Some said that they were on good terms until the end, but Merill's closest friend back home told the police – apparently very convincingly – that her friend had told her, in a brief telephone conversation, that she was terrified of a young man who was staying with her and that she feared what he would do if she made him leave and what he would do if she didn't.

"I really don't know what to think," Merrill had said. "Maybe I'm just being silly. He's been so nice sometimes; he's very sweet and everyone else likes him, too. But, I don't know, he seems to like me more than I like him . . . or at least he seems to be pretty set on getting me in bed. We've fooled around a little, but I really don't like him that much. And another thing bothers me. He seems to always have reasons why I should give him money. It's really crazy. They seem to make sense at the time when he's telling me and I give it to him. It's just been a little at a time and I didn't mind. I sort of knew he was taking advantage, but I just also felt like it would be mean to refuse. But now he really owes me a lot and I feel stupid. I asked him to give me some money back, but he didn't. And, really, the only thing that gets me is just how he looks sometimes. It's not like he ever threatened me or anything or even like he ever looks really mad. But this morning when I wouldn't give him more money I saw a look in his eyes that scared the hell out of me. I don't know how to explain it. This sounds pretty weird, I know, but all I could think of was that it reminded me of how people back home would look at their chickens when they were getting ready to bring them to the butcher, you know, counting them and figuring how much they'll make."

"Oh, my God," said Nancy. "Please get him out of there. I don't care how good looking he is or how much people like him. You've got me really scared for you... I have an idea. Make the other girl do it. Make her tell him. Maybe she won't mind. If he doesn't care as much about her maybe he won't get mad. Oh, my God, Merrill. He's scary. You're scaring me. He reminds me of that horrible boy from high school, Howard whatever his name was, the one who ended up in jail, the one who got poor Janey Adams pregnant and went around the school laughing about it. Remember? He forged his boss's name on checks and got caught. Oh, please, honey! Get him out of there!"

"I've got to get off. He's coming in now," was the last thing Merrill ever said to Nancy.

"Okay, but promise me you'll get him out!" was the last thing that Nancy ever said to Merrill.

Perhaps Merrill took her good friend's advice. Perhaps that's what led to her death. Perhaps she didn't. Perhaps *that's* what led to her death. No one knew then; no one knows now.

What her parents knew was that they were informed of their daughter's death by telephone. It was not until they came to New York that they were told by police authorities that they would not even have an intact body to bring home with them. Her mother later described how she had felt herself becoming dizzy, feeling as if she were watching the scene from somewhere else, before she passed out. Awakening in a hospital bed, awakening from what doctors called a "profound shock reaction," she thought she had dreamed being told that her daughter's body had been decapitated and dismembered, that the flesh had been pared from the bones. Had she not been sedated, she might have passed out again when told that it was not a dream but a cold, horrifying reality, an act of butchery by David either in an attempt to dispose of the body or, perhaps, just for the amusement value. One can only speculate how she would have reacted if she'd been told that some of her daughter's flesh had been cooked – cooked and served in sandwiches to David Reardon' blissfully unknowing acquaintances.

Of course, it is not a certainty that he actually fed her to his friends. Virtually nothing that David Reardon says can be taken at face value. Still, his story about fostering cannibalism, offered to authorities when trying to evade criminal responsibility for the murder by winning an insanity acquittal, did find some support in the memory of one of his friends. This young man told of how he and another friend had lunch in David's apartment a few days before the arrest. He remembered finding it hard to understand at the time why David seemed to have such trouble suppressing a smile after serving them what he said were chicken sandwiches. Certainly, he may have invented the story in order to support his insanity claim; but then, why would one doubt that he would relish the opportunity to round out his adventurous encounter with Merrill by putting one over on his friends in what he'd have seen as an inviting and entertaining side benefit of murder.

* * *

How does the world understand, how does the world cope with, how does the world protect itself from the likes of David Reardon? Difficult questions. No area within the realm of psychiatry is more suffused with confusion than that of the kind of personality and behavior that he exemplifies. Antisocial personality disorder, psychopathy, sociopathy – often employed with very unclear or conflicting meanings and connotations – are labels applied to behavior such as his. What is it? How does it develop? What can be done to prevent it? What can be done to cure or manage it? How can its effects on society be minimized? The apprehensive reader may be assured that no attempt will be made here to provide anything like comprehensive or definitive answers to these questions; I will merely offer a few observations and musings on the topic.

One of the first and most influential books on psychopathy was entitled The Mask of Sanity. It is my assumption that the author, Hervey Cleckley, a psychiatrist writing in the 1930s, chose the title carefully and cleverly. Psychopaths, as described by Cleckley, do not hallucinate; they do not have delusions; they do not speak irrationally, they do not speak incoherently. Furthermore, although (as Mr. Reardon clearly demonstrates) they persistently engage in antisocial behaviors, their behavior is not odd or strange in the same sense as that of mentally ill individuals; they are not psychotic. Psychopaths wear a mask of sanity. One might argue, though, that it is not really a mask as much as it is an actual sanity – of a kind. In point of fact, psychopaths, as described by Cleckley, have a number of seeming psychological strengths. They are usually not unintelligent and they are notably free of anxiety and other uncomfortable feelings; in Cleckley's words, there is an "absence of nervousness or psychoneurotic manifestations." They are in perfect contact with objective reality and read people quite well. In fact, they are remarkably capable of seeming affable, pleasant and congenial. They win people over with ease. They are, if anything, charming.

In attempting to understand such individuals, it may be helpful, as it often is in understanding psychopathology, to start with the basics: What is it that David does? What can we say about his behavior that holds across the years from his early childhood through his murder of Merill Baskow and includes his comportment in Kirby?

We might say, as an overall characterization of his behavior, that David does whatever he feels like doing; he does whatever amuses him. He does this at all times and at all costs, regardless of consequence to himself or others. When being punished for his actions, when suffering confinement, deprivation or physical assault, his only concern is putting an end to the experience and going on to find his next source of amusement. Never does he seem to have a second thought about his pursuits; never does he seem to regret his actions. He occasionally suffers very unpleasant consequences for his deeds, but never does he seem to learn. Having brought down upon himself the repercussions of his conduct, when paying a heavy price, he does not pause to ask himself – as another might – "How can I avoid being incarcerated again? How can I avoid being ostracized and hated? How can I avoid being beaten up?" Such considerations are foreign; what matters is to extricate himself from the unpleasantness of the moment and seek more amusement. Never does he seem to learn; but, perhaps more importantly, never does he seem to want to learn. Needless to say, never does he feel remorse for the suffering he has caused his victims. No remorse, no regret. Not for what he has brought upon himself nor for what he has wrought upon others. The only question: what's next?

But, you may well be thinking, there is surely something particular about the ways that he chooses to amuse himself. While he may enjoy prosaic human activities - sex, eating, sleeping, watching television or taking hot baths, these certainly do not suffice. Nor do the more run of the mill vices such as drinking or gambling, or thrill-seeking behaviors such as auto racing or parachute jumping. Even the more mundane forms of crime - theft, for example, with its potent amalgam of adrenaline and profit - are inadequate. Certainly he engaged in many of these endeavors, but they were time-fillers. Who knows, he may even find some enjoyment in productive activity. Perhaps he likes to draw flowers, play the cello or write long stories about psychopathology and macabre crimes. Perhaps not. But regardless of his feelings about any of these occupations, they are not what make David David. They do not provide the amusement that he craves. That amusement is derived from what he perpetrates upon others - injuring them, humiliating them, frightening them, conning, beguiling and bamboozling them - by many and varied means, malevolently exercising his power over others and making them suffer at his hand.

So David kills, injures and inflicts pain upon animals; David injures, mutilates, hurts and humiliates people; David lies to and otherwise deceives people; David attempts to charm and "put things over on" people. Although in one way the most notable thing about David is that, on at least one occasion, he killed a young woman and visited abominations upon her corpse, we may omit this from our list of what makes David David due to its inclusion in one of the above categories of behavior. Moreover, there is a possibility that this atrocity was a one of a kind enterprise for him; murder may not be a constant of his behavioral repertoire. Yet, of course, any explanation of the workings of David's mind would have to be consistent with and allow for the act of murder.

In a certain sense, in terms of their most fundamental nature, David's behaviors are of the ordinary human variety; that is, pleasure-seeking and aggressive urges are universal. Most people are able to enjoy a feeling of power and many can enjoy putting something over on someone – consider April Fool's Day, a day specifically set aside for such enjoyments. In another sense, in the sense of their wildly amplified form, his behaviors are bizarre, outlandish, grotesque and reprehensible almost beyond words; they are anything but ordinary. His behaviors are remarkable in degree, not in kind. Our task, then, is to attempt to account for their gross exaggeration relative to more customary conduct. That is, if David's urges are universal, how do we account for the fact that his behavior, thank the heavens, is not?

We are faced with at least two possibilities: It may be that David's urges, while typical in kind, are atypical in their quantity or their strength; it may be that he has been burdened by an excess or overabundance of these urges or that they are somehow of such power that they are unstoppable. Or, alternatively, it may be that the urges are more or less normal in both kind and degree, but that the problem is a lack or deficiency of inner controls which might render them less disastrous in their effect.

It is my belief, and that of many others, that, to a large extent, it is the latter of these possibilities which we have to thank – so to speak – for the unfortunate presence of David Reardon and his like in our prisons, our hospitals and, even more unfortunately, our homes and our streets. That is, it is not necessarily that David Reardon and others of his extreme character are burdened by excessive pleasure-seeking or aggressive urges, urges which, owing to their great and irresistible forcefulness, cannot be contained. It may be, rather, that they are lacking in the psychological function which, more effectively present in the vast majority of people, leads to the partial inhibition of these urges and helps to channel them and modify them into socially acceptable forms. This function is the task of a particular psychic organ, the organ which is the indispensable guardian of civilization; it is most commonly known as the conscience.

The observation that the lack of a conscience is the essential, defining characteristic of psychopathy is commonplace; it is well-charted psychological terrain and the reader likely considers it a cliche. Far less commonly understood is the nature of the thing we call conscience, even less so the issue of how one comes to be without one. It may be that the two questions are best tackled in tandem.

It seems unlikely that a child could be born without a conscience, as he might a limb; nor is it feasible that, in the manner that a child might be born with a deformity of one or another body part, that the mind could suffer a similar affliction, with the faculty of moral sensibility somehow stunted, crippled or dwarfed. These ideas, in fact, are absurd on their face, failing even the most cursory test of logic. Given that no infant, and much less a newborn, is possessed of a conscience, it makes little sense to warrant that the psychopath is born without one; in this, he would in no way differ from others.

A conscience is something that develops over many years. It is part of the process of becoming a human being, and many have thought and written about how this process unfolds. In the psychoanalytic world, the discussion focuses on what is known as the superego, an agency within the self that encompasses, but extends beyond, that which is usually called the conscience. The conscience sits in judgement of the self. We say, "my conscience would not allow me to do that." Or, we sometimes say, "I can't let myself even think that," or "I feel guilty just for feeling that way." Thus, the conscience renders judgments not only on our overt behavior, but on our internal, covert activity, as well. But we do not think of the conscience as sitting in judgement of the actions of others; we do not say, for example, "My conscience makes me feel that murderers should be punished for their crimes." The judgements pronounced by the conscience apply only to its owner; its purview is limited to the self and its comportment. In this way, we control our own behavior; a good thing, that.

The superego, by contrast, takes a wider perspective, in fact a universal viewpoint, adjudging all of human conduct, overt or covert, sifting all it encounters through a moral filter and making assessments of worthiness, of goodness and badness. Many are familiar with the Freudian nomenclature for the several parts of the psyche – the id, the ego and the superego. Freud, of course, wrote in German, and it is my opinion that of all the misunderstandings of his ideas caused by their imperfect translation into English, one of the most unfortunate

– and unnecessary – is the use of these awkward locutions, ones which, for most who think and speak in English, suggest nothing, have no commonplace connotations, no resonance of meaning. The German words employed by Freud actually are closer to – and much more helpfully translated as – the It, the I and the Over-I.

The I, unsurprisingly, refers roughly to what we mean when we say I or me. It is the executive of the personality, directing activity and making decisions; and it is the center of subjective experience, the experiencer, feeling the range of sensations and emotions to which humans are subject. It is the agent that does and the subject that is done to. What Freud observed, however, is that the I or the ego is often woefully mistaken in its beliefs about what motivates its decisions or causes its subjective experience, going through life blithely and blindly unaware of the powerful influence of the It and the Over-I. The It, or the id, is the seat of the passions; largely unconscious, it is the source of the fundamental, instinctual drives and needs. Even the parts of it of which we are aware seem, in some way, not to be part of what we mean when we say "me." We say, "something made me do it," or "I couldn't help it," or "I knew it was foolish, but I just couldn't resist." The sense that people are often pushed or pulled by something that is within them yet in some way foreign, that they are influenced by something within "me," but *not* "me," is patent in the way we speak. The ego and the id, the I and the It, have been discussed at great length in psychoanalytic writings, but we will here set them aside and focus on the superego, the Over-I, the part of the mind which, in discussing David Reardon, draws our attention by its absence or, at least, its gross deficiency.

The child wants, the child needs; and the young child, the infant, is motivated by nothing other than his most immediate wants and needs. As David Reardon dramatically and unfortunately demonstrates, at least a few adults never progress far beyond this state of affairs. Most of us, however, not only outgrow this stance toward the world around us but feel a contempt for those who don't. In regarding such a person, depending on the severity of the developmental defect, the attitudes which accompany it, and our relation to the emotionally and morally stunted individual, we may be repulsed, we may be enraged or we may simply wish to avoid any association with him.

The rudiments of what will be the superego have their roots in the earliest days of life. Frame-by-frame analyses of video recordings of mother-child interactions demonstrate clearly that, in the earliest days of life, the newborn is attentive and responsive to faces. We apparently come factory-equipped with the neurological capacity to recognize the human face and a tendency to focus on it. Not only do newborns attend to the face, but they react to it, as well. They make and break eye contact and show other signs that they are, in some manner, influenced by the actions of the face which they so closely observe. Almost from birth, there seems to be a powerful drive – of whatever nature and derivation – to relate in some manner to other human beings. It hardly seems necessary to state that children and parents have profound and highly complex emotional attachments and reactions to each other. However, for our purposes, we need look at only one aspect of the relationship and a relatively simple one, at that.

For all the infant's interest in and attachment to the mother, she has little or no capacity to elicit self-directed behavior of any particular kind from the child in the first months of life. The child simply does not have the physical or psychological equipment necessary to be aware of or exert control over his own behavior. He sucks, he screams, he sleeps, he flails; he looks, he touches, he eats, he clings. What he wants, he wants, and he wants it now. He does not understand "later," and wouldn't care about it if he did. Only very gradually, with time and maturation, does he comes to understand that he can, at least in certain ways, be consciously in control of his own movements and behavior. And, at some point, fortuitously, he becomes aware of the fact that his actions have consequences. He learns that certain behaviors lead to things that are good – such as lollipops or hugs – and others lead to things that are bad – such as no lollipop or a smack on the rear end. This is surely a crucial moment in the transformation of an unthinking child-beast into a civilized human being. But, in this period, behavior is controlled or influenced by a basic and elemental paradigm of reward and punishment and no one would argue that this level of behavioral control involves anything like what we know as a conscience. And yet it seems that it is this simple paradigm of reward and punishment that is the very essence of conscience; it is only the nature and source of reward and punishment that changes as lollipop-seeking/smack-avoiding is transformed into adult, human morality.

In the first phase of this development, the lollipop or the smack is the reward or the punishment. As the child develops and has experience, he becomes better able to predict which outcome is headed his way based on many repeated instances of perceiving the precursors of lollipops or smacks – a smile or a frown on the parent's face. The child learns that, predictably, when Mommy smiles, a lollipop or some other pleasant event may follow, and that when Mommy frowns, the opposite is likely to occur; thus the smile or the frown takes on great importance as an indicator, a weather vane, so to speak, signalling which way the wind blows – and whether it brings fair weather or foul. Over time, however, the smile and the frown assume a meaning, an importance, of their own. No longer are they mere harbingers of lollipops and smacks; they carry inherent, powerful reward or punishment, independent of any pleasant or noxious event that may follow. The parents' approval becomes a thing to be sought after in its own right. In fact, the importance of approval, in its various forms is endless – endless in the sense that it is immense, and endless in the sense that it generally continues throughout life.

During childhood and adolescence and into adulthood, a further shift occurs – the locus of this approval gradually shifts from the parent to within the self. The more mature adult internalizes the approving/disapproving mechanism, diminishing the need for parental approval and becoming more dependent upon his own approval of himself. Of course, the values that lead to approval or disapproval may be derived from and closely related to those of the parents, but the dispensing or withholding of approval is – optimally, for the adult – the province of the self, not the parent. This process, like most other aspects of human psychological development, is not an all-or-none affair; it occurs in greater or lesser degrees. What is internalized, it should be emphasized, is not merely the capacity to dispense or withhold approval of one's self, to be the administrator of one's own sense of self-worth, but the totality of the values and standards by which an individual judges himself and others and his criteria for acceptable and unacceptable behavior in general. In other words, the individual develops a superego. This superego, this Over-I, this judging agent, becomes a structural part of the self, but it has been absorbed from without and contains not simply the values and attitudes of the parents, but those values and attitudes as modified and expanded upon by the values and attitudes of other important individuals and entities – relatives, friends, teachers, books, films and the other many and varied transmitters of culture.

This is a brief and somewhat simplistic synopsis of the development of the superego – the development of the motivation to abide by standards of conduct as the consequences of behavior transform from physical rewards and punishments through parental approval. The process eventuates in an internal judge, a judge who dispenses approval and disapproval – a feeling of being at ease with oneself or a feeling of guilt and dysphoria, an unpleasant emotional discomfort. I have spoken of how this is a slow and long-term process, occurring over a period of years. But if we examine David Reardon through the lens of that understanding, we find that he failed to complete even the earliest steps toward developing a conscience; he jumped the train almost before it left the rail yard.

There have been many abstruse and complex theories about how this failure might occur. But having some mercy on the reader, I will mention only a few ideas on the topic. It is my hope that these tidbits will shed sufficient light on the behavior of our subject to enable the reader to feel that he has gained at least some degree of understanding of psychopathy and make him content to allow me to move on to my personal acquaintance with the no-longer-so-young David Reardon and a few of the more telling examples of his behavior in Kirby.

I must, however, delay a moment to make clear that what I will say does not apply to all individuals with antisocial tendencies, nor to all those who might meet the criteria for Antisocial Personality Disorder as described in the Diagnostic and Statistical Manual of Mental Disorders (DSM). Psychopaths are but a small subset of this group. Furthermore, what I will say does not even apply to all those whom one or another mental health professional might declare to be a psychopath or sociopath. As I said above, these terms have been used in many ways over the years. The disparity between the term psychopath as I am using it and the DSM description of Antisocial Personality Disorder is unambiguous: of particular note is the fact that the DSM criteria allow one to be considered to have ASPD even if that person feels deep remorse for his actions, whereas a lack of sincere remorse – deep or otherwise – is the essence of the kind of individual with whom we are now concerned. Although there might be better names, David Reardon and others of his ilk might be termed Cleckley psychopaths, psychopaths who conform to the thorough and clearly-stated descriptions offered by Cleckley in his book, also mentioned above.

Among the most salient traits of the Cleckley psychopath are lack of remorse, relative lack of anxiety, failure to learn from experience, superficial charm and intact intellectual functioning. Cleckley also refers to "inadequately motivated antisocial behavior," by which he means that, for the type of individual he is describing, the slightest whim has the force of law. Intelligence has helped many a psychopath, by no means excluding David Reardon, to be more successful in his shenanigans, his transgressions great and small against mankind. But what make David the person he is are his lack of remorse, his failure to learn from experience, his tendency to act on almost every whim and his enjoyment in conniving, manipulating, using, abusing and inflicting misery upon others, employing his charm as well as whatever other means he finds to be conveniently at his disposal in the service of these goals. The reader may recognize that neither violence nor overt criminality are necessarily inherent in this description. It is true that psychopaths of this type are far more likely than non-psychopaths to be violent and criminal, and it hardly need be said that David Reardon is both criminal and violent in the extreme. Many other psychopaths, however, are not; in fact, one of most eminent contemporary experts on psychopathy, Robert Hare, has published a book entitled "Snakes in Suits," focusing on the "respectable" members of society who, under cover of their profession, cheat, connive and find delight in taking advantage of the vulnerable at every opportunity. Neither the shedding of blood nor a criminal record necessarily qualifies one as a psychopath, nor are they requisite for membership in the category. Violence and criminality are neither necessary nor sufficient to entitle one to the label "psychopath."

Before returning to the question of the lack of a conscience and the resultant lack of remorse, it might be helpful to consider another very pertinent aspect of David Reardon's behavior – his failure to learn from experience. As I discussed above, the earliest stage of the individual's control of his behavior is not a function of conscience, but is instead based on his fear of or concern for externally-imposed consequences – the lollipop and the smack. David's evident lack of concern for such consequences sets him apart from the more run-of-the-mill criminal or antisocially-inclined person. Many an antisocial person, lacking a well-functioning conscience, learns from experience and, while perhaps continuing in his criminal ways, at least makes an attempt – however feeble – to avoid repeating his mistakes. It is true that many people – both criminals and law-abiding individuals – have great trouble changing self-defeating patterns of behavior, but both the non-criminal and the ordinary (non-psychopathic) criminal, even if unable to change their behavior patterns, at least *show a concern* for the consequences. Generally speaking, the inability to change their behavior is a result of that behavior being powerfully motivated. When the consequences land on them, they are likely to say or feel something along the lines of, "Damn! I did it again!" Not David Reardon; not the Cleckley psychopath. He may not enjoy consequences such as deprivations and confinements, but his behavior tends to be motivated by momentary whims; and while he may fight to put an end to his confinement or other punishment, he shows no interest in changing his future behavior. The whim is felt at the moment; the consequence comes later. And later simply does not matter.

How is this to be understood?

Modern science, science unavailable to Cleckley, has helped us to understand this characteristic of the psychopath. Experiments in recent decades have demonstrated – intriguingly – that psychopaths tend to have extremely low reactivity of the autonomic nervous system. The ANS controls such bodily functions as heart rate, respiration rate, perspiration and other aspects of bodily arousal – it controls, that is, the physiological underpinnings of the unpleasant feeling of anxiety. In the presence of danger, we experience a surge of anxiety, a signal: "Watch out!" If the feeling is within limits and accompanied by a knowledge that the danger is under control or is not fully real, we can enjoy the anxiety – the arousal and excitement – as we do, for example, on roller-coasters and while watching horror movies. If the anxiety exceeds a certain limit or is not accompanied by a sense that the danger is unreal or under control, it exerts a powerful force impelling us to stop what we're doing or to take action, depending on the nature of the threat. Through the use of sophisticated physiological measurements, we have learned that this warning system, with its obvious adaptive qualities, is impaired in the psychopath. The presence of danger simply does not have the effect on him that it might on another. This impairment helps to account for two traits often found in psychopaths. Firstly, it helps account for the tendency to engage in various forms of thrill-seeking behavior; the roller-coaster and the horror movie are insufficient to arouse the sense of excitement that he craves. Secondly, and probably more importantly, it helps account for the characteristic failure to learn from experience; the psychopath may have some recognition that his behavior may lead to a smack rather than a lollipop, but, as compared with others in that circumstance, he simply doesn't care.

This interesting discovery may help us to understand the psychopath's lack of concern for externally imposed consequences, his failure to learn. In controlling his behavior, he seems to lack a healthy fear of consequence and it may well be that considering such consequence simply does not set off the internal alarms necessary to motivate him to refrain from doing something that he wishes to do. In fact, based on our above discussion of the functioning of the superego, one might well posit that the malfunctioning warning bell helps to explain the failure of the psychopath to be guided by the internally-based system of rewards and punishments, as well. That is, perhaps he has a superego, but its punitive power is inhibited by this same relative unresponsiveness of the ANS; perhaps he has a superego but is unable to use it for guidance of his behavior.

However, this hypothesis ultimately falls short: the psychopath is unable to utilize a healthy fear of external consequences in the service of controlling his behavior, but he most certainly feels the sting of such consequences, having brought them down upon himself. David's history is replete with examples of his willingness to make significant and often quite clever efforts to avoid or terminate unpleasant consequences, nor was he at all shy about voicing his unhappiness with New York State's insistence on his remaining its guest in Kirby. In contrast, however, nothing resembling a conscience either guided his behavior or inflicted its post-behavioral retribution upon him; never did he seem to feel even a trace of guilt. Any word of remorse ever expressed by

David was strictly in the service of attempting to connive his way out of some all-too-justly-deserved punishment.

So now, at last, we come to the issue of the conscience – the lack of which is the sine qua non of psychopathy. The conscience, as discussed, is a component of the superego, the "Over-I." As I've said, the superego, in essence, is comprised of the standards and values of the parents as absorbed into the child, internalized and accepted as one's own. The process of superego development has two requirements, one obvious, one less so. The obvious requirement is the presence of the parents. The second requirement, while less obvious, is equally indispensable: superego development requires that the child care about, feel related to, *identify with* the parent.

The impact that parents have on their children is obviously profound and multi-faceted. But much of it hinges on the nature of the child's attachment to the parents, the quality of his emotional connection to them. The child, and more so the infant, is dependant upon the parents for his survival and that reality allows the parent to exert great influence on the child. But – again – many important aspects of development are contingent upon the character of the emotional interaction between parent and child. Typically, while he may – in fact, must – sometimes hate his parents, the child feels an intense emotional attachment to them, an attachment which shows itself in many ways. The child clings, the child turns to the parents for protection and comfort. And, normally, the child has a deeply-felt identification with the parents as is indisputably demonstrated by the ubiquity of the cliched statement, "I want to be just like Daddy (or Mommy)." Absent this identification, many things may go awry in the child's development including – most unfortunately – a failure of the child to internalize the feelings, attitudes, values and standards of the parent. That is to say, the failure to develop a superego.

How or why it is that a child would fail to identify with the parents is a question I cannot adequately answer. Many have said that antisocial people, especially violently and criminally antisocial people, tend to have grown up in situations of abuse and/or neglect, environments which may make identification problematic in varying ways. This is undoubtedly so. But some very interesting research findings seem to imply that the type of individual I am describing, the psychopath who is charming, and seemingly calm and at ease with himself, completely untroubled by feelings of guilt or remorse and given to allowing free rein to every passing whim – the Cleckley psychopath – may come from the most normal of homes, homes with loving, supportive parents. It is as if this group of individuals, this sub-group of antisocials, are somehow born without the capacity to form normal human relationships, regardless of the fact that the term "normal human relationships" takes in such wide territory. For a relationship between two individuals to be normal in any meaningful sense of the word there must be at least some minimal emotional connection between the two, some feeling – however slight – of concern by each for the other. The Cleckley psychopath seems incapable of this. It may be that, much as the person whose lungs do not function cannot breathe regardless of the quality or quantity of air surrounding him, the psychopath-to-be cannot develop a sense of human relatedness regardless of the quality or quantity of loving care, nurturance and parental devotion available to him. As a student once remarked to me during a discussion of a psychopath, "It sounds like he was just born without the chip."

The nature of the chip is open to debate. In considering causation, in attempting to find the essential, underlying characteristic or impairment in psychopathy, many of the most prominent researchers in the field argue that there is some as yet unknown genetically-based brain abnormality, present from birth and affecting very elemental aspects of the person's way of experiencing himself and his relation to others. There seems to be a problem in the wiring that leads to a fundamental misunderstanding on the part of the psychopath. Or, to use my student's language, there may be a chip, but its circuits are crossed. The psychopath's wiring problem, his cross-circuited chip, prevents him from feeling that he is a creature of the same order as his fellow human beings. J. Reid Meloy, another contemporary expert on psychopathy, put it quite well: the essential problem in psychopathy is a "fundamental disidentification with humanity."

Thus, David Reardon gets to do whatever David Reardon feels an urge to do. To oversimplify things a bit, his fundamental disidentification with humanity, and the lack of conscience to which it leads, allow him to treat others as if their feelings do not exist, and his sluggish autonomic nervous system allows him to act without concern for the consequences to himself. It is as if David sees himself as a human being, a center of subjectivity, a creature with feelings, while he sees all others as objects to be used for his own purposes, his own amusement. He treats others as I might, perhaps, treat a pair of shoes; I walk on them for my comfort and convenience and, when I feel like it, I discard them. To me, they are an entity of a different kind than myself; I use them for my purposes and, beyond that, have no concern for their existence or their "feelings."

But things are not so simple. The reader may feel tired of being told that all things in the realm of the psychological are relative, that all our traits and characteristics exist in varying degrees. But I must repeat my statement in anticipation of those who may observe, "But David Reardon does seem to care about the feelings of others. In fact, it's indisputable that he does. He consistently shows that he cares about the feelings of others in that he wants to make them feel miserable; he wants to inflict pain and suffering!" And the observation is entirely valid. In this way, he does care about the feelings of others. He cares about them insofar as he is able to use them to make himself feel superior. He cares about them insofar as he is able to use them to make himself feel powerful and victorious. It is of the utmost importance to him and I would assert, in fact, that his wish to exercise control over others, to give himself the feeling that he can take whatever they possess and use them at his will, is of greater importance than the infliction of pain. I believe that this is what enables him to take on long-term projects, such as his victimization of poor Mary Alice McDougall, in which he seems to be so uncharacteristically delaying gratification of his wishes. His grand triumph had to be delayed, it is true, for a matter of months, but his feeling that he was putting something over on her must have delighted him at every step along the way. The urge to satisfy this malevolent, grandiose narcissistic need seems to be almost as central to psychopathy as is the lack of a conscience, and it certainly implies that others have an importance to the psychopath.

Further, it seems true that David not only relates to but, in some way, identifies with human beings. Are they not his preferred target? There was a time in his life when he seemed involved mostly with tormenting small animals; but he, in his very own way, grew and developed; he matured and became more of an adult. He reached an adulthood in which his identification with his fellow humans is perhaps demonstrated by his realization that they are, indeed, the most satisfying and appropriate victims. This does, truly, imply an identification – of a sort. On an intellectual level, David is as capable as anyone else of recognizing that he is a human being, a member of the same species as other human beings. It is a lack of emotional identification which creates the problem.

I may, in fact, have further misled the reader by implying that what causes David and his brethren to carry out their mission of destruction is not an excess of malevolent motivation, but rather the lack or deficiency of the inhibiting force – the superego. This may be only a partial truth. It is likely that on a conscious level, the former comes very close to capturing David's experience; that all he feels is a desire to put something over on people, to con them, to get the better of them, to injure and inflict pain upon them and that he sees no reason to restrain these urges.

But there may well be more to David's insides than he consciously experiences. It may be that the same relative inability to identify with others that leads to the failure of superego formation has other equally disastrous consequences. We must wonder about the sense of apartness and alienation that is the inevitable companion of this disidentification. It may be that this failure to identify, this experience of living amongst human beings but being unable to feel that he shares in their world or that he is fully in and of the human race, not only allows him to perpetrate his destruction but, in a sense, propels him to do so.

Consider that this apartness is beyond any commonplace sense of rejection that one might feel; many easily injured people stew in their own juices, alone and angry with nothing to comfort themselves but their righteous indignation and their tightly-embraced and ever-growing accounting of the injustices visited upon them by those whom they eventually excommunicate from their world. David's apartness is of a more fundamental kind. Excommunicated though his friends and relations may be, the isolate at least recognizes the ongoing presence of others of his kind in the world he inhabits, and the angry, lonely collector of injustices has at least the theoretical possibility of putting aside his grudges and grievances and reviving old relationships. David's apartness holds no such possibilities; it is definitional, it is a permanent, unalterable exclusion, an apartness determined by his basic nature, by his lack of the chip.

Looking at David's behavior, it is easy to believe that he is driven by a need to tear from others that which he himself is incapable of feeling; he seems determined to steal from others their feelings of goodness, of wholeness, of contentment, of comfortable belonging, of the warmth of kinship in a world of their fellow beings.

One might ask, "How does it help David to take from others things that he will still not have for himself?" A reasonable question, but one which overlooks the power and motivating force of a particular feeling, the feeling of envy. And I can think of no better way to illustrate this feeling and its potency than by retelling a story that helped me to understand it. With apologies to the story's unknown originator for any unintentional revisions:

There were two neighboring Russian peasants, Boris and Ivan, who had in common their dire poverty. Barely able to feed themselves, living in mud and thatched huts which failed to provide shelter from the elements, they were equally impoverished and miserable with but one exception: Ivan possessed a goat – an old, flea-bitten, malnourished, filthy, mangy goat. One day, a genie came to Boris and told him that he would grant him one wish. It could be any wish of any kind, but one and only one wish would be granted. Boris's unhesitating request? "I wish that Ivan's goat should die."

If you are thinking that you would have made a wiser choice, providing for your own abundant prosperity rather than depriving Ivan of his meager portion, you must be reminded: for David, no such choice is imaginable. Closed to him is the experience of membership among his kind, of closeness or warmth or affection from others, leaving him with no option but to relate to them as alien objects – objects to be malevolently manipulated, defeated and destroyed. Given the impossibility of warmth and wholeness, the unattainability of a comforting sense of kinship with his fellow creatures, all that is left to him is to strip such feelings from others – to despoil in them what he cannot feel in himself.

David Reardon, goat-killer extraordinaire.

* * *

It was my first day at Kirby. I had spent the morning completing paperwork in the first floor administrative offices and, in the early afternoon, I was about to take the elevator to the sixth floor and see, for the first time, 6-West, my assigned ward. I was somewhat anxious about my first day on the job and all that it entailed – meeting many new people, familiarizing myself with the hospital, its culture, its routines and rhythms and getting my first taste of my new tasks and responsibilities. And I was somewhat anxious – perhaps a bit more than somewhat – about meeting and moving among the one hundred and sixty-something prisoner/patients of Kirby, a collection of murderers, rapists and other individuals whose care and containment required no less than a maximum-security forensic hospital – a hospital for the criminally insane. A close friend of mine had taken her place on the hospital's staff just a few weeks earlier and she was kind enough to spend some time preparing me for what I might face. It was not a very comforting conversation. I heard tales of matricide and patricide, fratricide and filicide, pyromania and erotomania, of subway pushing and eye-gouging, and of dismemberment and cannibalism – which latter categories included some discussion of David Reardon, our protagonist and one of Kirby's more illustrious occupants.

Near the main entrance of the hospital is the elevator lobby which houses four sets of elevator doors. The elevators are of considerable size, having the capacity to transport a ward-ful of

266

patients plus several aides, a group numbering as many as thirty. These elevators shuttle the patients to and from the wards, the recreation floor, the treatment floor and the basement, from where patients are escorted into the fenced and razor-wired hospital yard. Patient "movements," I had been told, are frequent and the elevators run almost constantly. Yet I was surprised and taken aback when, for the first time, I saw the wide doors slide open and was confronted by an elevator full of patients, my first exposure to my new acquaintances.

My most vivid impression, however, was not of dangerous or psychotic-looking men. I was new to the forensic setting, but not to psychiatric hospitals, and I was accustomed to the appearance of the residents. For the most part, this group was typical. The blank stares, slumped shoulders, and stiff and awkward postures were predictable; the unclosed mouths, unshaven faces, uncombed hair and unkempt clothing, all too familiar. Even the few whose slovenliness was capped off by the drool dripping from their mouths and covering their shirts failed to capture the greater part of my attention or arouse my strongest emotional response. I knew that a certain anti-psychotic medication had the unfortunate side-effect of producing overabundant saliva, and that the classically psychotic indifference to personal hygiene prevented any interest in the aid of the handkerchief, however sorely needed by consumers of Clozapine, the offending, although often-necessary, medication. No, my strongest reaction was reserved for, my attention seized by, one particular man, a man situated in the front of the crowd. Standing quietly, he was tidily and spotlessly dressed in well-coordinated shirt and pants. Hair perfectly coiffed, he was immaculately groomed, with evident attention to every aspect of personal hygiene. He stood with perfect posture and almost regal bearing, his head tilted just slightly upward, looking poised and at ease; his hands were held at his waist, fingers interlaced neatly together. Almost immediately upon the opening of the doors, this man glanced at me and with a quick look of recognition, smiled amicably, nodded politely and said, in clear and mellifluous tones, "Good afternoon, Dr. Sternberg. Welcome to Kirby."

The hospital grapevine was active, and patients often knew when a new clinician was hired. Whether this man had some idea of my physical description or was simply able to read into the situation, perhaps sniffing out my first-day-on-the-job tenseness and smoothly combining the elements of the information at his disposal, I did not know. But, owing to the incisive portrayals of some of Kirby's more notable personages imparted to me by my friend, I knew instantly: Reardon.

Such was my introduction to our subject. Although it was but the first of many encounters, it was of a piece with all the others in that David Reardon was, unvaryingly, David Reardon. One might wonder if it could become tiring to maintain the facade of pleasantness, affability and charm, and suspect that it might be a relief for him to openly and without reservation reveal himself as a vicious miscreant. But one would be fretting needlessly; Mr. Reardon evidenced no such need. Of course, there were moments when his smile faded and his irritation came through; after all, he was certainly not happy about his retention in a secure and highly-restrictive facility, one in which he could not pursue girls or drink or take drugs, to say nothing of the ways that he was stymied in his attempts to perpetrate insult and injury upon others; he had to content himself with minor misconduct, mischief of a sort that he might hold in contempt were he free and unfettered in the world at large. He could lie to his fellow inmates, stirring up unpleasantness, animosities and, on a good day, a brawl, but this was as nothing compared to his glory days. His plight was similar, perhaps, to that of an aerospace engineer, a builder of rocket ships who, having lost his position, is reduced to repairing cars in a gas station. Or, more in keeping with his remarkable creativity, we might compare him to Michaelangelo had he, after completing the Sistine Chapel, somehow been reduced to painting houses; an almost inconceivable debasement and degradation.

But David was one to seize opportunity and to do what he might with the materials at hand. So, in addition to creating a bit of excitement on the ward, he would do what he could to try to con clinicians and other hospital personnel which, I imagine he hoped, held out the possibility of a double reward: earning his way toward release, while feeling the sheer joy of manipulating others. In this attempt, though, his whims sometimes derailed his purpose. He might, for example, after devoting considerable energy to convincing a member of the professional staff of his deep remorse for having taken poor Merrill's life, enjoy an interlude with a fellow patient, telling him of how he has murdered and devoured dozens of people and will be sending his army of fellow cannibals to make a meal of this overwhelmed and fearful patient should the pitiable wretch ever be released from the hospital. On occasion, staff would get wind of such menacings and David would then feebly attempt to cover his obvious pride in his cruel handiwork and insist that the "joke" was harmless and had no bearing on his assurances of profound repentance for past actions. David, it must be understood, was not constrained in his protestations of innocence by issues of feasibility; if he wanted to say something, he said it. If his interlocutor believed him, it was a success. If not, he would internally shrug his shoulders and proceed, fully unabashed, to the next outrageous lie.

On one particular occasion, an occasion which will forever endure in my memory, David demonstrated this remarkable "ability" to me. Perhaps it was early in my acquaintance with him; perhaps it was my naivete that made the instance so striking. Or, perhaps, considering the comical brazenness of his claim, it would make a similar impression on me to this day.

"When am I getting out of here?" he demanded of me on this occasion.

"I can't say. As you know, it will only happen when a judge decides that you are no longer dangerously mentally ill."

"But I'm not dangerously mentally ill. I never have been and this hospital is holding me unjustly and illegally. I've never hurt anyone in my life."

"You admitted that you murdered Merrill Baskow, remember? You had to admit it before the judge would agree to a plea of not guilty by reason of mental disease or defect. You know that, and you know that's why you're being held here."

"But that was one incident and I've told everyone here how remorseful I feel about it."

"Yes, you've told us that, but only after you saw that no one believed any of your other stories."

"I never told any other stories. I've always accepted full responsibility for what I've done."

"What about last month when you told Dr. Javits that it wasn't you who killed her, it was a bunch of other guys who were going to rape her. You tried to fight them off, but in the process, you were injured and poor Merrill was killed!"

"Oh, well that was just a joke. Anyway, I'm telling the truth now and it's not fair that no one will believe me. And anyway, aside from that I've never hurt anyone in my life."

"Mr. Reardon, we have records. We know about some of the things you've done to other people – like that girl who you taunted into killing herself. Or what about that other poor girl whose fingers you cut off, just as one example?"

"Oh, she did that to herself. She was crazy. She liked doing shit to herself and then trying to get other people in trouble for it."

"David," I said, "I don't believe that for a minute. Not only that, the entire staff here knows very well that you lie like other people breathe; no one believes a word you say. Ever. About anything."

Any discomfort that I felt in having to make such a statement was certainly not shared by Mr. Reardon, who continued without skipping a beat.

"Well, it's very important for me to get out of here and as soon as possible."

"Why is it so important?"

"Because there are horrible people in this country who shoot defenseless animals, like ducks and geese, with shotguns. And I'm going to start a movement to put an end to hunting. It's mean and unfair and people shouldn't be allowed to do things like that. I certainly wouldn't!"

I opened my mouth to speak, but soon closed it, unsuccessful in finding a response.

David Reardon, like many another Kirby inhabitant, was there when I came and there when I left. He introduced himself to me upon my entrance and, shortly before my parting, provided me with another indelible memory.

David was being held in Kirby – in the custody of the New York State Commissioner of Mental Health – on successive two-year Orders of Retention. Each time a patient's order was to expire, he was entitled to a court hearing. Typically, in such hearings, the hospital would present one or more witnesses, usually clinicians who had submitted reports for the hospital recommending either retention or release. Sometimes a clinician with an opposing point of view would testify. Even if no clinician supported release, a case for it would be made by the Mental Hygiene Legal Service lawyer provided to the defendant by New York State for legal representation.

Today was David's hearing, a hearing he would have been free to waive and which, in all practicality, he might as well have; but making things easier on people was not David's way, and he would have his day in court. The witnesses would offer testimony by answering the questions put to them by a representative of the New York State Attorney General's office, a lawyer whose job it was to represent New York State's official position – in this case, that David should be retained in the facility. The testifying clinicians offered their opinions, fully supporting David's continuing retention in Kirby. Questions covered David's pre-hospitalization history, the murder of Merrill Baskow – the crime which led to his incarceration – as well as his behavior since his admission. David's lawyer then cross-examined the witnesses, bringing out whatever she might that could possibly help his case, help the judge to feel that maybe he should be granted his freedom or, at least, a transfer to a less secure facility. A valiant effort, but clearly to no avail. I do not believe that a person in the courtroom, with the possible exception of David, believed there was any chance for him to win the day. Nevertheless, the case proceeded to its conclusion in a thorough and orderly manner. Most of the audience – Kirby clinicians and administrative personnel – were not terribly attentive; they chatted quietly among themselves and seemed somewhat bored; there was little suspense regarding the outcome. But David Reardon, in a comment that was pure David Reardon, awakened the room.

At the conclusion of the testimony, the judge, as was her custom, asked David if he had anything to say before she closed the hearing. Sitting at the defense table, neatly dressed, the very picture of polite civility, hands folded neatly on the table, David responded:

Thank you, your honor. I have only one thing to say: This case has now been in the legal system for over ten years. Through those years, I have been dealing with police officers, district attorneys, judges, psychiatrists, psychologists, social workers, medical doctors, nurses, aides and others. And I find it sad to say that of all these people, all these people who have arrested me and prosecuted me and treated me and interviewed me, all these professionals, all these people who are supposed to be helping others, not one – not one! – has shown the compassion and concern that I have for poor Merrill Baskow.

* * *

But I would not wish to end our story on a note of absurdity. As preposterous as this astounding statement by David Reardon is, it speaks volumes about the extent of his psychopathology, of his lack of human connectedness. Faced with the inevitability of again being denied the right to his freedom, David felt he had nothing to lose by making a claim that might earn him some sympathy or feeling of kindness from the judge, some feeling on the judge's part that he is really not such a bad guy after all, that he might be shown some leniency. That he could make this statement with that intent is surely remarkable. Earlier, I spoke about his ability to read people, a necessary skill for one who derives such joy from conning, defrauding, putting something over on people. I maintain that David possessed this skill in great measure. He used it flawlessly with Mary Alice McDougall and many others. But in this instance, addressing a judge familiar with his case, a judge who had read the reports of hospital clinicians, he was faced with a far more difficult task. In reality, there was no possibility of his saying anything that would significantly change the judge's opinion of him and his suitability for freedom. So he tried what he could. He gave in to the whim to try, once more, to connive, to defraud, to manipulate, to finagle. But the fact that he was capable of making such a statement – and with a completely straight face – was yet another indication that, regardless of the fact that he showed no signs whatever of psychosis, he lived in his own world.

Hervey Cleckley spoke of the "Mask of Sanity" of the psychopath. Is there a mask or is the psychopath actually in many ways sane? Some have called psychopathy "moral insanity," implying that the psychopathic individual is otherwise sane. It would certainly be hard to quibble – using David Reardon as an example – with the notion that the psychopath is morally insane. In the end, I suppose, much depends on one's definition of sanity.

We often speak of "looking someone in the eye" in an attempt to know the person's true nature. And the notion that the eyes are the "window to the soul," is a common one. But what is it that one would see in David Reardon's eyes? Merrill Baskow thought that her terror, her primitive, visceral, deep-in-the-gut fear of David was the result of looking into his eyes. What did she see?

Some writers, in discussing psychopaths, have spoken of a reptilian state of being and a "reptilian stare." Reptiles differ from mammals in any number of ways, but two are of particular interest: reptiles do not hoard food – they are apparently interested only in what they can eat at the moment and have no concern for the future. And most reptiles do not tend to, do not care for, do not show any concern for their young – for the flesh of their flesh.

Sometimes in speaking with acutely psychotic individuals, individuals who are lost in hallucinatory or delusional experience and incoherent thought, one gets the feeling that the person is unreachable, absent. We flippantly say that the individual is "out to lunch." That is, one cannot make oneself or the world of shared experience understood to him. Such was not the case with David Reardon. In most senses, he was right there; he was present. But what did Merrill Baskow see in his eyes?

Psychopaths are not oblivious in the same manner as the person who is lost in psychosis; they know what is happening around them; they can converse with others; they are sharp, they are on the ball. But in another way, in terms of being capable of feeling a sense of kinship, an attachment to, an identification with others, they are absent. Merrill Baskow had been terrified by the reptilian look that she saw in David Reardon's eyes, a look that told her that to him she was an object and nothing more.

We don't know how she died, but we can imagine how she felt in the moments immediately before her death, moments when she might have sought mercy from David Reardon. She might have pleaded, she might have begged. Looking into her murderer's eyes, try as she might, she would have found no sign of sympathy, no glimmer of concern for her or for decency itself, no hint of even a simple recognition of her as a sentient creature, a fellow human being. She must have hoped, hoped against all reason, to find a trace of some such feeling in his eyes – in the window to his soul. Despairing, terrified, she would have searched those eyes, searched with feverish desperation. Perhaps she cried for help. If so, it was to no avail. She was alone. Alone with a man with the eyes – and the mercy – of a crocodile.

CPSIA information can be obtained
at www.ICGtesting.com
Printed in the USA
JSHW022209270920
8259JS00005B/11